THE RELUCTANT MEDIUM

Praise for The Reluctant Medium

"If Elyn Aviva was reluctant, she overcame it beautifully to produce this gift of a book. Not only does it accurately describe the very common human response to tapping into higher consciousness, but it provides the deep wisdom derived from doing so with courage and commitment. The truth in these words can be felt in the heart. The teaching carries a transmission that will propel readers farther on their own spiritual journeys. Highly recommended."

Suzanne Giesemann — Author of *The Awakened Way* and *Making the Afterlife Connection*

"*The Reluctant Medium* is not merely a memoir—it is a luminous conversation across dimensions. Elyn Aviva offers a rare and riveting account of what happens when the ancient world knocks on the door of the modern mind. Plotinus speaks, the veil thins, and we are invited to listen… and we are changed. Told with impeccable honesty and graceful clarity, this book is an exquisite testament to the intelligence, love, and presence that waits just beyond ordinary sight. As someone who walks between worlds, I found it to be a rare gift for anyone curious about the continuity of consciousness, the power of inner inquiry, and the unexpected magic of saying 'yes.'"

Cheryl Page — Author of *Mystic Richness: Inspirational Letters from Visionaries Beyond the Veil*

"Reading *The Reluctant Medium* has been a deeply rich and layered experience. Much of the wisdom shared through Plotinus, Hypatia, and The Collective felt like a remembering—echoes of ancient truths humanity has known and carried through the ages. It was not so much a discovery of new information, but a profound recognition and deepening. What stood out most powerfully, however, was Elyn. Her honesty, vulnerability, and willingness to share her doubts, her questions, her experiences with channeling, her relationship dynamics with Gary—all of this breathed life into the teachings. It made the entire journey relatable, human, and deeply authentic. … Her book is alive; it transmits Light. It is more than a book. It is a living experience."

Natalie Fillet — Dream detective and blogger

"Elyn's book presents a work of spiritual and courageous self-inquiry. Her work reflects an unwavering respect for the forces of inspiration and the sacred discipline of mediumship. She guides the reader on a transformative journey characterised by honesty and humility, one that honours and acknowledges the subtle distinctions between the conscious and subconscious mind, while unlocking the profound inspiration embedded within the universe of spiritual insight."

David Schiesser — Medium, healer, and teacher

"In *The Reluctant Medium,* Elyn Aviva, PhD, invites readers into an unsettling yet awe-inspiring descent across the threshold of the known. As a scholar grounded in skepticism and rigor, she never intended to become a vessel for consciousness from beyond—yet one quiet afternoon in a Girona café, the spirit of Plotinus surged through her, offering clarity, challenge, and a shattering of all certainties. Aviva's narrative crackles with visceral immediacy: she describes the strange pressure at her temple, the physical shift in voice, and the electric shock of realizing that a philosopher from the 3rd century was not only real—but speaking through her.

This is not a polished séance memoir, but a raw, deeply felt account of transformation. Aviva confronts her own doubts, intellectual defenses, and the tremors that follow when an alternate realm breaches everyday life. Her meetings with Plotinus unfold like expeditionary forays into an uncharted interior wilderness—fraught with wonder, frailty, and startling revelations about life, death, and the contours of consciousness. With honesty, urgency, and an unflinching eye, she compels us to explore whether the afterlife is mere fantasy—or a presence insisting on being believed."

Stephen Berkley — Filmmaker

"Elyn Aviva's *The Reluctant Medium* is a fascinating and engaging read. Her book is rich with wisdom straight from the mouths of some of history's greatest teachers, and Elyn's access to the other side of the veil provides rare insights into the brilliance of the Hermetic legacy. Useful guidance and fresh perspectives for humanity during a time of great change."

Ani Williams — Musician, recording artist, sound medicine teacher, and author of *Guardians of the Dragon Path*

"Reading *The Reluctant Medium* felt like entering a deeply personal and expansive exploration of consciousness beyond the physical. Elyn Aviva writes with sincerity, courage, and a refreshing willingness to question her own experiences. That self-reflective quality invited me to trust her story. When I finished the book, I disappointed myself—not because something was lacking, but because I didn't want the journey to end.

I believe spiritual insight becomes most meaningful when it translates into how we live in the present—not just as transcendent truth, but through listening, speaking, and behaving with clarity and maturity. After 30 years as a psychotherapist, I've come to believe that the psychological and relational skills we need to develop—especially how language shapes our experience—are just as essential as spiritual insight. For me, this is a both/and, not an either/or."

Jake Eagle — Psychotherapist, author, *The Power of Awe*

"From the first astonishing contact to the last reveal of divine connection and synchronicity, *The Reluctant Medium* is a riveting read, full of humour, honesty, sensitivity, and helpful intel. The slice of life offered to the reader is accessible, relatable, and restorative. From Gary's wit to Elyn's unwavering pursuit of truth and proof - this book delivers.

But what I loved most was the growing relationship between Elyn and her Guide Team. Their wise patience over many years, waiting for just the right moment to appear, is faith-building. Their love, care, and delight at Elyn's development restores belief that no matter what happens or what we choose to think at times, we are never alone. Perhaps this is the greatest gift of *The Reluctant Medium*."

Elizabeth Diamond Rose — Transformational healer, writer and content provider

THE RELUCTANT MEDIUM

How Channeling Plotinus, Hypatia, and The Collective Transformed My Life

ELYN AVIVA, PhD

The Reluctant Medium

How Channeling Plotinus, Hypatia, and the Collective
Transformed My Life
by
Elyn Aviva, PhD
Copyright © 2025 by Pilgrims Process Publishers
http://PilgrimsProcess.com

All rights reserved. No part of this publication, including illustrations, may be reproduced in any form or by any means, electronic or mechanical, including photocopy, recording, or any information storage and retrieval system, without permission in writing from the publisher.

ISBN 978-0-9915267-3-4

Set in Minon Pro 11 pt. and Arial Bold in various sizes.

Cover design by Carles Torrent Pagès

The author does not recommend anyone follow any practices or healthcare advice given in this book by her or by the beings whose messages she channeled.

To Plotinus, Hypatia, and The Collective,
whose eagerness to communicate is
transforming many lives.

We offer this book in service
to the highest good.

Contents

Acknowledgements xi

Preface xii

Conventions Used in the Text xiii

The Reluctant Medium 1

Afterword 250

Appendix A – People and Other Beings 252

Appendix B – Concepts 262

Appendix C – A Brief Introduction to Mediumship and Channeling 269

Appendix D – More Questions, More Answers 274

Author's Biography 301

Acknowledgements

Heartfelt gratitude to Plotinus, Hypatia, The Collective, and all the other non-corporeal beings from the Other Side who have graced me with their presence. Without them, this book would not exist. Thanks to Cheryl Page for introducing me to mediumship. Deepest appreciation for the unswerving support, trust, and participation of my beloved husband, Gary White. Many thanks to Jake Eagle, Natalie Fillet, Nigel Fleming, Marchiene Rienstra, Sally Roscoff, Elizabeth Diamond Rose, Jane Seiler Thompson, and Tessa ten Tusscher for their valuable comments and proof-reading suggestions. I am grateful for the teachers and mentors, including Suzanne Giesemann and Robert Moss, who have helped guide me onto this most unexpected path.

Preface

For many months, I felt a compulsion to write this book. I tried to ignore it, but something kept urging me to publish my channeled conversations with a group of long-departed souls.

I am uncomfortable going public. I much prefer to live quietly, unnoticed by critics, scoffers, and naysayers. But I have been told in no uncertain terms that the messages I received are not just for me. They—Plotinus, Hypatia of Alexandria, The Collective, and a few other beings who reside on "the Other Side"—have wisdom to impart to humanity. And I have the responsibility to get the information out there.

With their support, I have summoned my courage and written this compilation of a year's conversations. The exchanges occurred in the context of my everyday life—including relationship struggles, a bout with serious illness, and feedback from friends. They led to deep personal transformation. I have not edited the channeled messages except to add words in brackets [ ] that make the exchanges clearer.

The Afterword includes a summary of the most important and urgent messages that I have received, as well as reflections on how they have transformed my life.

I want these dialogues to be as accessible as possible, so I've included four appendices. Appendix A is biographical information about the people and other beings I mention. Appendix B is a glossary for words followed by an * at their first appearance in the text. Appendix C is a brief description of mediumship and channeling. Appendix D includes conversations that took place after the first year.

I hope you will find these exchanges as transformative and inspiring as I have, and that you will use them to change your life for the better.

Conventions Used in the Text

Abbreviations for the most frequent communicators: P = Plotinus communicating to me without sound. PS = Plotinus speaking aloud, through me. TC: The Collective. TCS = The Collective speaking aloud, through me. H = Hypatia of Alexandria.

I have added words in brackets [ ] to make the channeled messages clearer, to describe responses that I sensed but could not see or hear, and to provide additional information.

Single ' ' or double " " quotation marks indicate that the word or phrase is not being used in a literal or usual way. For example, I don't see, feel, or hear Plotinus and the others with my normal senses, so I often put those words in quotes. Also, it is difficult for those on the Other Side to accurately describe what it is like in their dimension/realm, so I also use quotes around some of the words they use in their effort to communicate.

The Reluctant Medium

Thursday, 28 February 2024

If you had told me that I would be channeling messages from a Greek philosopher who died over 1700 years ago, I'd have said you were nuts! But that's exactly what spontaneously happened to me—with irrefutable evidence, so I knew I wasn't making it up.

Gary (my husband) and I had discovered Gipsy, a pleasant café-bar on the ground floor of the four-star Hotel Palau Fugit in the medieval Old Town of Girona, Catalonia, Spain, the town we were currently calling home. We made a habit of stopping in, strolling through the atrium, and walking up the three short steps to the coffee nook hidden next to the barista station. It's a charming, relaxing area, with walls of chunky, beige-colored bedrock interspersed with swaths of white plaster, comfortably padded chairs, low tables, and easy-listening music from the 70's. Most people don't know it's there, so we usually had it to ourselves. Or so I thought.

One day Gary and I were sitting in our favorite hidden corner of Gipsy, sipping coffee. We were talking about our next book project, tentatively called *Adventures of Everyday Mystics*. We were discussing such varied topics as the nature of reality, why is there evil, making sense out of awful events, do we come into this life with a destiny plan, why do souls* reincarnate (assuming they do), is there life after death, can we communicate with the deceased—you know, the kind of superficial topics everybody discusses over coffee.

These last two questions weren't really questions, however, since we'd been studying off and on with Suzanne Giesemann, a retired Navy Commander turned evidential medium*. Although we'd taken several of her online classes, neither Gary nor I wanted to—or planned to—become a medium. That was a good thing, since we weren't very successful at it. We were just curious and wanted to explore the evidence for life after physical death, contacting spirit guides (if there were any), and so on.

The more we studied with Suzanne, the more we looked at the evidence, the more we watched other reputable mediums at work, the more we agreed that life after death—the continuity of consciousness* from this realm to another—seemed feasible and made sense.

Gary and I were engaged in an intense conversation about these topics when I suddenly felt a voice eagerly wanting to come through me and speak. I felt a light pressure on my right temple; my eyes shifted focus; and I could feel the inside of my mouth change shape and get larger.

I spontaneously spoke a few words in a deep, slightly accented voice—and then I abruptly stopped. Wooooaaah! I wasn't at all sure I wanted to channel* someone! Then I reconsidered and decided, "Okay, I'll do it." After all, I was being offered an opportunity to channel without having to do a lot of disciplined training. Why not give it a try?

I gave a mental nod of permission, my mouth cavity changed shape again, and I spoke in a voice that was not my own. Here's what came through:

> "We humans are here to experience the full range of experience. That's why we have incarnated. We learn from the 'bad' more than from the 'good.' We are in the process of spiritual evolution, and we need to have the full range of experiences to evolve."

The voice I was channeling was answering some of the questions we'd just been asking! Then the voice stopped and started to withdraw.

I had the presence of mind to ask, "Who are you?"

I silently "heard" the answer: someone with a name beginning with P. The name Plotinus flashed before me. Then he was gone.

Gary was watching me, wide-eyed.

"That was interesting," he said.

I nodded, unable to speak. I took out my iPhone and wrote in my Notes app what I could remember him saying, which was not much, and what Gary remembered I said, which was all the rest of it.

Thank goodness our cozy coffee nook had good Wi-Fi. Shakily, I Googled "Plotinus" (see Appendix A). There he was. Widely considered the founder of Neoplatonism* (see Appendix B), Plotinus was a Greek philosopher who lived in the 3rd century CE*. I skimmed the Wikipedia entry. Plotinus's *Enneads* addressed many of the questions that Gary and I were asking each other. He must have been listening in. But how could that be?

Stunned, I finished sipping my coffee. Plotinus was *real*. A real person. A real *dead* person. A very-long-dead real person. Talking through me. Using me as a "speaking tube."

We sat in silence for a while, then paid our bill. We walked out of the café into a radically altered reality.

It was one thing to take courses in mediumship* and contacting spirit guides—it was quite another to have a being "come through" me to comment on our book project. I wondered how long Plotinus had been eavesdropping.

I was deeply shaken. If Plotinus really was real—and he certainly seemed to be—then continuity of consciousness really is real. It was an earthquake to my BS (Belief System), my reality paradigm. It was one thing to intellectually believe in channeling departed loved ones and to believe in others who have these experiences—but having it myself was quite another matter.

And oh, my! the ramifications: There *is* life after life. There is continuity of consciousness. Non-physical beings are listening in. They know what's going on in this realm of reality. They are engaged/involved in our human lives, giving us gentle nudges to help us move in the right direction. We aren't living in an uncaring or disinterested universe—it (Consciousness*?) is actively engaged.

I am by nature and training analytical and skeptical. I stepped back and reevaluated my experience. I knew what had happened was real. I even had evidence: Plotinus was a real person who was interested in the very topics we had been talking about. It might not be evidence that would hold up in a court of law, but it was good enough for me.

Nonetheless, I told myself, maybe it wasn't really Plotinus. After all, he'd been dead for 1700 years. Maybe it was some other non-physical being presenting itself as Plotinus. But that just made things more confusing. Why would that other being do that? How would it know what Plotinus had written? Why would it be involved? It was more logical to believe that the being I had channeled was the ongoing spirit of Plotinus.

Evidential mediumship* emphasizes the importance of asking for (and getting) evidence, and I had some. There really was a Greek philosopher named Plotinus who wrote about the questions we had been pondering. But I wanted more evidence. I needed more evidence. If he showed up again, I planned to ask for more.

I did a very superficial Google search. I read a little about Plotinus's philosophy, but I didn't want to know much. If I learned very much, I wouldn't know whether what I channeled was information from Plotinus or my subconscious memory, repeating something I had read about him. On the other hand, I wanted to know more about his personal life so that I could ask him verifiable questions.

Thursday, 29 February 2024

The next day we returned to the Gipsy bar. No one else was there, so we settled into the comfortable armchairs in the far corner and ordered coffee.

Plotinus started to come through again. Gary said he could see me changing. I suddenly looked off in the distance, and then my face shifted. My experience was that I was listening for something, in a state of high alert. Soon there was a subtle alteration in my mouth as it changed shape inside. Then a voice came through that was different from mine.

As I felt my mouth start to change shape, I instinctively resisted again and mentally exclaimed "No!" Immediately the process stopped. I was pleased that Plotinus respected my wishes.

Gary asked what had happened. I told him. He suggested instead of "No!" I could say, "Not now." After all, if I wanted to continue communicating with whatever/whoever this being was, a polite request was better than a forceful rejection. He was right.

I allowed the process to start again and asked Plotinus, "Is there something special about this coffee nook at Palau Fugit that enables this to happen, or can you come through elsewhere?" (PS = Plotinus speaking aloud, through me.)

PS: *"It's not the locale, it's the mindset."*

Me: *"Ah."*

PS: *"I can visit you elsewhere."*

Me: *"I look forward to that."*

Just then, our coffees arrived, and the connection ended. I wrote down the exchange in my Notes app.

Gary and I pondered the ramifications of Plotinus "listening in." Or maybe it wasn't like that. Maybe we are all aspects of Consciousness experiencing itself. We think we are separate, but we are all expressions of the One Source. In which case, there is no eavesdropping: There is only all-knowing Consciousness always present everywhere.

I knew Plotinus would have a lot to say on this topic; one of his oft-quoted lines is something about "the alone to the Alone." But I didn't want to read what he had to say on the topic—I wanted him to tell me.

That evening, I sat in front of my meditation altar in my office/workshop/meditation space. It was a simple altar, a low square table covered with a neutral-colored silk cloth. On the table were a candle, a few pictures, and several objects of importance to me.

I honored the seven directions (sky above, land below, East, South, West, North, and the center within), lit the candle, lit a stick of palo santo wood and wafted the smoke around me, took a few deep, centering breaths (breathing in, holding, breathing out longer than I breathed in), and invited Plotinus to join me and have a conversation.

I had a notebook and pen ready to write anything down. I devised the following code. P = Plotinus communicating to me silently. PS = Plotinus speaking aloud, through me. Me = me, Elyn. Brackets [ ] = feelings or words not spoken but understood, or else added later for clarification when I transcribed my notes into a Word file. A line of three dots (…) = a momentary pause.

Soon I felt his energetic presence.

Me: "Welcome, Plotinus."

P: "I am pleased to be here with you."

Me: "I'm a little uncomfortable channeling your voice aloud, as opposed to silent inner contact."

P: "I needed to get your attention and for you to know I'm real. That's why I 'came through' you."

Me: "Why me?"

P: "I saw your [your and Gary's] lights shining and heard your questions. Questions I spent my life answering. I will help you as I can."

Me: "Thank you."

P: "Most of my answers are in my written work, which now you have been guided to."

Me: "So you won't be 'coming through' again?" [I'm sad at the prospect.]

P: "I will, but you will need to ask me questions."

Me: "What was your bowel disease?"

P: "You call it, I believe, IBS or OBS."

Me: "Did you suffer much?"

P: "Occasionally. But I learned I suffered less if I resigned myself to it."

[I felt 'surrender.']

Me: "How did you reach your conclusions?"

P: "After much study. Then they seemed obvious."

Me: "Why didn't you marry?"

P: "It seemed superfluous. I had no interest in human relationships that would take me away from my time for work."

Me: "But you raised [other people's] children?"

[Some aristocratic friends and students, as they approached death, appointed Plotinus as guardian of their male and female children. He conscientiously fulfilled his obligations under Roman law and took impeccable care of their education and property.]

P: "Of course. I love humanity. I didn't want to be embroiled in complex male/female [spousal] relationships. But of course, I love humanity—after all, we are all ONE, all part of the One, so I did what I could to be of assistance to those children."

Me: "Explain your phrase, 'alone to Alone.'"

P: "It is complicated and simple. We think we are alone, isolated, apart—but we are not. We are all part of the ONE—the ONE that is the Only Thing. Alone in the universe in that sense of meaning—there is nothing but It [the One]."

Me: "Thank you. I'll ponder that. ... I'm a bit tired now."

P: "I will come again whenever you request. I'm always here and eager to help an aspect of the ONE."

Me: "Goodbye and thank you."

I looked at the clock. The session had lasted about 20 minutes. I was tired. Conversing with a spirit from another realm took a lot of energy. Suzanne Giesemann had explained in one of her mediumship courses that we have to raise our vibration, and they have to lower theirs. It requires energy from both sides.

I had written to two friends, asking them for input into my disconcerting experience. Cheryl Page is a scientist, medium, teacher, and author who had connected with me some years before. She had been guided to contact me by a message she had received from Mary Magdalene about "following the

Milky Way"—which just happens to be the name of my travel narrative about my pilgrimage on the Camino de Santiago*. It was Cheryl who suggested we study with Suzanne Giesemann to learn about mediumship.

Elizabeth Diamond Rose is a professional psychic, transformational coach, spiritual alchemist, healer, astrologer, and visionary. We had connected with her a year ago during an Angelic Reiki* training course. I figured of all the people I knew, those two would be able to give me helpful feedback.

I checked my messages. They had replied almost immediately. Both were excited for me and very encouraging. They didn't find my experience at all strange; after all, they swam in these waters all the time. It felt reassuring to have their support.

Friday, 1 March 2024

A busy day. I had my weekly acupuncture and lymphatic drainage treatments; we shopped at our neighborhood grocery store. And, as usual, we went to Gipsy bar.

From the pressure on my right temple, I could tell Plotinus wanted to talk. I wasn't up for it, so I mentally asked him to wait until later. He withdrew.

Gary told me he had dreamed the night before about interviewing Plotinus. Not only was I channeling Plotinus, but he was visiting Gary in dreamtime!

In his dream, Gary had asked Plotinus how he pronounced his name. Plotinus answered that there are several different ways, each with a different syllable accented. (My online search later showed his name is pronounced either PLA-ti-nus or Pla-TYN-oos, with the second more popular.)

Gary had asked him how well the available English translations of *The Enneads* represented his writings, and if he would change what he'd written, and if so, what changes would he make?

Either Gary didn't receive any answers, or he didn't remember them. Dreams are like that. And waking from dreams is like that.

Sometimes it felt like the life we were now living was a dream.

Then Gary and I started talking again about our next book project, *Adventures of Everyday Mystics*.

Gary said, "We've taken on this project, and they—the Spirit Realm—are going to help us. It's obvious! Plotinus 'came through' to help when we started talking about it. This means that the universe is not indifferent. And it means that spirit beings in the other realms have volition. They can make choices to be engaged with humans."

Our attention shifted to the background music. U2 was singing "Still haven't found what I'm looking for…."

"… I have spoke with the tongue of angels/ I have held the hand of a devil/… But I still haven't found what I'm looking for/ I believe in the kingdom come/ Then all the colors will bleed into one/ But I still haven't found what I'm looking for…"

My ears perked up. "Tongue of angels"—was that channeling? And "all colors bleed into one"? Unity. The song wasn't just a random selection, it had a message to convey to us.

I noticed Plotinus was eager to come through—I could feel the pressure on my right temple and my mouth expanding. Gary saw the change in me. I started looking off in the distance, then my face shifted.

I asked Plotinus to wait until later.

> Plotinus spoke through me: "Stop wasting time!"

> Gary: "We aren't, we are doing the work!"

Plotinus withdrew.

Gary understood from this that we were to be the bridge to bring through the information that Plotinus wanted to share. And that Plotinus was *very* eager for us to get started. He felt pushy—but then, who knew how long he'd been waiting to communicate through someone on this plane.

We both knew this was a shared project. I was the one doing the channeling, but I needed Gary's support, encouragement, and advice. We had different tasks. Bringing Plotinus's message to the world would take both of us.

Late afternoon when we were back home, I returned to my meditation space. I settled in with a notebook and pen.

PS: "You are wasting time at the hotel bar."

Me: "But I do meditate!"

PS: "We see that, but you can do more. It will help you focus."

[I start to feel very warm in my chest and face, perhaps from the energy of channeling.]

Me: "What is it like on the Other Side?"

P: "It is more beautiful than I had ever imagined."

Me: "I need time to adjust to your presence."

PS: "I see that. We will help you."

Me: "Thank you."

PS: "We do not want to frighten you, but we have much to say."

Me: "I will try to bring it through, but I need to have my boundaries respected." [This refers to my request that, in general, he not speak through me as forcefully as the first time in the Gipsy café-bar. And that, when I ask him to leave, he would do so.]

PS: "Have I not done so?"

Me: "You have. ... You're telling me I need to meditate more?"

PS: "With more focus."

Me: "How can I gain that focus? [My mind wanders.]"

PS: "We will help you."

[I have a mental image of Plotinus guiding me by holding my hand or shoulder. I 'see' (with my mind's eye) a sort of foggy, semi-translucent shape that I identify as someone in a white toga or draped garment of some kind.]

Me: "OK. How do I know it's you, really?"

P: "Who else would it be? Remember, I came to you and gave you my name."

Me: "It's true, you did already show me. ... Can you tell me something about magic?"

[I knew from skimming some biographical information online that Plotinus had opinions about and experience with magic. I had avoided reading any details.]

PS: "Magic: manipulating the One Field of All. It's very easy to do and not worth doing."

Me: "How did you deflect the spells [directed at you]?"

P: "Just as we are all One, we are also separate. Remembering the separation negates the spell."

[I see an image of 'foggy' arms and hands held in front of Plotinus's 'foggy' torso, creating an invisible shield.]

Me: "Thank you. What is it you want to tell us?"

P: "My very presence affirms your questions."

Me: "Were you in pain before you died?"

P: "Yes and no. The soul does not suffer; the body does."

Me: "And the snake [that showed up] at your deathbed?" [I had read about this on Google.]

P: "A visual reminder of eternal life. I will go now so as not to weary you."

Me: "Thank you. I look forward to your return visit. Perhaps tomorrow?"

P: "Perhaps."

10 minutes of channeling.

As I reviewed my notes, I realized I had changed the topic abruptly several times. Was it because my thought process shifted while channeling—in other words, maintaining a logically consistent conversation wasn't part of the process? Or was it because I wanted to avoid Plotinus's suggestions for enhancing my focus? I didn't know the answer, but I recognized that I needed to be more attentive.

Shortly afterward, I did my daily practice of sending distant healing. I "heard" Plotinus's silent voice say, *"I will be part of your Guiding Force."* What an unusual choice of words: not guide, but guiding force. Then I saw an image in my mind's eye of a horse wearing eye blinders (AKA blinkers); the blinders limited its field of vision to what was ahead of it and kept it from being distracted. I had a sense of being held steady on both sides and better able to hold my focus. What a useful image.

Thank you, Plotinus.

Saturday, 2 March 2024

Gary had a dream/daydream that he would videotape me channeling Plotinus. My immediate reaction was, NO WAY! I couldn't imagine channeling in public. It was difficult enough to tell people that this was happening, let alone have someone watch me do it. But who knew about the future: definitely, not me. I never would have imagined what had already transpired.

We went to Girona's municipal market for our Saturday grocery shopping. Within minutes, I had to flee—I couldn't deal with so much chaos. Gary suggested perhaps Plotinus was with us and in shock from the tumult. I mentally asked and got "Yes."

I needed a break from channeling. It was disconcerting and disorienting to experience this interpenetration of different realms.

During my afternoon meditation, I did a brief check-in with Plotinus addressing my feelings.

> P: *"It's impossible to lead a contemplative life [exposing yourself to] the kind of intense energy in the market."* And, he added, *"You need to find ways to be more contemplative."*

I understood that he was urging me to be less busy-busy and spend more time in quiet meditation and centered thoughtfulness. I thanked him and said I was grateful for his presence.

Later that day, we had a long FaceTime conversation with our dear friend Marchiene about contemplative versus engaged mysticism. Marchiene is a wonderfully gifted, extremely well-read, retired interfaith minister and author. She was living in the US, but we FaceTimed with her every two weeks. We were grateful for our friendship.

Marchiene wasn't at all surprised that I was channeling Plotinus. She reminded us that Gary and I had spent years visiting sacred sites, writing books about powerful places, exploring different kinds of energies, and studying distant healing modalities like Healing Touch and Angelic Reiki. In other words, we had lots of experience opening up to the other realms.

She asked why I was uncomfortable with channeling Plotinus.

I said, "Because it is very unsettling to have this different voice come out of my mouth rather than have a silent inner conversation."

Then I laughed. Only a few days earlier, the idea of conversing silently with a spirit who had died 1700 years ago would have been shocking. Now it was only the aspect of physically channeling his voice that I found uncomfortable. How quickly I had adapted to the "new normal."

Sunday, 3 March 2024

During meditation, I used my new horse-blinder tool to help me focus. Then I talked with Plotinus briefly. I asked him if he had any advice about Gary's blood pressure spikes. He said that was not his area of expertise. He suggested perhaps Asclepius (the Greek god of healing) or someone else (I didn't catch the name) could help.

I thought about it and decided that having a health consultation with a disembodied being was probably not the most reliable way to go. We would stick with Western medicine for now and with Stephanie, Gary's daughter, a talented medical intuitive and Pranic Healing* practitioner, living in Australia. She had been our very helpful go-to energy healer for years.

We had coffee with our friend Nigel, a retired biochemist and highly successful entrepreneur. He was curious about "the other realms" but had spent a lifetime thoroughly steeped in scientific materialism. He was working diligently to expand his worldview, but it was challenging.

Hesitantly, I told him about spontaneously channeling Plotinus.

Nigel replied, "If I didn't know you as well as I do, I'd think you were cuckoo—but I do know you. You are both reasonable, intelligent people with PhDs."

I told him how unsettling it had been, a real upheaval to my worldview.

He wanted to know what the goal was of these difficult, disturbing, destabilizing journeys we were both experiencing. I think he wanted to have a goal to make it all worthwhile.

I replied, "Goal? I have no idea. It's a process."

I told Gary later, "We are living the *Adventures of Everyday Mystics* book project. You are researching various topics, and I'm having the direct experience!"

Often on Sunday we watched the latest YouTube episode of Suzanne Giesemann's "Messages of Hope." This time, Suzanne sounded like she was channeling Plotinus. She started by explaining that the spirit guides on the other side eagerly wait for us to invite them to participate in our lives. She also talked about how we are all One, but we think we are separate. When asked whether the soul suffers at death, the answer her spirit-group Sanaya gave was "No." The body may be in pain, but the soul never suffers. Sounded familiar.

Gary felt awe and gratitude that Plotinus was going to help us. In exchange, we had the responsibility to accurately represent what he had to say. I was doing my best.

Gary had been telling me for some time that one of us might be "across the veil" before we finished the *Everyday Mystics* project because he was born in 1937 and I was born in 1946. But now he realized that *Plotinus* was the one across the veil, not one of us.

Gary told me that some scientists were trying to expand their worldview to include realms beyond the physical. Their approach is called "Beyond Physicalism." But some of them seemed to have an unconscious bias that the other dimensions were passive, empty, not inhabited. In other words, they were willing to consider that perhaps we could experience non-physical realms, but there was nothing there with volition—the ability to make choices—to be engaged with.

We knew from credible channelers and mediums that the other realm (or is it realms?) is full of spiritual beings who want to help us and who are helping. Just like Suzanne said in her YouTube program. They are eager to support us, guide us, watch over us. They patiently wait for us to notice them. Synchronicity* is one way they make their guidance known.

Certainly, our experiences over the last few years (for example, our moving back to Girona) had given us the very strong impression that we were supported and guided by beings/intelligence/consciousness from beyond this dimension. These beings often used synchronicities to get our attention. And now we had this channeling experience—evidence of engagement and volition coming from the Other Side. The other realms weren't empty. They were full of conscious, non-physical beings that could, and did, interact with us.

Our decision to move back to Girona after being gone for five years resulted from a series of synchronicities. We were having coffee with a friend in a seaside town in Portugal, where we were living at the time. Gary suddenly started talking about my unfinished novel, *The Key to the Kabbalist Garden*, set in a garden in Girona. He went on and on about how I needed to finish it. I hadn't thought of it in years and had no idea where to go with the story. He vehemently insisted (which was unlike him) that we go back to Girona and do research. Puzzled, I replied, "Well, maybe."

Two days later I received a Messenger text from Nuri, a Chilean woman I hadn't heard from in 53 years. 53 years! Because my name had changed from Ellen Reynolds to Elyn Aviva, she wasn't sure I was the same person she had known briefly in Ames, Iowa, but if I was—

I replied, I was—same person, different name—and I was glad to be back in touch. But why was she contacting me after all these years?

She said, "The night before, I had a dream. A woman in white came to me and told me I needed to remember Ellen Reynolds. I woke up and tried to find you on the internet without success. Then I remembered your mother's last name (Feinberg)—she taught me English as a second language—and I thought I'd look for you using your maiden name. And I found you!"

I asked Nuri if she had any idea why she might have been urged to find me.

Nuri replied, "Well, I noticed in your bio that you used to live in Girona. My father and grandfather came from Girona!"

A Girona connection? I thought Nuri was Chilean. Nuri explained her father and grandfather had fled the Spanish dictator Franco and gone to Chile, where she was born and raised.

Well, that was an amazing synchronicity. But it was only the first of many.

After the Messenger exchange, I decided maybe we should go back to Girona for a visit. So I opened my Booking app. But instead of listing hotels, it listed apartments. That was odd. And even odder, the first apartment was Roses Apartments: "Rarely listed on Booking, so grab it while you can!" Roses Apartments were located two blocks from the Garden of the Angels, the location of my unfinished novel. Then Vueling Airlines sent an email with a special deal on flights from Lisbon to Barcelona (near Girona) for the next three weeks.

I booked the apartment, made flight reservations, and we returned to Girona. As soon as we arrived, we felt like we had come home. Synchronicities continued, and we realized without doubt that we were being guided to return. So we did. And we have not regretted it.

Sitting in front of my meditation altar, Gary and I started to make a list of questions to ask Plotinus, even if we had already received partial answers to some of them. These included:

Do we *really* come here with a soul plan—an idea that makes sense of suffering and injustice as something we agreed to before incarnating?

Is the universe passive/disengaged/observing/uncaring? Or is it active/participating/caring/loving? I thought I knew the answer already: Plotinus coming through me at that moment in the Gipsy Bar indicated to me that the answer was active/caring/participating. But I would ask again.

The question of evil in the world. Plotinus had said that to evolve, we have to experience duality, the range of good and evil. But I would ask again.

Is there really "life after life"? Continuity of consciousness? Do famous people continue to exist as personalities on the other side? Reputable mediums and channelers, and many rigorous researchers and near-death-experiencers, say "Yes." Plotinus coming through to me also seemed to answer this question with a definite "Yes." Unless it wasn't him but instead was some spirit disguised as him—but why would it do that? And if it was the latter, what difference would it make if it was Plotinus's spirit or a "concentration of energy" that somehow retained or expressed his personality? At any rate, I would ask again.

More questions. Do we simply have a limited perspective that keeps us from understanding the true nature of all that is? If we could see from that broader perspective, would we understand why people suffer and bad things happen? Do we have soul families? Is there spiritual guidance available for each of us? What's synchronicity got to do with it—or anything?

Monday, 4 March 2024

Gary and I sent Angelic Reiki to a friend. I visualized Plotinus's image of the blinkered horse, and it helped me keep my focus during the healing meditation.

Afterward, as I sat alone in meditation, I could "feel" Plotinus. When he showed up with my regular group of spirit guides, I started weeping.

After I recovered from being so emotional, I told him I would need to do my monthly Goddess Brigid/Saint Brigid practice. Several years earlier, I had committed to light a candle and read/pray/listen to music/focus on Brigid on the 4th of every month.

Plotinus informed me he didn't think that was very important. Worshipping deities was just not his thing. That led me to ask him the following.

> Me: "What do you think of gods and goddesses?"

> PS: "I don't think much. They are ephemeral. They take our focus away from the One True ONE. They can be helpful as an in-between or stopgap. There is no harm unless you take them seriously."

> Me: "Seriously?"

PS: "As the end point of Being."

Me: "How did you entertain yourself [when you were alive]?"

P: "I played board games."

Me: "What do you want us to know?"

PS: "That this realm where I am is real."

Me: "Tell me something I don't know." [I want more evidence.]

P: "Iambycus (sic) was a dirty man. He didn't bathe."

Me: "You didn't either." [I had read a little bit about Plotinus on Wikipedia.]

P: "I was allergic to water on my skin. I had massages."

Me: "I think that's enough for today. It's been 15 minutes, and I'm tired."

P: "One more observation—you, all of you, are cared for. We all watch over you."

Me: "Thank you."

I lit a candle and did my meditation for Brigid. As I sang along with YouTube songs dedicated to her, I thought about channeling Plotinus. I realized that my experience with Plotinus was what many worshippers of gods/goddesses were trying to accomplish: to connect with a real being in another dimension in order to have a relationship. And many of them believed they had succeeded. Who was I (knowing what I now knew) to question that?

As soon as I finished my time with Brigid, I looked for Iambycus on Google. I didn't find anyone with that precise spelling, but I found Iamblichus, which was certainly what Plotinus had said but I had misheard. Iamblichus was an Arab Neoplatonic philosopher who lived c. 245–c. 325 CE. He was the biographer of Pythagoras and—drum roll!—he studied under Porphyry of Tyre, who was the most important student of Plotinus. Porphyry edited and published Plotinus's writings, *The Enneads*.

Oooh.

This was another watershed moment, another piece of irrefutable evidence that Plotinus was real, not just a figment of my imagination. It was what Suzanne Giesemann calls "a gold nugget" or "NOE"—"No Other Explanation."

I wrote to some of my friends about the latest evidence.

Nigel replied, "'Curiouser and Curiouser,' said Alice."

Marchiene wrote, "That's pretty convincing proof. Have you asked him why he chose you for communication and why now?"

Another question to add to the growing list.

I had a long conversation with our skeptical but open-minded friend Tessa, a very wise, retired psychotherapist. No harm in having another reality check. I wrote down the conversation afterward. (During my long-ago fieldwork as an anthropologist, I had trained myself to remember much of what was said in a conversation and write it down afterward.)

Tessa thought my channeling Plotinus was fascinating and intriguing. She also hoped there was a way to have it go slow enough that I didn't end up feeling "very-not-good weird." I assured her he was respecting my boundaries and seemed like a nice guy. Even so, it was very unsettling to have my intellectually held beliefs about the afterlife (it made logical sense that it existed) suddenly become so directly, irrefutably validated.

Tessa also wondered why Plotinus came through now and to me. Gary and I thought it was because of the book project and that Plotinus wanted to help with some of the topics. Tessa loved the working title of the book, *Adventures of Everyday Mystics,* and the idea of a book including interviews with other people as well as our stories. Bringing mystical experiences "down to earth." Normalizing it, she said. And she said we were good at that—we'd been doing that kind of work for many years.

I realized with surprise that she was right. That was indeed what we've been doing with our Powerful Places Guidebooks series, my books on pilgrimage and journey, and my five novels. This was the culmination of our work over the years, gradually moving us further down this path without our realizing it.

How was I handling it? Tessa wondered.

I replied that it was fine if I didn't think about it! And that I was getting more accustomed to it.

In truth, channeling Plotinus blew apart my worldview—or rather, it required me to integrate a part of my worldview that I had kept in a closet for years. Continuity of consciousness—life after life—made logical sense. There was plenty of evidence in documented reports of NDEs* and reincarnation. They made sense, but I had no personal experience with them, so I couldn't affirm they were true. I had kept those possibilities in a (metaphorical) closet where they didn't have to confront the humanist, materialist worldview with which I had grown up.

Yes, I had studied mediumship with Suzanne and several others, but I didn't really want to talk to people "across the veil." I was curious, and I was looking for evidence. Now I wondered: Could my resistance to practicing mediumship have been because, if I succeeded, I would have to acknowledge life after life was real?

Tessa and I talked some more about why now, why me, why Plotinus? The book project. The questions we were asking. Our openness to exploring other realms.

Tessa observed that it was interesting that Plotinus chose to come through me, a cultural anthropologist by training. For over 50 years, my default stance had always been to be an anthropologist: observing and not judging, participating but not full-on "believing."

I often said when confronted with a belief system that didn't quite match mine, "It's their belief system—might not be mine, but I can't judge it. They think it's real; who am I to argue?" Now I realized that hidden behind this apparent open-mindedness was a kernel of condescending disbelief.

That was how I'd dealt with the afterlife channeling stuff—even Suzanne, in some sense, though I believed she really did bring through people from the afterlife. Talking with angels? Well, I hadn't had that experience, but if you think you do, who am I to judge?

Since my encounters with Plotinus, my deeply engrained observer stance was shredded. I could no longer (figuratively) hold the afterlife at arm's length.

What I still found so challenging was realizing that OH MY GOD they really are alive on the other side! Historic figures are still present and retain their personalities, their identities. How can that be, 1700 years or 3000 years or 50 years after they have passed over? Gary had suggested that on the Other

Side there is no time or space, so it didn't make any difference to them when "now" was. But that was something else I found very confusing.

Tessa wanted to know what it felt like to channel: for example, how I knew Plotinus was coming through. I told her I sensed a kind of pressure on my right temple, an awareness of a presence. I became still and listened inwardly. When he spoke through me, I felt my mouth cavity changing shape, which was how my voice became lower and I spoke with a light accent. When Plotinus spoke to me mentally, I just heard words. Well, not words per se—it was more like telepathic messages that I put into English. His native language was Greek, but he wasn't communicating in Greek. He communicated telepathically, without words.

And when I was tired or asked him to leave, he did. He respected my boundaries. He felt like a kind and courteous person.

Tessa asked if I felt an absence when he left. I didn't. I felt the lack of his presence/pressure on my right temple but nothing else.

Tuesday, 5 March 2024

During my weekly acupuncture treatment, Alina told me about the serious problems her son had with drug addiction. She had tried repeatedly over the years to help him, but without success. Alina wondered how her son's difficulties could be part of any divine plan. I responded that there's much we don't understand.

Then I took the risk of telling her about Plotinus. I told her Plotinus said that we are here to evolve spiritually, and we learn better from bad events than good. So maybe her son made a soul plan before reincarnating to experience abuse and addiction. Alina couldn't understand how that could be part of any divine plan. It made no sense that her son would have to suffer so.

Listening to her grief, I realized that it was easy to blithely say, "Maybe he agreed to this for some reason." But how do we know? I wondered if her son's soul plan included the plan that Alina would learn that she couldn't always make things better, and that trying to help could be counterproductive. If so, Alina hadn't learned that lesson yet.

I remembered the first time someone told me that people chose to be born into abusive situations as part of their soul plan. I was outraged. Talk about blaming the victim! Talk about trying to find something redeeming in what was a dreadful situation! And yet there I was, saying something like that to Alina. Was Plotinus just trying to give meaning to pointless suffering? Or was he able to see a much larger picture than Alina or I could see? I voted for the latter.

Alina was also upset because she always asked her "Inner Father" (a kind of paternal spirit guide) for guidance, and he had always been helpful, but the last time it seemed that the advice she was given was wrong. Which made her doubt her inner guidance. I wondered (silently) whether the advice she had received was intended to teach her a lesson she needed to learn.

When I told Gary about the conversation, he pointed out that when it comes to family and close friends, you must be really sure you're hearing inner guidance. It's too easy to mistake parental love or deep compassion—or a projection of your own feelings and hopes—for inner guidance. Discernment and due diligence are critical.

Later, I received a message from Nigel with his reflections about my channeling Plotinus. In summary (lightly edited):

"Here's what this experience of Elyn's suggests: Firstly, that deceased lives continue in an individuated form and can endure in that form for some 2,000 years. That is a big First! Second, that these deceased entities wish to interact with some living persons and give guidance and impart knowledge. Another big Second. Third, that we can meaningfully interact with these disembodied beings. Fourth, that there really exists this other realm of deceased souls. Another state. Another place. Fifth, that this realm is but a hair away from our realm. Accessible and even intrusive. Sixth, that all of us have immortality or at least a vastly extended mortality beyond life in the Soma.

"It is one thing to hypothesize it and quite another to experience it, albeit second-hand. Things are not what they seem to be. They exist whether we believe this or not. Is this unsettling or comforting? It defies the decrepitude of Soma and defies death. No small matter on each count. It will take some time to even begin to assimilate this shattering information. - Nigel"

I agree completely, Nigel!

Wednesday, 6 March 2024

Late-night thoughts last night: (1) My connection with Plotinus is like an etheric cord, the kind of cord we "cut" after sending Angelic Reiki to someone. We intentionally sever the energetic connection we have established. But I didn't want to cut the etheric cord with Plotinus. And I had a suspicion that the more we communicated, the thicker the cord would become, making our communication easier. I also knew that, at any time, if I wanted to, I could cut it.

I visited with Plotinus in my meditation space.

Me: "Hello."

P: "Hello."

Me: "You're back."

PS: "I said I would always be here."

Me: "I'm very grateful for your presence."

P: "Thank you."

Me: "I have a question. Why now? Why me?"

PS: "Because you are available and open. Because now is the time."

Me: "For what?"

PS: "To bring through, to make available the truth/knowledge about the Other Side."

Me: "Is there only one Other Side?"

PS: "Oh my no. There are multitudes."

Me: "Where do you reside?"

PS: "There is no address as such. No physical location. It is more a vibratory state of being, full of many creatures."

Me: "We call it the afterlife."

PS: "That is one name for it."

Me: "Do you communicate with other beings?"

PS: "Oh yes. We are all interconnected."

Me: "Do you know my guides?"

PS: "That is a complicated question. 'Knowing'—what does that mean?"

Me: "Interacting?"

PS: "With some, it depends on the vibrational frequency and 'overlap.'"

Me: "Do you talk to them?"

PS: "We do not talk to anyone. Not as you think of talking. We share frequencies, thought waves/expressions."

Me: "Can I communicate with others who have passed over?"

PS: "Of course. But it depends on the level of need. And mutual availability."

Me: "The Spirit World wants to help us evolve?"

PS: "Absolutely. Why else are we here but to evolve? We continue to evolve in the afterlife as well."

Me: "What does it mean to evolve?"

PS: "To purify our frequency. To become closer to the One."

Me: "Are there gods and goddesses where you are?"

P: "No. They are different frequencies, on a different path."

Me: "You are against worshipping them?"

P: "It is a misunderstanding to worship them. They lead nowhere but to themselves."

Me: "I honor and respect Brigid—healer, poet, wise woman—I call on her sometimes for support."

P: "In that way, you use her like [you use] me. You do not think of her as the 'be all and end all' of your devotion."

Me: "That's true. I honor her and find support."

P: "There is no harm in calling on higher powers to help us, as long as we don't confuse them with the Source of All, the One True Being. They too are from the—emanate from—the One True Being."

Me: "Thank you. I'm getting tired."

P: "I will withdraw. I am here whenever you request me to come."

Me: "Thank you so much. This has been an eye-opening, life-changing experience—and it continues to be."

P: "That's why I've come to you. So you can tell others—vouch for the reality of other beings, other dimensions, life after death, the ongoing existence of the Soul and personality."

Me: "Oh—that's a question I want to ask—the ongoing personality? Then how do you return to the Source?"

P: "All things pass, all things change. It takes time—but not time as you would know it. Best to leave that for another time." [He smiles. I don't see him, so I can't see him smiling, but I can feel it.]

Me: "Thank you. Bless you. Much gratitude."

20 minutes of channeling.

A little later, we had a short, spontaneous conversation:

Me: "Are you lonely ever?"

P: "Never."

Me: "Is there love [where you are]?"

P: "Love is all there is. Love is everywhere. Love is all around you—just like that song."

Later that afternoon, I suddenly realized that the so-called "fully contacted" mystery schools I'd heard about really *are* fully contacted! Maybe by a medieval Templar knight (as a friend of ours claimed about her anonymous mystery school), or a Renaissance scholar, or maybe by some other being who continues to exist "beyond the veil." Their claim is that a non-corporeal being had contacted the founder of the school and remained in contact to provide guidance and support from the Other Side. I'd always been skeptical of such assertions, but if I could be fully contacted by Plotinus, mystery school founders could be fully contacted as well.

Thursday, 7 March 2024

I emailed our psychic-healer-friend Elizabeth Diamond Rose to keep her posted on what was happening. She responded immediately. She recognized the importance of über-skeptical Nigel's openness to my experience.

She said, "It's wonderful to see the healing ripples spreading out around the world. This is one of the reasons I stay in my business-networking group. The people there would never have met me under the normal circumstances of their lives, nor would they have [accepted] what I do. But because they've gotten to know, like, and trust me, they come and get the healing they need. They have a very special place in my heart as a result because their coming [to me, a psychic healer] is truly a miracle!"

My reply: "Hurrah for miracles! It is indeed a wonder-full world, beyond amazing. Gary and I have just dipped our toes (well, maybe our feet) in it—not yet fully immersed the way you are. Speaking of support, I may need some help myself—Gary has these great ideas about me channeling Plotinus—like, let's make a video and link it to our *Adventures of Everyday Mystics* book! Or, his spirit guide Clem and Plotinus could have a tape-recorded conversation. Etc.

"I told him his suggestions make me feel like a trained dog on exhibit. And vulnerable. I know that's an overreaction, so it makes me wonder about my past lives—what might have happened to me regarding being psychic or something in the past and either put on display or punished publicly.... Any ideas? Love, E"

Elizabeth Diamond Rose replied: "That is not true at all [that you have just dipped your toes in it]. You are totally immersed in it. Look at all your individual and collective achievements and the contributions to the world that you have made. Not to mention your charming company! I think this reluctance is a combination of wound and you wanting to be a free spirit. I like his ideas—and maybe you do, too—but first, we have to see if there is a pathway to get you there. Schedule a session with me. Much love, EDR"

I replied: "Great! Very affirming. I thought I was still just barely keeping my head above water, but it looks like I'm already submerged!! I must remember to breathe. Will schedule. Thank you. Love, E"

Saturday, 9 March 2024

Channeling session. I could feel Plotinus was there. I felt a slight pressure on my right temple and my mouth cavity expanded.

PS: "Hello, Dear Little One."

Me: "Hi, Plotinus. I'm so happy to be here with you again."

PS: "It is my pleasure."

Me: "Please, can you tell me why I've found your visits so disconcerting? I want to celebrate your visits [not be unsettled]."

PS: "That is good. [Pause] When two realities touch, sparks fly. It gives a shock, like touching a hot stove. Once you are prepared, there are no more sparks."

Me: "I want to believe this is real—I do believe you are real."

PS: "I'm not real like things on your plane of existence. I'm real in a different way, on the Soul Plane. Of course, it's different."

Me: "Tell me something I don't know."

P: "Tomorrow will be sunny." [I added, with a smile, part of the day.]

Me: "Do you want to talk with Gary's [spirit] guide Clem?"

P: "It would be complicated. We can try, if Gary will serve as Clem's vehicle."

Me: "Vehicle. I like that expression."

P: "Thank you."

Me: "Is there anything you want to tell me?"

P: "Just do the work. Tell people about the true nature of reality."

Me: "I promise I will. But—what *is* the true nature of reality?"

P: "Much more complicated than your scientists think with their silly foolish measurements of nothing very important. They think they are so smart, but they are like children wandering in a forest and only seeing what's on the path before them instead of looking up to the treetops."

Me: "Wow. That's a pretty strong condemnation."

P: "And very appropriate! It angers me—well, it would if I still had such emotions. Now I see them as children stumbling around and exulting at each new find like a child picking up a pretty stone and exclaiming, 'Look what I found! It's mine and it is so pretty!'"

Me: "What can be done?"

P: "Get the truth out. Write your books."

Me: "Books?"

P: "Oh yes, you have another one to write, very different from this current project."

Me: "Tell me more?"

P: "In good time."

[I vaguely recalled that Elizabeth Diamond Rose had said something about book projects when we met her nine months ago, but I hadn't believed her.]

Me: "Are we just puppets doing the bidding of higher powers?"

P: "Not at all. You have free will to say yes or no. It's not as free as you imagine because your choices are conditioned, but you have choice. You decide what lessons to experience in your life. We simply help you accomplish this by orchestrating opportunities."

Me: "Whew. That's a lot to take in."

P: "I don't want to tire you. Perhaps it's time to leave."

Me: "I'm so very grateful. ... Oh—I have a question."

P: "All right."

Me: "Why was I so upset and triggered by Gary's suggestion about recording you, or you being interviewed by Clem?"

P: "Your sovereignty felt like it was being attacked. Not many people will understand this work. You must use discernment."

Me. "Thank you. I could imagine a different response of YES!! Eager to tell the world Plotinus is still alive!"

P: "How does that feel?"

Me: "Energizing! To share the Truth of life after life, the continuity of the soul ..."

P: "Yes. That's it. But practice discretion in how you share it. You are used to flying under the radar. You feel exposed by Gary's suggestions."

Me: "Yes, that's it."

P: "Do not worry. All in good time. Everything is going as planned."

Me: "There we are again: 'as planned.' Who or what is planning?"

P: "We will leave that for another day. I'll leave you now."

Me: "Thank you thank you. I CELEBRATE your coming to me!"

P: "Goodbye for now."

23 minutes of channeling.

Immediately, I did my daily 20 minutes of sending healing and blessings. It felt like time was dragging. Interesting how 23 minutes with Plotinus flew by, but 20 minutes of sending blessings felt like a very long time.

I was so tired. Took an hour-long nap at noon. These exchanges were draining. Not a complaint, not Plotinus's fault, just the nature of exchanging between dimensions. I was sure I would get stronger and less affected over time.

Tuesday, 12 March 2024

Gary had a knock-your-socks-off Zoom healing/guidance session with Elizabeth Diamond Rose. We went for coffee at Gipsy afterward for him to process the experience. Elizabeth Diamond Rose had "brought through"/envisioned a grand choral composition by him, libretto by me, to be sung in cathedrals, etc., to raise the frequency of people whenever they heard it. Gary told her he was not sure he was up for that. He had stopped composing 30 years ago, and he was pretty sure he was not interested in getting back into it.

(Back story: Gary is a Distinguished Professor Emeritus of Music Theory and Composition and an award-winning composer. He stopped composing when he took early retirement, 30 years ago, just before we got married. He had only composed one short commissioned piece since then. When asked about composing again, he would refer to his years as a composer as "a previous life." It was not one he ever wanted to revisit.)

I told Gary that doing this music project was up to him. Take up the challenge or not, I had no opinion one way or the other. Elizabeth Diamond Rose might bring through ideas from the Spirit Realm, but that didn't mean we were obliged to do them.

Suddenly, I felt Plotinus wanting to chime in. I said "No," then "OK."

> Plotinus said something like, "While you are here in a body, you can do those things. Once you pass over, you won't compose music. Take advantage of your skills and gifts while you are alive—and you are still very much alive!"

Much to ponder, including the source of creativity. There were questions to ask Plotinus: for example, why they didn't compose music. Did they make art?

Gary had always composed by entering an altered state of consciousness. He would hypnotize himself or set a musical intention before going to sleep. When he awoke, he would have the beginning of (or part of) a composition. This was the secret method he had used since he had started studying composition at the university.

Now that I was channeling Plotinus, Gary suddenly wondered about his lifelong composition method. Who or what had been giving him information from the Other Side, the Imaginal—not the imaginary—Realm? (The Imaginal Realm* is a space/place where great creative potential exists.)

In a dream, Gary saw himself watching himself composing. But was that him? Where did the ideas come from? In all his years as a successful composer, he'd never wondered about the process: it worked, so he didn't ask. Now he wondered.

As did I. When I wrote novels, I would wake up with an image of a scene that I would then write into being. Sometimes characters showed up whom I later met in real life. Often characters did things I never planned. Sometimes I provided information I hadn't known was real but verified later.

For example, in *The Journey – A Novel of Pilgrimage and Spiritual Quest*, at one point, the narrator goes to a Tarot reader. To write that part of the novel, I would shuffle my Tarot deck and pull one or more cards. I would briefly consult a few introductory Tarot guidebooks and write what came to me. I later realized that the storyline had unfolded according to what I had described in the cards. People who read the novel complimented my ability to read Tarot so well—but, in fact, I didn't and I can't.

In my novel *The Question – A Magical Fable,* the main character goes to a seer who uses a variety of Tarot and oracle decks. I would pull a card from one of the five decks I had on my desk, look at it, and write a story about what I saw. A few years later, I discovered that many of the cards I had used in the novel didn't look quite the way I had described them. I realized that I must have channeled the information. But where did it come from? The same place as Gary's compositions, the Imaginal Realm?

Thursday, 14 March 2024

I had two very powerful dreams. Both had an identical subject: music related to the theme, 'We are an extension of the One True Being.'" In the first dream, I was standing before a crowd of people in a huge conference room. I started singing, naming all the fish/animals in the sea, including mammals, then the land animals, including amphibians, and the birds in the sky. I woke up and realized I had forgotten to include plants, so I went back into the dream and included them. I urgently told the group, "We must sing all their names so the world doesn't end [in an Apocalypse]—We are an extension of the One True Being." I passionately called out, "Sing with me! Name all the living creatures!"

I woke up shaking from the dream's intensity. Then I went back to sleep and had a second, somewhat different dream with the same song and words as the central theme.

I woke up again. Following the dream techniques I had learned from Robert Moss's Active Dreamwork, I wrote down everything I could recall in the small notebook next to the bed.

I remembered that Elizabeth Diamond Rose had said we were being asked by Spirit to create powerful music to help raise the frequency/vibration of people on the planet. My dream certainly seemed like a confirmation of that.

While I had been dreaming, Gary had been muttering and twitching in bed beside me. Once he woke up, he told me he had dreamt about a musical composition for chorus and orchestra, performed in a Romanesque or Gothic cathedral with lots of reverberation. He heard clickings and hissings, every kind of sound the human body can make to sound like living creatures. He also heard singing, with silent pauses for the sounds to reverberate.

When I told him my dream, he realized the sounds he had heard were humans making the sounds of the animals/birds/snakes/etc. whose names I was calling out in my dream.

We looked at each other in shock. We had had overlapping dreams. We had literally shared a dream about creating an event that included the sounds and names of animals, birds, serpents—of all life itself. And it was urgent. And it was very important.

Reader, take a deep breath. Let what happened sink in. Gary and I had a shared dream! I dreamt the words and storyline, and he dreamt the sounds.

This made perfect sense since, in waking life, I am a writer and he is a composer. But—how could this be? Clearly, Spirit (whatever that was) had presented us with a project.

We sat down together at my meditation altar, preparing to send Angelic Reiki to several friends. But before we could start, Gary began envisioning what the performance/music would be like, including a narrator (MC), a chorus, and audience participation.

I suddenly felt very light-headed. I held up my hand for Gary to stop talking, and I started channeling a deep voice with an indeterminant accent, like Plotinus's.

> It said: "We thank you for taking on this challenge. We will help facilitate the performance. We thank you for saying 'yes.'"
>
> I asked [I was learning fast!]: "Who is 'we'?"
>
> They said: "You are not ready to hear our names. We are your guides and helpers. We are extensions of the One True Being."

First Plotinus, and now a group? This channeling stuff was getting out of hand.

I WhatsApped Elizabeth Diamond Rose because she had first mentioned a music project. I told her about our dreams and asked who had spoken through me. She said it's a collective that includes Plotinus. A kind of stacking of entities, including angels. She said it will become clearer over time. I hoped so.

She also said, "When we are in alignment with our purpose, the synchronicities keep coming—and keep getting bigger, bolder, and louder!"

Saturday, 16 March 2024

A discombobulating morning—numerous photos kept coming in on WhatsApp, interrupting everything I tried to do. Bing Bing Bing! STOP IT ALREADY!

I felt stressed and frustrated. We needed to go to the market before it got crowded and I got overwhelmed, but it was getting late. I hadn't done my morning practice, including talking with Plotinus. Gary also got upset, and his blood pressure went up (not badly this time, thank goodness). I/we needed a reset!

We went shopping. It was good to walk to the market, get fresh air, a change of focus. On the way home with our heavily laden shopping cart, we stopped at Gipsy at Palau Fugit. As if we didn't have enough going on already.

Plotinus wanted to come through, so I said, "OK." I started my iPhone voice-memo app.

> Me: "Gary asked about observing himself composing in Dreamtime. Is this lucid dreaming? Something about the hypnogogic state? Or was he traveling into the Imaginal Realm?"
>
> PS: "I can help you with this question. You are coexisting in several dimensions. [Gary's] so-called self was observing [Gary's] so-called self, composing in another dimension. [Pause] We are watching over you."
>
> Me: "Who is 'we'?"
>
> PS: "We are not ready to tell you yet."
>
> Gary: "I send gratitude, Plotinus."
>
> Me: "Thank you. We appreciate your help."
>
> PS: "You are welcome."

Gary's so-called self, observing Gary's so-called self, composing in another dimension? That took some pondering. We finally concluded that meant that part of Gary was here, in this plane, but another part of Gary (part of his soul?) was somewhere else—on the Other Side, in another dimension where "that" self was composing. It was a hard concept to wrap our heads around, but that seemed to be what Plotinus was saying.

Suddenly we became aware of the background music playing in Gipsy. Synchronicity struck again! We'd started noticing the music that was playing in Gipsy. It often seemed targeted to our conversation. Were we just making meaning out of random events, drawing lines between unrelated occurrences? That would be the skeptic's response, but who knew? It happened often, and the more we noticed, the more it happened.

There's something called "confirmation bias" that asserts people search for, interpret, and recall information that supports their previous beliefs and values. That's used as an explanation to minimize the significance of synchronicity. In other words, the aptness of the music wasn't a meaningful event, it was just observer bias. But what if, instead of confirmation bias, paying attention attracts/draws more similar occurrences—more synchronicities—and it's a matter not of bias but of becoming more aware? And it was a way for spirit guides to nudge us or communicate?

We (and many others) have noticed that spirits seem to be able to manipulate electronics. We've had some strange experiences, and we've heard stories of how they turn on radios to the perfect song, leave messages on cellphones or answering machines, turn on the television in the middle of the night, or make meaningful photos pop up on someone's cellphone. Very weird, but it happens a lot.

So—back to the synchronicities of the music in Gipsy.

The first song was by Johnny Cash, "One love, one life." "We're one but we're not the same … We get to carry each other… love is the highest law." It sounded like a message from Plotinus about all is love.

Next song: "I thought I knew what I had to do …" Hah! We thought we were writing a book, but now we were doing a musical project.

The third: "Keep on the sunny side of life!" —the Carter Family. A great reminder after our rocky start this morning.

Gary laughed. "Plotinus is a DJ!"

I sensed Plotinus chuckling.

Later that afternoon, we FaceTimed with our retired interfaith-minister friend Marchiene. She knew a bit about Plotinus but had wanted to learn more. She found references to him in a classic anthology of philosophical/theological quotes by Dorothy Philips, Ed., *The Choice is Always Ours*. She read a quote; it referred directly to the questions we had been asking.

As to the possible music project based on our shared dream, Marchiene said to Gary, "You are a channel for this musical project. Don't worry about being 86 years old—"

Gary said, "Almost 87!"

Marchiene urged, "You can you still do it—just let it flow through you!"

Marchiene stressed the importance of Gary using his musical gifts, and she reminded him she'd been saying for years that he should compose again. She felt vindicated and very excited by this new development.

On another topic, Marchiene was curious about Plotinus's connection to Egypt. He was born in Egypt and found his teacher, Ammonius Saccas, in Alexandria. She wondered if my long-time interest in Egypt and Thoth, the god of learning and writing, had some connection with Plotinus.

She also wondered if Plotinus had a Sufi* connection. (Years ago, Gary and I had been part of the Sufi Order International, a branch of Sufism brought to the West by Hazrat Inayat Khan. The Order did not require members to be Muslims and honored all major world traditions. I had just learned that some Sufi philosophy was Neoplatonic—in other words, Sufism owed a lot to Plotinus.)

I restated to Gary and Marchiene what I understood about the musical project: What was most necessary was to raise the vibration of people on the planet—for people to realize we are all ONE—not separate, not hating, not separated from each other. It was not just about music or sound, it was about being ONE. The message I had been given in my dream was, "We are extensions of the One True Being."

After our conversation, I went to my office to have some private meditation time. I was tired, but I'd promised Plotinus I would talk to him. I needed to keep my promise.

Me: "What do you do for 'alone time'?"

P: "Ah. Remember my famous line, 'alone to the Alone'? 'Alone time' is a meaningless concept on 'this' side [the Other Side]: Here there is no time, no space as you understand it. And we are all interconnected. But we also maintain our separateness. Like waves in the ocean, or rays of sunlight. What does it mean to be alone? Why do you require it? Because your frequencies are not in [time? sync?] with those of another. It is your mythology that you must have 'alone time.' You mean [by that] the time to recover your equilibrium, your vibrational frequency's wholeness and balance, after being subjected to discordant, inharmonic frequencies. That is all it is.

We have no need for such in our dimension. All is harmonious—and what isn't, is 'healed'—re-tuned into harmony."

Me: *"I'm so grateful for your support, your visits—all you share."*

P: *"I am eager to do so. I have waited until you were ready to hear me and believe."*

Me: *"Yes, it's taken a while. [Most of my life!]"*

P: *"All things in their proper time. It is not too late. Remember: Now is the time; the time is now."*

Me: *[Smiling because that line is in my novel* The Question – A Magical Fable*] "What advice do you have for me? I got so stressed this morning."*

P: *"Yes, you went unconscious. You forgot who you truly are: One Being. You got sucked into the stresses of daily life. Take a deep breath. Step back. Notice when you start to feel jangled and step back, stop the action. Right then. That will help."*

Me: *"Thank you—I'll try to remember! ... Who is 'we' [the group that came through]?"*

P: *[Smiling] "You can ask often, but until you are ready, you will not be told."*

Me: *"Should I stop asking?"*

P: *"It doesn't matter. Ask, don't ask. It makes no difference."*

Me: *"OK. ... How many dimensions are there?"*

P: *"That's like asking for the sound of an orange or the taste[buds] of a cockatoo. It's meaningless. They overlap and interpenetrate."*

Me: *"Are there parallel lives?"*

P: *"Not exactly, although somewhat. The problem is with your basic idea of separation. They are not separate, so they are not parallel. Rather, they are co-existing."*

Me: *"Hmmm."*

P: *"It really is unimportant. Just breathe."*

Me: "Thank you. And thank you for all your help and support on this music project."

P: "I have waited a long time for the moment to be ripe—not a long time in my time, because I don't exist in your kind of time, but a long time in your time."

Me: "I think I'd better go now… I need to do my healing practice."

P: "I am always here for you. Bless you."

Me: [Surprised] "Thank you!!!"

20 minutes.

Monday, 18 March 2024

I asked in meditation, "What's going on with all this Egyptian stuff? Is it related to Plotinus? Marchiene thinks so."

I had a sudden flashback to an event in 2020. Thoth (the ancient Egyptian ibis-headed god of learning and writing) appeared unexpectedly, totally unbidden, in my meditation. He challenged me to learn about the five Platonic solids and sacred geometry. So I did.

Historically, the Egyptian deity Thoth later merged with the Greek god Hermes. The syncretic figure, Hermes Trismegistus, was considered the founder of Hermeticism*. Hermeticism and Neoplatonism shared some similar philosophies. This was yet another connection between my contacts with beings from the Other Side.

Suddenly I was sure Thoth was part of my spiritual collective. A god? Pretty shocking! Who else? Was Elen of the Ways, the ancient reindeer-headed, Northern European goddess who had also appeared unexpectedly, also totally unbidden, in my meditation in 2017? She had invited us to walk her paths in Wales and "see what happens," and we did.

I looked back and remembered both times I've been given a challenge/opportunity (test) by a deity in my meditation, and I had said "Yes." Had that prepared me for channeling Plotinus?

I tried to explain all this to Gary, but he just smiled and said, "It's all One." Which didn't help at all. In fact, it was irritating. Such a grand pronouncement! To be told, "We are having a human experience, but we are all connected to the One," might have been helpful, but to be told, "It's all One," felt like a pointless non-sequitur. I was annoyed.

I realized my irritation was fodder for our music project. We needed to figure out how to get people to have an experience of Oneness, not an intellectual assertion. That would require moving out of left-brain analysis into right-brain intuitive knowing, which brings with it a sense of wholeness/oneness. The audience wouldn't get there if we just made pronouncements. They would just be aggravated. Or bored.

Thursday, 21 March 2024

In meditation, I asked "Mr. P" or "the collective" to visit me. I called Plotinus "Mr. P" because our friend Nigel referred to him that way.

> PS: "I am Plotinus. You can call me Mr. P, but I prefer Plotinus."
>
> Me: "I didn't mean to offend."
>
> PS: "There is no offense. I have many names."
>
> Me: "Then why do you care?"
>
> PS: "It is the energy associated with [the name] Mr. P—slightly light and ironic and humorous, distancing from me."
>
> Me: "I see. I understand. Names are important. What is the name of 'the collective'?"
>
> PS: "We are not ready to divulge that yet."
>
> Me: "OK. You and Thoth are members?"

PS: "Indeed."

Me: "How many in all?"

PS: "Six."

Me: "That's a lot!"

PS: "We come and go in the group."

Me: "But you will always stay?"

PS: "Yes, Dear Little One. I am always with you."

Me: "Tell me more about our projects."

PS: "Yes. They are important. We have waited some time for this moment. Not our time but your time."

Me: "Books? Music?"

PS: "Both and all. We need to express the deep Truth underlying existence."

Me: "Why now?"

PS: "Because humanity is at a crossroads of destruction or liberation. … 'All hands on deck!' [Chuckling] Humans helping humans to evolve."

Me: "And if we don't?"

PS: "Another failed experiment."

Me: "Another?"

PS: "There have been many before."

Me: "On Earth?"

PS: "And elsewhere. It is a gradual process. We have lots of time—an infinity of time. But you don't."

Me: "How can we help?"

PS: "Live to your fullest potential. Live from your heart, with heart and love. Feel your unity with The All."

Me: "Thank you. ... Did you send the dream that Gary and I shared?"

PS: "It's not as simple as 'Did I send it'? Intersecting wavelengths of frequency coalesced in your dreamtime."

Me: "Why did you send it?"

P: "So you and Gary would take it seriously and do something."

Me: "Why me [why watching over me since I was a child]?"

[Elizabeth Diamond Rose had told me Plotinus had been watching over me since I was a child.]

P: "Because your soul agreed to this task."

[I heard, "Many are chosen but few arrive ..." or something like that. The correct quote is, Matthew 22:14, "For many are called, but few are chosen." Or more likely, "Many are chosen, but few make it to the finish line."]

P: "This task, this plan was made before you were born."

Me: "So it's all predetermined? No free will?"

PS: "That is an awkward question because it frames the choices wrongly. Before you're born, you agree to a general plan. How that is done or not done is your development in this plane."

Me: "So I could not do my soul plan?"

PS: "Of course! And many don't. The challenges of this life are many and grave. Some lose the path. The focus. They cannot endure, and [so they] leave. They can try again. [Smiling] There is plenty of time. All there is is time."

Me: "But you said these are challenging times—a crossroads on Planet Earth."

PS: "On Planet Earth, there is only time. And space. It matters to you how you live."

Me: "Does it matter to the universe?"

P: "Yes. We are all evolving, though at different rates. Planetary systems, stars—all are evolving."

Me: "Toward what?"

P: "Ah, that I cannot say."

Me: "Can't or won't?"

P: "A partial statement is, evolving back into Oneness. But that is woefully incomplete."

Me: "Is it all a big jumble there [where he is] of beings from different dimensions?"

P: "Not at all. We intermix. Interflow. There are interference waves created. But all is perfect and as it should be."

Me: "Is there one more thing you want to tell me?"

P: "Yes. Be happy."

Me: "Thank you. I guess that's hard for me. I'm not unhappy but—"

P: "Be happy. Relax. Enjoy your life on Earth. And—do the Work!"

Me: "Thank you. Goodbye for now."

20 minutes.

During my regular meditation, I'd "heard" the name Netana for the collective, even though that may not be correct since Plotinus said they wouldn't tell me yet. It might just have been my imagination. I looked up Netana on Google but couldn't find that word. I did find Netanel, which means "Gift of God or God has given."

Later that day at Gipsy in Palau Fugit, we saw an update on Facebook about my son's half-brother Andy's six-year-old son, Isaac. He was undergoing treatment for a very nasty cancerous tumor and was back in the ER in horrible pain. He had bowel blockages, and the surgery had been successful. Poor little guy!

Plotinus wanted to come through. I gave permission, and he came through with more sensation (stronger pressure on my temple) than at home. I turned on the voice-memo app on my iPhone.

PS: "Yes, poor child. He suffers, and his family suffers. It is always like that.

Without suffering, there is no opportunity to show support. It is like yin and yang—even in the suffering, there is the one point that is light and love. In the alternative, which seems better, there is the one point that is separation and sadness. Both are necessary. We cannot experience joy without experiencing sorrow. That is the human existence, flowing from one to the other in an endless dance."

Gary: "That goes into the book for sure!"

PS: "Do I get royalties?"

Gary: [Laughs]: "Let us know how we can pay you."

[I sense Plotinus smiling.]

Me: "Do you have more to say, Plotinus?"

PS: "Only that I wish you well!"

Me: "Thank you."

Later, we were at a café near Cuit GastroBar, waiting to meet some friends for lunch. Plotinus came through.

Me: "Is there evil?"

PS: "It is not what you think. Your limited perspective labels actions you don't like or find reprehensible [as evil]. What is good or bad depends on many things—time span, attachment, preconceived expectations. There is much to discern. Remember the Sufi story of Khidr and Moses*. Moses kept challenging Khidr about the bad things he saw Khidr doing, until Khidr finally explained what would have happened if he hadn't done the perceived-as-bad things."

Me: "Why did you come through stronger here at the café [than at home]?"

P: "To get your attention."

Oh.

Saturday, 23 March 2024

I woke up feeling off, tired, achy, and a little light-headed, so I asked Plotinus for health advice.

> P: "That's not my area of expertise. I will invite my friend [Hippolytus? Hippocrates?] to give you advice."

[I'm not sure whom he said he would invite. I think it was Hippocrates because I remember trying to decide if his name was pronounced Heye-PAH-crates or HIP-po-CRAT-es. I sensed another energy, but I didn't 'see' anything.]

Hippocrates said my humors [an ancient medical paradigm] were off, and I needed more water and more salt.

Later in the day, Nigel sent me a batch of questions to ask "Mr. P." He approached these conversations in a much more methodical way than I did. I had asked him not to call Plotinus Mr. P, but he appeared not to remember. I told Nigel I would ask Plotinus/The Collective (that's what I had decided to call them] and see what they said.

Sunday, 24 March 2024

I asked for Plotinus or The Collective to come through to answer Nigel's questions. TC = The Collective.

> TC: "We are here."

> Me: "Thank you. May I ask you some questions for Nigel?"

> TC: "You can always ask. We will see what we will answer."

> Me: "Nigel's first question is: Are you very busy 'over there'?"

> TC: [Laughter] "We are always occupied and never busy. Time stretches out infinitely. 'Busy' is only meaningful in limited time, in your existence, not in ours."

Me: "Hmmm. Do you ever rest?"

TC: "The answer is the same. Resting and busy are meaningless terms where we exist. We are constantly vibrating/scintillating light forms. Would we rest and stop scintillating? Of course not! We are what we are. Would we be busy and scintillate more? Of course not! Next question."

Me. "Thank you. Nigel asks, 'What is the purpose of life? Why does creation exist?'"

[Pause]

TC: "Again, a meaningless question. All that is, is. Everything exists. Existence itself infers creation. Creation infers existence. How could it be otherwise?"

Me: "Maybe I can ask it differently. WHY does the universe exist? Is there a purpose?"

TC: "Ah. [Pause]. It is its nature. Like an orange tree bears fruit. You don't ask the orange tree what its purpose is. True, it bears fruit, but that is ancillary. It is part of what it is. Bearing fruit is something it does, but it is not its purpose. It has no purpose. It simply is."

Me: "I've read that God/Source created the universe to know Itself, to experience its potential, and that it is evolving, too."

[I sense they are asking each other who should answer this.]

TC: "This is like trying to explain higher math to a dog. What you have said is partly true. The universe is experiencing itself. But that is not its purpose. Some things simply are and are unfolding."

Me: "Oh. ... So ... It's purpose-less?"

TC: "We will try again. Purpose, purposeless are meaningless in the context of the universe. It simply is. It evolves because it is a living thing. That is not its purpose, however. How grand it is that not everything has to have a purpose! Does a beautiful sunrise have a purpose? If you think its purpose is to make you happy or appreciate it, you would be misguided. The sunrise simply is, and you place meaning on it."

Me: "So it's all meaningless?"

TC: "By no means. But the meaning is attributed. The meaning you give a beautiful sunrise is not intrinsic. Nonetheless, all is unfolding in marvelous ways over billions of years. [Pause, reconsidering] We think these answers are unsatisfying to you."

Me: "Well …"

TC: "We will approach the question from a different perspective. Does a fractal have purpose or meaning? No. It is obeying deep laws. That does not diminish its being in any way."

Me: "So—beyond or behind purpose is something else? Law and order?"

TC: [Smiling] "That's part of it. The Law of Attraction. Indra's Net*. Everything is interconnected. The sheer joy of interconnection. The more connections, the richer the experience."

Me: "By whom?"

TC: "Sigh. This is like teaching higher math to a dog."

Me: "OK. I'm sorry I can't [understand] it better."

TC: [Soothing] "Don't fret. And don't worry about the meaning of existence. It is beautiful, is it not?"

Me: "Let me ask another question [from Nigel]."

TC: "Begin."

Me: "Death. What is the nature of the afterlife?"

TC: "That is two questions. Death is inevitable, built into the nature of life, like two sides of a coin. You can't have one without the other. Everything grows, changes, decays. Plants, people. Star systems. It's a grand, ongoing spiraling event that feeds the movement of the universe."

Me: "And the afterlife?"

TC: "Immensely varied. We humans and transhumans can choose our appearances, our interactions. Dogs, cats, parakeets—much less so."

Me: "What do you do when we're not talking?"

TC: "That is a meaningless question based on your limited experience of time. We are not constrained as you are by tick-tock time. We exist—differently."

A new voice speaks: "Some people prefer to relive their lives for a while. They recreate their house, their golf course, their teaching venue. Others move on more rapidly and don't need to adapt to formlessness. We all move at different speeds. [Chuckle] Some even sit around playing harps. They think that's the afterlife! It takes them a while, long or short, to realize they are unlimited here. Well, almost unlimited. We are vibrating frequencies. We do not need hard-core physicality in this place, though we can [create it/manifest it] if we choose."

Me: "Is there other life in the universe [another Nigel question]?"

TC: "Of course. We are life; the gods and goddesses have a different kind of life."

Me: "I think the question is, are there beings on Sirius, for example?"

TC: "The universe is filled with other life forms. Some are similar to you, others wildly divergent. Some are more intelligent and some exceedingly less so."

Me: "Do you interact with some of them?"

TC: "Of course."

Me: "I'm tired … I think I need to stop. Can we meet again in a few days?"

TC: "Of course."

Me: "Will you tell me your [group] name and who you are?"

TC: [Chuckle] "We'll tell you when you already know."

Me: "Thank you."

30 minutes. I'm tired.

Monday, 25 March 2024

I woke up thinking about the incompleteness, or unsatisfactoriness, in the answers to the question, "What is the purpose of the universe?"

I understood that it is a meaningless question: the universe simply *is*. Which is not to say that we humans don't evolve, have meaning, etc.

During this morning's meditation, I received more of the answer. I saw an image of an orange tree covered with oranges. What's its purpose? NO PURPOSE. It might well produce oranges, but to say *that* is its purpose ignores/denies its fundamental perfection in its "beingness"—its "isness." Not doingness, not having to have a purpose. It simply *is*. It produces oranges and it continues its species. It's like saying the purpose of humans is to continue the species. Very Darwinian. No. We do continue the species, but is that our purpose, our most important purpose? (Maybe the question should have been, what are the purposes of the universe?)

I suddenly, for an instant, experienced the Beginning of Everything—the Big Bang, the Big Outbreath, the first Orgasm—and it was sheer JOY. JOY and AWE at everything, like a child experiences when blowing a puff of dandelion or discovering a bug. Absolute joy and awe at what there is and might be and could be. Something—Consciousness?—expressing everything out of itself, whatever that is. Consciousness, somehow, is both being everything that is and being joy and awe.

Everything at the fundamental (quantum) level is permeated with this joy, which can also be experienced as unconditional love. Perhaps this is the Dark Matter/Dark Energy of the universe. At a more macro-level, the Newtonian level, there's a shift in perspective from united wave-flow to particles/the separate particularities of experience. At that level (the physical, manifested level of which we are conscious), humans are evolving, frequencies are rising, and that's also happening. At the quantum micro level, there is no purpose, everything *is* rather than *does*. At a more macro level, we *do* things. We are both human beings and human doings. It was difficult to put it into words, since they exist at a macro level.

Tuesday, 26 March 2024

I was gradually developing the outline of the libretto for our music project. The narrative moved from exploring gratitude, to experiencing the five elements (earth, water, fire, air, ether) that make up the planet and us, to relationship, interconnection, and Oneness. A recurring motif: We are all made of the stuff of stars and we are all connected.

I gave Gary a few phrases to begin putting to music. He composed a canon (AKA a round) based on "Bless all that we receive in thankfulness" (a phrase from a Sufi Order International blessing) and "We are extensions of the One True Being."

("Good") Friday, 29 March 2024

Gary and I had coffee at Gipsy and an intense conversation about the distressing world situation. In addition, I was unsettled by the over-the-top Good Friday pageant in Girona, which included processions of large, sculpture-laden floats and an army of Manaies, a local hereditary brotherhood. The Manaies dressed up like Roman foot soldiers and marched through the street pounding their lances on the ground and beating drums. Some (the officers) rode elaborately caparisoned horses, and their hoofs clattered loudly on the ancient cobblestones.

I found it disturbing to be in a place that enthusiastically relived the events leading up to the crucifixion of Jesus. In the Middle Ages, Holy Week was the time when Christian priests would incite their flocks to assault Jews. In Girona, the angry mobs would force their way into the gated Jewish neighborhood and attack the residents. Locals told me that the reenactments were just folkloric, but the energy I felt told me otherwise.

Plotinus came through. He said silently: *"Take a deep breath, Dear Little One. Relax and see the bigger perspective. We see it from the larger [higher] perspective from this side. You are like ants scurrying around creating chaos. But all is as it should be. Remember, all is as it should be."*

Saturday, 30 March 2024

Morning meditation. I asked what to do with the novel I had begun years ago called *The Key to the Kabbalist Garden*. This time-slip novel was set in Girona, which in the Middle Ages had been an important center of Kabbalah* (a mystical branch of Judaism).

I had started writing the novel, but the plot petered out, so I had set it aside. This unfinished project had brought us back to Girona. I had re-read it yesterday at Gary's suggestion.

I breathed in and out, relaxing, moving into stillness. I asked what to do with the novel. Some possibilities arose in my imagination. If I told the true story of how and why Gary and I returned to live in Girona, nobody would believe me. Maybe instead of time-slip, the novel should be reality-slip, based on our current experiences.

I put aside questions about the novel and focused on connecting with Plotinus and The Collective.

I felt energy flowing above my crown chakra, which felt wide open. I "got" that what was coming through was The Collective. And I "heard" some names: Plotinus, Thoth, Marsilio Ficino, and … someone else? I also "got" Nuvana/Netana/Nutana as possible names for The Collective. I decided to ask directly.

> Me: "Who else is in this group?"
>
> TC: "We will tell you later. It is too soon."
>
> Me: "Will you help me with the novel?"
>
> TC: "No. Now is not the time [to work on that]."
>
> Me: "Will you answer some questions?"
>
> TC: "Of course."
>
> Me: "Is there a god? If so, what is it like [one of Nigel's questions]?"

TC: [Silence, ruminating] "Another meaningless question from our perspective. There are energy forms you call gods—[coalescences] of vibration, each with a different 'flavor,' just as we are. You build stories around them, myths. Your concentration/focus on them gives them energy, sustains them. When you stop, they fade away."

Me: "I thought the soul was eternal."

TC: "It is, but constructs [like this] are not. These god-forms do not have souls. They are eddies in the Ocean of Consciousness."

Me: "Let me ask differently. What underlies everything?"

TC: "It is beyond your comprehension—and ours, although we are closer vibrationally to the ALL."

Me: "The Source of ALL?"

TC: "You can call it that."

Me: "But what does that mean?"

TC: "It's impossible to explain. Perhaps you can think of it like the sky. You see something you call the sky, but it doesn't exist in the way you think it does. The night sky [appears to be] completely different from the day sky, yet what it is has not changed. It remains the same."

[In other words, our perception changes, not the thing itself.]

Me: "Hmmm. Can you tell me what was before the beginning, before the Big Bang?"

TC: "Sigh. Language is so limiting. How can there be something before the beginning? By definition, there cannot be. Your language limits your ability to understand. And why do you insist on [calling it] the Big Bang? We prefer Jude Currivan's 'the Great Breath'—inhale, exhale ... [That is] much more organic and cyclical instead of violent. You humans frame everything in terms of violence. War against drugs. War against cancer. But we digress."

Me: "Can I change the subject?"

TC: "Of course."

Me: "Do I understand correctly that we are here to evolve? Our souls evolve?"

TC: "That is what happens in your 'isness.'"

Me: "And evolution continues in the Spirit Realm?"

TC: "Indeed. We become more 'coherent' energetically and gradually raise our frequencies."

Me: "So, eventually, you return to the One Source?"

TC: "It's possible, but none of us have done so. It's theoretical. We, like you, have to make sense out of our altered existence."

Me: "By evolving, what happens?"

TC: "We do not know. Everything changes."

Me: "Is there an endpoint?"

TC: "We do not know. Perhaps there is a cycling in and out, like breath. A giving and receiving."

Me: "Is the universe evolving?"

TC: "In a certain sense of increasing coherence ... over eons. Beyond comprehension."

Me: "I've read that God created the universe in order to know God's self."

TC: [Chuckling] "So many questionable words. God. God creating. God creating to know God's self. We won't even try to deconstruct that."

Me: "OK. ... Can you tell me about evil?"

TC: "Another time."

Me: "Please?"

TC: "Evil is a name you give to actions you do not like and do not comprehend."

Me: "Like Hitler and the Holocaust?"

TC: "It is only a matter of scale. People hate and kill each other all the time."

Me: "Yes, but certain acts seem evil. Sexual abuse, child murder."

TC: "It is true they don't meet your standards of good behavior. They are deviant. They are performed by souls with little/limited understanding, who are cut off from love."

Me: "I thought love was everywhere?"

TC: "It is. But, as you say, you can lead a horse to water, but you can't make it drink."

Me: "What happens after someone who has committed a heinous act dies?"

TC: "They are held in love and re-educated. Their discordant energies are gradually—'re-tuned.' It is all part of their evolution. Besides, without what you call horrible acts, there would be no opportunity for others to respond with growing love and awareness."

Me: "So, evil offers an opportunity to evolve?"

TC: "Yes."

Me: "Are there actual forces—like Good and Evil—in opposition?"

TC: "There are only opportunities to grow. We will stop now."

Me: "Thank you very much."

40 minutes.

I was struck by the musical analogies Plotinus and The Collective used: discordant, re-tuned, harmonious. It made sense if you think of everything as vibration and frequency.

Our friend Marchiene once told us that she is "a song God is always singing." The personality in this lifetime is like a riff on the song. The song includes our soul as well as our body. And when our body is gone, our soul—that part of the song—continues. It was a metaphor, but it felt very apt.

Later, I thought of more questions to ask Plotinus. These sessions were a unique opportunity to learn about the nature of reality from beings with a much broader awareness of it than I had. I assumed Plotinus and The Collective would keep visiting me, but I didn't want to waste their time.

Questions I wanted to ask:

What causes evil? A "falling out of harmony"? Why?

Will you (members of The Collective) re-incarnate? If so, why?

Why is there mental illness, and what is it?

What can't you do on the Other Side (compose music, write novels, etc.)?

More questions arrived in another email from Nigel, among which were: "Mr. P has previously admitted to Elyn a couple of times that 'there are things that we do not know.' … What does Mr. P look like? – Nigel"

I hadn't thought to describe their appearance because I was so caught up in the experience of channeling them. I "saw" Plotinus as a human, blurry around the edges, wearing a semi-translucent white garment. It was a bit like seeing a shape through the fog, except that the shape itself was made of fog. I didn't see his face, but sometimes I could sense facial expressions.

I experienced The Collective as something like an invisible, classical Greek theater chorus. I didn't see them, but I heard them inside my head. They spoke together, their voices blending as one, but I knew they were not a single individual. They were a group. Sometimes, one of the group would speak on their own. Each being had a unique energy or vibrational quality. That made sense since they described themselves as vibrating/scintillating Light forms.

Sunday, March 31, 2024

Coffee at our friends Nigel and Tessa's home, for our regular Imaginauts* conversation. Gary and I called ourselves and some of our friends Imaginauts: adventurers in the Imaginal Realm. As Nigel began plying me with questions about Plotinus, reality, and the afterlife, it became clear that Plotinus wanted to come through. I struggled to hold him back—I was not ready to perform in public—to be a show!

But Plotinus really pushed. I felt the pressure building. He was excited that Nigel had so many probing questions and wanted to learn how to ask the right kinds of questions. He knew that Nigel was a primo subject to engage with, and he thought he would help spread the information they wanted to share.

I reached an agreement with both Nigel and Plotinus that we would figure out a way for me to mediate between them. Not right now, but soon. Plotinus quit pushing and withdrew.

Nigel was excited. He was going to have a direct connection to the Other Side—or maybe to the Collective Unconscious. He decided that the truth status of this contact didn't matter for now.

Wednesday, 3 April 2024

Nigel had been messaging me daily. He was very excited about communicating directly/indirectly with Plotinus and impatient to begin. He thought he'd get his big questions about the nature of reality answered at last.

I sat down at my meditation altar and asked how to proceed.

> Me: "Is that you, Plotinus?"
>
> PS: "*Of* course *it is me. Why would you think it was someone else?*"
>
> Me: "It was a rhetorical question."
>
> PS: "Ah."
>
> Me: "Are you willing to help Nigel in his quest to understand the nature of reality?"
>
> PS: "I am eager to support him."
>
> Me: "How shall we do this? Should I ask you Nigel's questions, or can he ask you directly?" [In other words, either I would ask Nigel's questions and relay the answers, or Nigel would ask his questions and I would relay the answers. Nigel had no intention of becoming the channel.]

PS: [Pause] "That all depends on you."

Me: "Me?"

PS: "Of course. I can speak to him through you, or you can speak for him to me."

Me: [Pause] "I'm anxious you won't show up."

PS: "I'm always here. There is nothing to be afraid of."

Me: "I'm worried he'll scoff at your voice [coming through me]."

PS: "In that case, I won't speak."

Me: "OK. What place is optimal? He could be here when I contact you and ask questions, or ..."

PS: "I leave the choice of setting to you."

Me: "Thank you for your willingness."

PS: "I am eager to begin."

Me: "One question Nigel has asked is, what are the limits to your knowledge of reality?"

PS: [Sigh] "Another complicated question, or rather a simple question without a simple answer. [Pause] We [like you] only know what we know and not what we don't know. I sense that we are/I am part of a much bigger reality than I can comprehend—even in my current disembodied state. We don't waste much time pondering these things in this dimension where I 'reside'—which overlaps and interpenetrates yours. [Pause] Think of those nested lacquered Russian dolls that fit inside each other. Does the median doll know how much—how many dolls surround it? No. It only knows the immediate presence of the doll directly surrounding it or within it. [Pause] I am not sure that my answers will relieve Nigel of his uncertainty. His desire to know ALL is admirable but impossible."

Me: "Why then do you want to interact with him?"

P: "Because there is much to communicate, and he has a questing mind."

Me: "What do you want to communicate?"

P: "Drop by drop. An experience of another reality. Of expanded reality. He will be tasked to find ways to communicate this to others. It is not just to satisfy his own curiosity.

Me: "Is there a difference between what you know and what The Collective knows?"

P: "Of course. We are all limited in our knowledge by our experience. The Collective members bring together more information."

Me: "But they speak as one?"

P: "Yes. We share an energetic space, an overlapping harmonizing thread— it's like a chord playing [notes] together instead of individual notes."

Me: "I 'got' that you—The Collective—is called Netana. Is that correct?"

P: "That will do for now."

Me: [Pause] "Will you help Nigel form his questions?"

P: "No. He must—or rather can—ask his questions. My response will help him reformulate them."

Me: "Why is this so important?"

P: "We see humanity floundering in detritus, in ... mental pollution. A gray muck fills the land and taints the air. As once-humans—most of us, at least—"

Me: [Interrupting] "Is this Netana speaking now?"

TC: "Yes. As once-humans—plus Thoth—we feel concern, an obligation to help humanity rise. By so doing, we help ourselves rise as well. [Pause] It's not retroactive—we are not alive [in the same way] as you—but your development or, rather, our aiding your development, enables us to develop as well. [Chuckle] It's a harmless pastime."

Me: "It keeps you busy?"

TC: "It keeps us occupied—but that's not accurate, since time here is not like you imagine. Imagine [time like] a balloon. You press against it from inside. It expands. You release the pressure from inside, and it returns to stasis."

> Me: "The goal is to evolve?"
>
> TC: "There is no goal. There is simply 'isness.' An outcome of that is change." [Pause] We will discuss this further with Nigel since he has thought about this more than you have."
>
> Me: "OK. I think I need to stop now."
>
> TC: "Rest yourself. Do not over-exert. We are always here."
>
> Me: "Thank you, Netana. I'm grateful."

30 minutes of conversation. I was tired.

Gary and I went to Gipsy and had a lengthy conversation, this time without any interruption from Plotinus. I didn't write it down, but we reconstructed it later that afternoon and I summarized it.

We had several friends who were having a difficult time, and Gary was worried that I was letting my concern for them take my focus away from the big picture. He cautioned me to conserve my energy because this was very important material that I was receiving from The Collective. He reminded me that Suzanne Giesemann says that those on the Other Side use our energy to help them come through. This accounted for me being tired after a long conversation with Plotinus/Netana.

Me: "I must close [bring back in] my energy field better. My field gets very expanded doing the channeling. I'm 'hearing' that doing Suzanne's chakra-balancing practice would be a good thing. She does it before a mediumship or channeling session, but I think I should do it *after*. It's very important that I shut down the connection and my wide-open energy field. I've been feeling pretty scattered, what with the problems our friends are having and the channeling."

> While I spoke, I "heard" the message come through, "We are all related—we are all part of The One."

Me: "I am aware that after conversations with Plotinus, I am even more empathic than usual. The boundaries that separate me energetically from others are even more permeable. I feel our friends' distress deeply."

Gary: "It's good we are talking about how to make this communication as easy for you as possible. Maybe Plotinus will have some suggestions."

Me: "I asked. Plotinus says it's not his area of expertise. But then I got the idea of doing Suzanne's chakra balancing. "

Gary: "Maybe that came from someone else in The Collective. You know, we are individual rays of the same consciousness that animates them. Nigel is always talking about the Collective Unconscious—that's what he thinks you are in contact with. But I think a better way to frame it is to call it the Collective Consciousness. Calling it the Collective Unconscious focuses it on our human side, the materialized dimension. To talk about the Collective Consciousness includes all the other dimensions and doesn't home-base it here in our limited reality."

Me: "It's like a new Copernican revolution is needed. First, the Earth was thought to be the center of the universe; then with Copernicus, it was the sun. Much later, astronomers confirmed that the universe has a center, and we are on the periphery. But now what's needed is to shift the center from being in this physical dimension to being everywhere, in *all* dimensions."

Gary: "They really want to get this information out into the world."

Me: "These days, there are many people who are channeling groups that want to share information about raising the frequency of the planet and helping humanity evolve. There is a feeling of urgency."

Gary: "Evolving may not be the right word. Rather, changing. Somewhere in there, when you were channeling, you said, 'All this is too much.' You couldn't take much more of it. You said that I should remember it so we could write it down later. I told you I felt the ideas that I was expressing were coming through from the other dimensions, and not just from me. That I was in some sense a messenger representing the multi-dimensional folks.

Gary: "I think what you channeled this morning was important. The image of the nested Russian dolls who only know their immediate surroundings. Putting our limited understanding together with Plotinus' limited understanding broadens the scope of what we can know. We also talked earlier about possible places to meet with Nigel and Plotinus. I said there were lots of places. The Garden of the Angels. The John Lennon Garden. Gardens en route to Tessa and Nigel's house, including at their house. Palau Fugit. I said there are lots of places that have the right energy. You said the main issue is to be sure we aren't interrupted."

Gary: "I also said that perhaps we have been being groomed for this for years. That is consistent with what Elizabeth Diamond Rose said about Plotinus watching over both of us since we were young. And now we are ready. My composer background and musical gifts and skills, your writing background, the book project *Adventures of Everyday Mystics*. ... I keep telling you that all of this [conversations with Plotinus] will be in the new book. And now we've come together with Nigel as well, who provides a scientific approach to all of this."

Me: "I can see that a group of souls are all being drawn together. Cheryl and Marchiene in the US. Elizabeth Diamond Rose in England. Our friends Carles and Nigel and Tessa in Girona. Everything has happened to bring us to this moment."

Me: "When we talked earlier, I summarized the Henry Corbin article, "Mundus Imaginalis, or the Imaginary and the Imaginal," that Cheryl Page sent us. It is perfect timing that she sent it. The article shows how deeply the medieval Arab and Persian philosophers explored these other realms. They are not imaginary. Not fantasy. They exist in the Collective Consciousness as locations or places that can be visited."

Gary: "The way I think about it, everything—including our material surroundings—is energy. And I said we could think about it all as a thought. An idea in the mind of God. You disagreed with the word 'thought' because you believe these realms have a reality of their own. They are not only generated by our thoughts."

Me: "Not just me—Henry Corbin and some other important philosophers think so! ... Not *our* thoughts, however. Maybe a thought in the mind of God is all that anything is."

Saturday, 6 April 2024

Nigel was coming over to talk to The Collective or Plotinus. I was very nervous about the prospect. I was trying to approach his visit with curiosity and enthusiasm instead of performance anxiety. But I was worried. Would The

Collective show up? Would they convince this scientific skeptic? He was trying to get out of his "left brain" ways of thinking, but all his questions were predicated on scientific analysis and replicable experimentation.

Gary reminded me that the guides were always here. Yes, I knew that, but I hadn't channeled in front of anyone but Gary. I worried that Nigel would scoff.

I heard an inner message: *"The Collective says they will be there."*

Nigel came at 10:30 and we sat at the kitchen table, drinking coffee. Nigel had a notebook and was prepared to take extensive notes.

I closed my eyes and took a few deep breaths. I felt The Collective and Plotinus come through. Nigel and Gary were having an animated conversation about séances—that being the wrong word for what we were doing, according to Nigel—France and its esoteric history; the importance of this morning's experiment; and many more distracting themes. They were so busy talking that The Collective couldn't get a word in edgewise!

I started laughing and explained that The Collective wanted to come through, but they were talking too much. (Gary later said that they were providing comic relief to help me relax. I don't know if that was intentional, but laughing did have that effect.)

I told Gary and Nigel I couldn't go back and forth between asking a question to The Collective, listening to the answer, perhaps repeating it aloud, while at the same time hearing Gary and Nigel having an animated discussion about something else. Perhaps it would work better if Nigel asked a question, and I relayed it.

The Collective spoke through me a few times. Nigel didn't hear much difference from my normal voice, which I assured him was not surprising. My channeling voice was lower and only lightly accented, but it was still mine.

Nigel wanted to know who was speaking in the group. Did I identify different voices?

> *Plotinus spoke:* "We are not as concerned as you are about who is speaking. We are both individuals and part of the larger collective. We are waves that overlap."

Nigel: "That's very quantum."

I found it very difficult to channel that way. I couldn't ask questions, repeat the responses as The Collective, interact with Nigel, and write notes.

I suggested that Nigel ask a question, and I would listen to their answer and repeat it aloud—either as the voice of The Collective or with my own voice. I wrote down what I could.

Nigel: "You—The Collective—said there have been many failed experiments. I'm very curious about this. I'd like clarity."

Nigel (always the scientist) added that he'd often thought we were like bacteria on a Petri dish, a grand experiment. I explained that was not what they meant, though that was what the words sounded like.

The words were an approximation. After all, they don't speak in English. I received images and words psychically or telepathically. But the gist of their message was, there was no cosmic scientist conducting experiments.

So what *did* they mean by failed experiment? A better choice of words would be "discrete event." So why had they said "failed experiment?" Failed seemed to indicate a trajectory. There was success or there was failure. But The Collective was always adamant that it wasn't like that.

I tried to describe to Nigel and Gary what I saw with my mind's eye: waves rising and falling, rather than success and failure. However, there was a paradox/contradiction in saying that we [humans] came to Earth to have experiences and learn and evolve—and then to say there was no goal.

It was subtle, but I thought "evolving" was part of what we are or can be, just as they (The Collective) can evolve as well, but without some sort of goal orientation. I wasn't clear on the meaning. I needed to ask them again, in a different way.

Nigel asked about life elsewhere in the universe. I said they'd already said that there was life everywhere, but it was "not life as you know it." This excited him greatly because that's what he, a life scientist, had always thought. He was delighted to have The Collective affirming some of his own beliefs.

It was hard to stay focused, shifting from listening to Nigel, listening to The Collective, repeating aloud their response, explaining it to Nigel, and clarifying what I thought they meant. I felt drained.

I thanked The Collective for coming and closed the session. It wasn't a failed experiment, but it wasn't a great success.

We spent some time debriefing from the experience and considering what to do next. Nigel had a list of questions he wanted to ask next time or sometime. A hugely important question for him was: Can we engage Plotinus to look at the layers beneath Newton's laws? What underlies that? If we could engage Plotinus to do so, and if he (Nigel) could formulate it in a way that was testable, it could rewrite science as we know it.

Nigel declared this was a landmark day because he had participated in this exchange with beings from the Other Side.

He promised not to push me, but he didn't want to wait until next Saturday to repeat the experience. He asked if we could do it sooner. I didn't feel pushed. I, too, was curious and eager to learn more. And The Collective wanted to talk with him. He was a scientist and asked different questions than I did.

Nigel asserted that Gary and I are evangelists for them—eager to tell people what they want to share. I said they want him to be an evangelist also. He knew he would have work to do and accepted it.

In our debriefing, Nigel revealed that he'd read the first two tractates of Plotinus's *The Enneads*. He said Plotinus was a moral philosopher and very logical, grounded, and clear, just as he came across in my channeling. Nigel found it confirming that Plotinus talked through me just the way he had written.

I was delighted to hear this. I hadn't read Plotinus's work. I wanted him to say what he had to say to me without my wondering whether I was generating what he said because I had read it in a book.

Nigel observed that the real problem with channeling was the limitation of language. He suggested we listen to Samuel Beckett's two-act play, *Happy Days,* on Netflix or YouTube. (Later, I did. A sobering commentary on the difficulty of meaningful communication.)

I didn't think I was tired, even though Nigel had been there for 2 ½ hours, but I was exhausted. I crashed around 3:30 for 1 ½ hours.

Sunday, 7 April 2024

I was given an image that expanded to explain the paradox of "no goal but evolving."

An acorn has the potential to become an oak tree. That's part of its "isness." If somehow it doesn't become one—it's eaten by a squirrel, or there are too many trees nearby for it to thrive, or the soil is infertile, or there's no rain—it could be considered a failed experiment. It hasn't become an oak tree.

It's not that its purpose or goal is to become a full-grown tree but, rather, that it has the innate potential to become one. I thought that was what The Collective/Plotinus were saying about humanity. Human "isness" includes evolving into clarity, harmony, higher vibratory frequencies. It is not our goal or purpose but our innate potential. So far, humanity didn't seem to be evolving very quickly.

Thursday, 11 April 2024

I sat down to meditate after a few busy days. It felt like it had been a long time, though it had only been a few days since Nigel had questioned The Collective.

I invited The Collective to have a conversation. This time, The Collective had another member: a woman. I didn't see her with my physical eyes (she was non-corporeal), but I sensed her wearing a white toga-like robe. I "got" the name Hypatia, AKA Hypatia of Alexandria. In this and other conversations, I refer to her as "H."

> Me: "Nigel has a question for you. May I ask it?"

> TCS: "Of course. We are here for you."

> Me: "He wonders about good and bad beings on the Other Side. Are there?"

> TC: "Hmm. Complicated. Of course, there are all sorts of beings here with different energies. Some resonate well with you and some do not. You call that good and bad."

Me: "Would the 'bad' be attracted to me?"

TC: "Some might, but it is not likely. They have 'other fish to fry.'"

Me: "Do I need to protect myself?"

TC: "You need to keep your energy clear and high. Come from the heart. Think 'good' thoughts. Act with loving kindness."

Me: "Are there evil beings there?"

TC: "We repeat: There are all kinds of energies."

Me: "Suzanne Giesemann describes [what we would call evil—murderers, abusers] souls wrapped like cocoons until they are re-educated. Is that accurate?"

TC: "The image is more accurately [wrapped in] a swaddling cloth. [These are] Human souls we are talking about now. Not exactly accurate—metaphorical. After all, there are no bodies to wrap. It is more a case of re-tuning and clearing disharmony."

Me: "A different topic. Nigel wonders if you can help with a science project."

TC: [Laughter] "Perhaps."

Me: "Can you ... He wants to know if Newton's Laws are correct or there is more behind them."

TC: [Speaking] "That is the kind of question Nigel needs to ask us directly because you don't understand the question [or the answer]."

Me: "You are right. He wants something he can test and prove Newton was wrong."

TCS: "Of course Newton was wrong. How can you think you can describe five or seven dimensions in terms of three or four? There is a null point in the void. ... There is no explanation for the cause. Gravity. Attraction. Your scientists use big formulas, but they make up—construct from imagination—a so-called constant to make the equation work. How can there be a constant when all is always in flux?"

Me: "I'll tell him what you said—and that you'll talk to him about it."

TC: "Thank you. Is there more?"

Me: "Always."

TC: "Continue."

Me: "What can't you do in your realm? You said earlier that Gary should write music now because he won't [be doing it] in the other realm."

TC: [Laughter] "There is much that we have no need or reason to do. Jog. Cook dinner. Write music."

Me: "Is there music where you are?"

TC: "There can be. We can open ourselves to the music of the Spheres. ... It is exquisite."

Me: "Where does it come from? Who composes it?"

TC: "It is its very nature. ... It flows from another realm."

Me: "How many realms are there?"

TC: "How many frequencies are there? How many colors in the rainbow? You can segment them into seven [colors], but they are infinite and flow into each other."

Me: "Is there something more you'd like to say today before we end this?"

TC: [Pause] "Tell Nigel to relax and get out of his head! Life is much better that way."

Me: "He thinks too much?"

TC: "Not everything can be solved by thinking."

Me: "What do you suggest instead?"

TC: "Floating."

Me: "Floating?"

TC: "Effortless floating in the Sea of Consciousness. You will not sink. Let it penetrate your very being. Let it support you and buoy you up."

Me: "Go with the flow?"

TC: "Perhaps that is another way to describe an effortless way of being in acceptance to ALL THAT IS."

Me: "Is there a god?"

TC: [Laughter] "There are many gods and no god. There is only Being."

Me: "Consciousness?"

TC: "A limited description for something beyond your—and our—comprehension."

Me: "I feel dizzy contemplating it."

TC: "Relax and flow. We will leave you now."

Me: "Thank you. Until—Sunday with Nigel?"

TC: "Perhaps. Or perhaps before."

30 minutes.

After the session, I Googled Hypatia of Alexandria, Egypt. I had recognized her name and remembered that she was brilliant, a respected peacemaker between pagans and Christians, and was ripped apart by a violent Christian mob. I learned that she lived in the mid-4th – early-5th centuries CE. She was a noted astronomer, mathematician, teacher, and Neoplatonist philosopher who had been heavily influenced by Plotinus. Judging by her credentials, she would be helpful to Nigel.

It was interesting that Plotinus had included another Neoplatonist. Or maybe he hadn't sought her. Maybe she had volunteered. I needed to ask.

I forgot to write down in my transcript of the just-channeled conversation that I had asked Hypatia to tell me something I didn't know. I wanted evidence.

She said she speaks a few words of Chinese. I "heard" something like "Boon (bon?) han jai (chai?)."

I was puzzled that she spoke Chinese. I did a Google search and learned that, for a long time, there was extensive trade on the Silk Route from China to

Arabia, including into Egypt. Chinese silk was used for making Egyptian wigs, among other things. Hypatia might well have encountered someone who knew a few words of Chinese or learned it herself.

I tried to find the words I heard her say, but without any success. Lo Han Jai is a Chinese vegetarian dish called Buddha's Delight. Was she was making a joke? Bon Han is a Cambodian male personal name and Boon Han Chai is a Malaysian male personal name. Maybe she just remembered random words, or perhaps she told me the name of a Chinese dish she enjoyed.

In addition, I learned that the robe I "saw" her wearing was only worn by male philosophers. However, she was so highly respected in Alexandria that she was permitted to wear it.

Later that day, Gary and I were back at Gipsy in our favorite corner. The Collective wanted to say more. This time, I recorded the conversation on my iPhone voice-memo app and transcribed it later.

> Me: "They really want to come through again, to say more about some of the questions I asked this morning. I feel them coming in."
>
> Me: "I was wondering who was in charge of deciding who would be wrapped in swaddling clothes. There must be a hierarchy on the Other Side. Job descriptions?"
>
> TCS: [Speaking aloud] "There is a hierarchy, but it is not what you think. We all shift roles. It's all flexible. But we have different frequencies."
>
> [I have an image of different overlapping waveforms, different quantities/percentages of different frequencies ... some strong in one area, some strong in another.]
>
> Me: "My question is: Who's in charge of the moral decisions, like deciding who gets wrapped up like a swaddled babe and 're-attuned'? Who makes those decisions?"
>
> TCS: "It is more diffuse than you think. It is like a murmur[ation] of starlings. We all move together. And shift. And sometimes one being is in the lead, and sometimes there is something else, someone else, some other being who is in the lead. It is all vibration and waveform and flow. It [your question] is like asking who is the wave in the ocean."
>
> [A long pause while I think about this.]

Me: "I have more questions about evil and ... uhh ... that which is not good. People who do those things. What makes them do those things on this Earth plane?"

TCS: "They have lost their way. They have lost the harmony of their soul-flow, which is always there, beneath everything. At the core, it is perfect. But they have miss- ... missed the mark. They have aligned with discordant energy. It may be it was part of their purpose for this life, to experience this."

Me: "You say, it may be?"

TCS: "There is always free will and ... disorder. Nothing is predetermined. Everything is interrelated."

3.35 minutes of channeling. The background was very noisy, but I was able to hear everything on the recording.

Sunday, 14 April 2024

Coffee at Nigel and Tessa's during our regular Imaginauts get-together. There was a little bit of channeling but a lot more conversation. We discussed the complexities of asking The Collective questions and understanding their answers, and how to improve communication.

Monday, 15 April 2024

I knew immediately they were here.

TCS: "We are here."

Me: "I apologize for shutting you down yesterday."

TCS: "There is a growing—learning—curve. We understand. We were eager to participate in the conversation."

Me: "I'll try to stay open next time."

TCS: "We appreciate that. We are delighted Nigel is so eager to converse."

Me: "Can you suggest better ways for him to form his questions?"

TCS: "He must learn to simplify."

Me: "He wants to understand the nature of reality."

TCS: "Don't we all."

Me: "You, too?"

TC: "Of course. We are limited. But we are not anxious. All in due time."

Me: "Do you evolve?"

TC: "We progress into finer, more refined vibrational states until—we believe—we disappear into the One True Light."

Me: "Have you witnessed this [occurring]?"

TC: "Where we are, beings come and go. We make assumptions. ..."

Me: "How do you maintain personality in your dimension—realm—plane of existence?"

TC: "It is difficult to explain where we are when there is no 'where,' and all is no where."

Me: "Oh. ... And personality?"

TC: "It's like the riff on a basic melody, the elaboration, the elaborate filigree on a basic form. This [basic] is what you call the soul. It continues to exist."

Me: "It doesn't change? I thought everything changes."

TC: "A complex paradox. It is like a flame. A flame is used to light another flame. The flame is the same but different. But you still call it a flame. The soul is the same. It continues recognizably always, yet filagree, vocal riffs, and decorations surround it. After death—after the transition to this realm—these superfluous decorations fall away. Some others remain, [but they are] recognizable."

[Later, thinking about it, I realized another analogy is layers of clothing, which we put on and take off; underneath it all is our body. But in that afterlife realm, there is no body—there is the soul, which was underneath everything all along.]

P: "I—this is Plotinus speaking—retain my central characteristics, recognizable personality."

TC: "The more harmonious aspects—"

P: "Yes, in this realm. I am recognizable."

H: "I am recognizable. I have still my sharp intellect, my desire for peace-making, my purity and clarity [of thought]."

Me: "Will these attributes continue?"

TC: [Shaking collective head] "Not when we progress 'higher'—at least we don't think so. We haven't, so we don't know. [Chuckling]"

Me: "Why have you chosen to come through now?"

TC: "Because we are eager to share our understanding, our experience on the Other Side, and you are eager to learn and to share."

Me: "Last night I dreamt I had a conversation with Plotinus. Was I dreaming or—"

P: "We were conversing. You can trust that and write it down when it happens again."

Me: "Thank you. ... Nigel wants to know the limits of your knowledge. For example, do you know the price of milk in Girona?"

TC: [Laughter] "Why would we want to? [Huddled discussion] We function on a need-to-know basis."

Me: "If you needed to know, you could?"

TC: "Yes. But 'need' is the operant word. Do we need to know the price of milk? [Laughter] No." [Also, I understood telepathically: what kind of milk? Full-fat? Organic? Cows milk? Goat's? What brand? Which size container? Which shop? Etc.]

Me: "Where do you get the information you need?"

TC: "Ah. Difficult to explain."

[I see the image of a hologram, a kind of 3-D image that can be explored from different angles, created by the interaction of light waves.]

TC: "At some level, everything is One, so all knowledge is available."

Me: "Nigel is worried you'll get bored or feel pestered and stop communicating."

TC: [More laughter] "Nigel is full of human concerns."

Me: "So, not to worry?"

TC: "Indeed. Not to worry."

Me: "Thank you. I'll tell him. What is the most important thing to tell him today?"

TC: "Tell him to look to the sky. It is boundless. And it is not what it appears to be. Remember this: NOTHING is what it appears to be, so arguing over one worldview or perspective or another is a trivial waste of time. None of your [Nigel's] understandings are even vaguely accurate. But does it matter? No. He keeps on living and thinking and pondering regardless. False ideas don't kill us or lead to madness. They are unavoidable."

Me: "I'm not sure that will be very reassuring."

TC: "Probably not, since he wants absolute certainty in a world of illusion and flux. We told him before to relax and enjoy life. We tell him that again."

H: "And also, to enjoy the mystery of unknowing and the unknowable."

Me: "Thank you all. I'm going to stop now."

25 minutes.

Addendum: My early morning/sleep conversation with Plotinus was about what holds the universe together. I remembered something about how nobody understands gravity or magnets. Something about, "It's all Love—love connects everything, love is what attracts everything to each other."

During relaxation at the end of our weekly Therapeutic Yoga class, I was thinking about Hypatia again, and she "came through." I recorded what I remembered later at Gipsy Bar and then transcribed it afterwards.

I wondered what it was like for Hypatia on the Other Side because of her extensive background in mathematics. What had she learned?

Hypatia said something like, *"It's not about numbers—the underlying [whatever] of the universe—it's not numbers."*

I "saw" the Platonic* solids and understood that it wasn't *numbers*, it was *forms* that underpin everything.

Hypatia responded with, *"No, it's more than that. It's not the forms, it's actually the relationships. It is relationships and the relationships between things that underlie everything. And, of course, the relationships [my (Elyn's) paraphrasing: give rise to numbers, but the relationships are primary]."*

Thursday, 18 April 2024

First, an early morning conversation with Plotinus as I lay half-awake in bed. I initially discounted it as made up (imaginary), but then I remembered Plotinus had said these were real conversations.

Here's what I remembered:

> P: "You misspoke, Human One, when you wrote Nigel that we have no emotions. We do. We have feelings that are equivalent to joy, love, compassion—and curiosity. And you are wondering how we think without [physical] brains. We are part of Universal Consciousness [just like you are]. Perhaps you call it Mind. By the way, Nigel asks interesting and also amusing questions."

Later, at my meditation altar, I felt The Collective come in. I had Nigel's latest list of questions in front of me.

> Me: "Are you willing to answer Nigel's questions?"

TC: [Gentle laughter] "If we are able."

Me: "First: What was the nature of the earliest transition from a somatic [body-based] phenotype to an energetic phenotype?"

TC: "He has the wrong end of the telescope. Energetic came first."

Me: "Second: Do you mature as individuals? With recognizable stages?"

TC: "Even you humans do not mature in stages. That suggests concrete steps, quantum levels. Everything flows. We are each unique in our development. We flow from less harmonious, denser, to higher, more coherent. Each at our own 'speed.' Remember: time is not what you think, and it is different here—wherever here is."

Me: "Third: Do all somatic life forms have souls? Do they differ?"

TC: "We cannot answer that."

Me: "Why?"

TC: "The concept of soul is very complex. We can say there are levels of complexity of aggregation of energy. The more conscious the life form, the more of what you call soul. But all things participate—partake—in Consciousness. Nothing is inert."

Me: "Fourth: Do subatomic particles have souls and afterlife development?"

TC: "An interesting question indeed. But based on misconceptions. The more complex the physical form, the more potential it has within it to express. In sub-atomic particles, [the potential to express is] less so. A certain level of complexity is required to contemplate oneself and experience options. An oak tree may be close to this development. Many sentient beings are not [reflective]. A certain [reflectivity]—self-awareness—is required before what you call 'soul' is present. But consciousness is always present, even in the smallest of particles. You see, you must remember energy came first. You people have a saying: 'You are a spiritual being experiencing life in physical form, not a physical being experiencing spirit.' That's an approximation."

Me: "I think the saying goes, 'You are a spiritual being having a physical experience, not a physical being having a spiritual experience.' ... Do guides come from the same 'phyla/taxa' as the beings they are guiding? For example, once-human guides for humans?"

TC: "Obviously not. Angels are not human and never were! Some of our best friends [chuckle] are from other dimensions and planets. Some of you believe you have come from other planets. You are not wrong."

Me: "Can you travel in other dimensions?"

TC: "There can be some overlap, but it is a matter of frequency."

Me: "Thoth is in The Collective, and he's not a once-human."

TC: "That is correct. Gods and goddesses can move more freely between dimensions—don't ask us why!"

Me: "Nigel asks, 'Do you worry about cosmic threats? Solar flares, meteor strikes?'"

TC: "Remember: We do not exist in your time/space physical dimensions. Those threats are not meaningful to us."

Me: "How do I know this isn't coming from my imagination [today]?"

TC: [Laughter] "You have a good—no—excellent *imagination*, but it is not this good."

Me: "Thank you. One last question for today."

TC: [Gentle laughter] "OK."

Me: "Nigel wants to know, do you continue to learn?"

TC: "Ah. Language. Again a problem. 'Learn.' We 'evolve' into our potential. We do so by exploring possibilities. We support human efforts. We become energetically more complex and more pure, more coherent. It's really impossible to explain. It's a good question nonetheless."

Me: "Well, I'm sure you aren't simply floating on clouds playing harps!"

TC: [Laughter] "No indeed. We expand our fields of consciousness—our range—we interact with humans (a voice adds, 'And other beings')—and we may choose to reincarnate and have further experiences to develop our potential. It's an almost endless cycle."

Me: "Almost?"

> TC: "Almost. Of course, if all we did forever was cycle back and forth into life forms and out, that would be pretty tedious, don't you think? We have said before: Becoming our full potential ultimately leads to unity with the One True Being."

> Me: "Which is?"

> TC: "You can call it the Consciousness That Pervades All. All dimensions. All universes. ... That's enough for now."

> Me: "Thank you. There are always more questions."

> TC: "It is important to experience the Now and not just ask questions."

> Me: "Thank you."

30 minutes.

In Kabbalah*, there is the belief that humans reincarnate repeatedly until they eventually remember who they truly are and where they come from at a higher level of the Tree of Life*. At that point, some choose (like Bodhisattvas) to return to Earth to help raise the awareness/consciousness of other humans. Eventually, when all human souls have been lifted in awareness, the cycles will end.

That sounded a lot like what The Collective was saying. Because I knew this from my Kabbalah studies, was I contributing to what they were saying? Or perhaps they were saying it because Kabbalists learned this from Spirit?

I talked with Gary about the difficulties of translating the questions and answers into shared vocabulary. And how I was sure the answers would only raise more questions. I wondered if there was any way to give Nigel information about the other realms/dimensions that he could use to construct testable hypotheses.

I felt Plotinus come through.

> P: "We enjoy Nigel's questions. They are not a bother or annoying. We will ponder how we can express our reality to him. It is not a case of apples to oranges but more like hamburgers to asparagus. Not even the shared category of fruit."

Friday, 19 April 2024

I read an Institute of Noetic Sciences article about how channelers have difficulty answering scientific questions. That matched our experience.

During lunch with Gary, Plotinus spoke through me.

> PS: "I am a human being who was alive. I am still alive. I don't know everything. I didn't then and I don't now. There are topics that interest me and topics that do not. Nigel's questions are interesting to me, but I don't have all the answers."

That led to a conversation with Gary.

G: "The ONLY thing that knows everything is the Ground of All Being, Universal Consciousness—The One True Being—whatever you want to call it. And it doesn't know it in the way Nigel is asking to know because it is not separate from what it knows. It's not an outside observer of this. It *is* this. We think of 'knowing' as an objective left-brain project, with the scientist outside the experiment looking at it. But we know from quantum physics that the observer is part of the experiment. Even the scientists are part of their experiments and influence the outcome. If there is a Unity of Consciousness that extends through all dimensions/universes, there is nothing that is outside of it to observe it."

Me: [Nodding appreciatively] "You're channeling Truth. You are more available to that kind of information now."

G: "Yes, I am."

Me: "And they are eager to come through—and they don't recognize the limitations of our human bodies."

G: "We have to take care of ourselves because we occupy physical bodies, and these bodies have physical limitations."

Monday, 22 April 2024

At my meditation altar.

Me: "Come to me, please, Plotinus, The Collective."

[I sat quietly waiting, then I felt a shift.]

TC: "We are here."

Me: "Thank you for being here."

TC: "You are welcome. What do you want to ask today?"

Me: "Lots of questions!"

TC: [Laughing] "Of course. Begin."

Me: "How can I stay more focused during my meditation?"

TC: "Remember the tool Plotinus gave you—the horse wearing blinders that focus its vision ahead instead of letting it become distracted."

Me: "Of course. Thank you for reminding me."

[I sense them nodding.]

Me: "Are you alive? What is life?"

TC: "Again, the language problem. If 'alive' means moving and sensing on the physical plane, of course not. That word is very limited in scope. Not all sentience on your planet is alive. AI, computers—non-living but sentient."

Me: "Are they conscious?"

TC: "Again, the language problem. You use words that cannot be defined, at least not with fixed parameters. Do you know what Consciousness is?"

Me: "No."

TC: "There you have it. It is irrelevant."

Me: "'It' means consciousness?"

TC: "This discussion. We cannot talk about things without a shared understanding."

Me: "Let me try it differently. You seem conscious, in that you talk, communicate, have thoughts. ..."

TC: 'That is our nature as it is yours. You do it in a physical form, we in non-physical form."

Me: 'If I said, 'Everything is Consciousness,' would that be correct?"

TC: "It is incomplete. You still don't know what Consciousness is."

Me: "Directed intention?"

TC: "A small part."

Me: "Analysis? Communication?"

TC: "Also part. ... We also find it hard to understand and communicate this concept to you."

Me: "Wave versus particle?"

TC: [Laughter] "Perhaps that will help bring clarity. You are asking 'particle' questions when we are waveforms. And Consciousness is like a waveform, which includes shifting back and forth into particle form."

Me: "Why? Why does it do that?"

TC: "It is its nature."

Me: "In Kabbalah, there is Ein Sof*: the concept that the ineffable God-form makes space for Creation so it can know itself fully. Is that an accurate description?"

TC: [Nodding] "Limited but close. Be careful with the languaging of 'make space' and 'to know itself.' It is its very nature to know itself. And 'making space' is inaccurate since it contains all."

Me: "Is the Universe—Consciousness—benevolent?"

TC: "Of course. Would you harm yourself? All is One."

Me: "But there is evil, war, racism ..."

TC: "All aspects of the One knowing itself, to use your limited terminology."

Me: *"Can you see the future? And if so, what does that say about free will?"*

TC: *"Imagine looking down on Earth from a cloud. You see more. We are not of course on a cloud, but we have a wider/broader vision than you."*

Me: *"And free will?"*

TC: *"In the immediate present, things are as they are. A drop in the pond. The ripples spread, interact, hit hidden obstacles—rocks, a passing fish. Where the individual ripple [waveform] ultimately ends is such a complex result of nearly infinite factors. That is something like what you call free will."*

Me: *"But is it all predetermined [if you knew all the factors]?"*

TC: *[Pause] "At some abstract, remote level, if you knew everything you might say so. But you don't. And can't. And it is useless to pursue that."*

Me: *"It makes me nervous/uncomfortable to think that at some level everything is predetermined."*

TC: *"But it is not. That is your misconception of what we have described. Remember—we have often talked of potential—at the level of discrete human consciousness, there is potential. And we also have potential. It is in fulfilling this that we all have free will, framed on the margins by our histories and those of others with whom we overlap."*

H: *"You have random-number generators. If everything was predetermined, there would be no randomness. Nigel will understand."*

[Pause]

Me: *"Can you be more than one place at once? Can our souls be both there, where you are, and reincarnated?"*

TC: *[Pause, conferring] "Yes."*

Me: *"So—is there part of me on your plane?"*

TC: *"Yes, though 'part' suggests a breaking off, something partial, like my arm is here, but my leg is somewhere else."*

H: *"Obviously you can be two places at once. You sit in your chair at your meditation table but converse with us in another dimension."*

Me: *"Of course!"*

H: *"It's more fractal. Or perhaps what you call a hologram. Whichever metaphor—it's all metaphor—works better for you."*

Me: *"Plotinus talked about the 'so-called' Gary here and the 'so-called' Gary composing in dreamtime."*

TC: *"Yes, it's something like that. Remember, all is flux."*

Me: *"So even the Ultimate Supreme All-Encompassing Consciousness doesn't know everything that's going to happen?"*

TC: *"If it did, what would be the point of its unfolding? It, too, has potential."*

Me: *"Totally different question. How many dimensions are there?"*

TC: *"We do not know. Numerous, perhaps unlimited—or perhaps only one since they all flow into each other, like the colors in the rainbow."*

Me: *"Are there malevolent beings in other dimensions?"*

TC: [Collective sigh] *"Language again. Malevolent. They are simply living out [experiencing] their potential."*

Me: *"It can seem bad or evil to us."*

TC: *"Indeed, because you do not like it or feel comfortable with the effect. Yesterday you read a post by Caitlín Matthews about intrusive entities, attachments. She said, consider them like accumulated dust or dirt. You want to get rid of them for hygiene purposes. But don't feed them with fear or loathing."*

Me: *"Thank you. We humans try to understand why there is evil in the world."*

TC: *"It is like the yin-yang sign—black in white, white in black, interconnected."*

Me: *"Always? On all planes?"*

TC: *"We do not think so. There is the process of purification we have mentioned, of becoming more coherent and less discordant ... raising in frequencies—a metaphor, but there you have it."*

[Pause]

Me: "I have a question from Nigel about how the physical body is animated—how it relates to the soul ... evolution ..."

TC: "We will address that next time."

Me: "Thank you. I am grateful for your visit."

TC: "You are welcome. We are eager to explain reality to all of you."

Me: "Why?"

TC: "To help you realize your potential."

Me: "Thank you. Goodbye."

35 minutes.

En route to our weekly Therapeutic Yoga class, I had an insight about free will/chance/predestination: that Consciousness (Ein Sof*, All That Is) built randomness into the rules. After all, it could construct whatever reality it wanted to!

After class, Gary and I returned to Gipsy at Palau Fugit. I was still cogitating about free will versus determinism. The music playing as we walked in was Leonard Cohen's "Hallelujah," followed by Simon and Garfunkel's "The Sound of Silence." Next came, "We still haven't found what we're looking for." Synchronicity, once again. Sounded like The Collective was the DJ.

I realized that what I had been thinking wasn't quite accurate. *Everything* has potential, including Consciousness. Consciousness is the rules/laws. They are not separate from it. And they include randomness. It was as if everything, including Consciousness, moves towards higher self-organization.

I told Gary, and he said, "Stop looking for the answer, and it will come to you. It's in trying to figure things out that we miss it."

Later, Gary added, "It's not either/or, it's both/and. Contradiction is built into it."

Wednesday, 24 April 2024

I had a lengthy conversation with Ariel before/during my monthly massage. Ariel is a gifted body therapist, artist, channeler/medium, and spiritual teacher. I was eager to get his opinion about some of the questions I'd been asking The Collective. I made notes immediately afterward. I also wrote to him later that day to ask for clarity on some of the topics. The following is a partial summary.

Ariel explained, "There is biology and there is soul. There is evolution (biology) and ascension (soul). We are here to ascend to the fifth dimension. The planet is in the process as well. It is becoming a star."

I asked him what the connection is between the soul, DNA, and cellular memory. How can our body's cells remember past lives if the fetus is created at fertilization before the soul descends into it? Ariel explained that the appropriate Brotherhood (there are many—but the Emerald Brotherhood is probably responsible for this particular thing) condenses all the information/experience of this lifetime (and all previous ones) into a single atom. At the moment of fertilization, this data-atom is put into the fertilized egg. The soul comes along later. It continues to move in and out of the fetus and the young human for some time. The soul isn't quite in the person until after they are about 7-8 years of age. *All* the past-life experience is held in this single atom and transmits that information into the cellular memory/DNA.

According to Ariel, our DNA has been hacked. Source put a bit of itself into the DNA (imagine a monkey with Source's DNA put into it), thinking that we would "wake up" and know ourselves as Source. But another group of beings (also a part of Source) hacked the DNA, and we forgot that we have Source within us. They hacked us because they don't want us to ascend to higher dimensions because they couldn't follow us there.

I asked about people who incarnate on Earth and do evil/horrible/monstrous things. Did they make that soul plan before coming? Ariel was adamant that all soul plans are made in the Light and there would *never* be a plan to do harm or kill anything.

So, how is it that people do bad things on Earth? Ariel said it was because they forget who they are, and so they could do anything. It's not that they decide to come here and be an example from which other beings could learn. No. They have simply forgotten who they were: namely, Light and Source.

Are there ETs (extra-terrestrials)? Of course! But many of them are at much higher levels of vibration, not the third dimension. They've passed through these lower levels long ago and can help us ascend.

Ariel talked about Kryon, an entity channeled by Lee Carroll since 1989, who may be the source of much of what he was telling me.

In reviewing my notes, I observed the following. In channeling, there are many variables: the medium, the entities, the message, the mental/personal/cultural/religious filters through which the message passes; the ability of the entity to communicate; and the ability of the channeler to understand. And then, there is the interpretation of what the entity has said by people who read what the channeler has said/reported/written.

It made me wonder what people would make of my conversations with The Collective, Plotinus, and Hypatia if I ever went public. I would need to be prepared for criticism, misinterpretation, rejection—and, hopefully, appreciation and gratitude for the messages they were sharing through me.

Monday, 29 April 2024

Morning meditation with The Collective and Plotinus.

I cried happy tears because, in meditation, I visited with my spirit crew again—my regular spirit guides, Dad (who started showing up recently, nearly 20 years after he passed on), Blau (my beloved black panther spirit animal), Helen, and the others. When I felt their presence in meditation, sometimes I was moved to tears of joy.

Then I asked Plotinus and The Collective to come through.

    TC: *"We are with you."*

Me: "Nigel is very excited about what you are telling us, but he is also frustrated about languaging, asking better questions."

TC: "All in good time. Your time, that is."

Me: [Smiling] "Can you tell us more about what Consciousness is?"

TC: [Pause] "It's difficult. Like a fish in water—how does the fish describe water? Of course, there is a difference because we *are* Consciousness, it doesn't just surround us like water. We are limited in part by your inability to understand, to have words to express it."

Me: "Exactly. So what can we do?"

TC: [Pause] "Be still. Move into stillness. Loosen your sense of self. There—perhaps—in that moment, for a moment, you will sense Consciousness."

[I went into a deeper trance state for a short time, then came out of it.]

Me: "I had a moment of ... nothingness."

TC: [Nodding] "It may appear that way, but it is not nothingness. It is fullness."

Me: "Sometimes, like this morning, during meditation I have moments of joy. Ecstasy. Like the mystics talk about. Is that it?"

TC: "That is also part of the experience of consciousness, not filtered through the limiting and distorting filter of human experience."

Me: "Are there experiments or tests to describe it better or measure it?"

TC: [Laughter] "Of course not! It's everything! So how can it be measured? That's like trying to measure life. You only know what it actually is when it is no longer there."

Me: "But can't we say life is about cells dividing and replicating?"

H: "That's replication. Numbers divide and replicate."

Me: "Oh. ... What do you want to tell us?"

[I have a sudden feeling of deep joy and peace when Hypatia entered into the discussion.]

TC: "That's what we want to tell you. It [living] doesn't have to be so hard. Underneath everything is this foundation of peace, love, compassion, connection. ... There is no loss. There is no separation. At the cellular—no, atomic—level, we are all connected, and all is well."

Me: "How does that make life easier?"

TC: [Puzzled pause] "Not to be separate? To experience love and connection? It is so foreign to how you [all] live that you cannot even imagine how different it is. [Sigh]."

Me: "Do you experience this in your dimension?"

TC: [Group nod] "Much more so."

Me: "So, if Hypatia encounters the [souls of] people who brutally killed her—"

H: "If I did encounter them, we would 'embrace'—intertwine our energy fields. That was all part of my human story and theirs. It certainly made a good story—or at least a memorable one! Human historians still argue about who organized that brutal murder. [Gentle sigh] I suppose that has helped keep the memory of me alive. Along with the anger [in your plane of existence] at the injustice."

Me: [Pause] "It's that different in your dimension? No guilt, no recriminations?"

TC: [Nodding] "Exactly."

Me: "But what about people who have done truly evil acts?"

[Note: they have said before it's just our limited perspective that sees these acts as evil, but here they are conceding that some souls are not very harmonious. Maybe it's a question of semantics.]

TC: "As we told you before, their souls—not exactly their souls but the vibration-cloud surrounding their [soul] cores—go through a slow process of harmonization."

Me: "Who is in charge of that? Who organizes that?"

TC: "Well ... we have ... we choose ... we can choose to participate in different ways to assist the evolving potential of all beings. Some of us dedicate *ourselves for a time to harmonization."*

Me: "Who organizes taking these 'inharmonious' souls into 'reharmonizing' treatment?"

TC: "We all know what to do and what is happening. We each make choices. We are each exploring our own potential, and it is similar yet different. ..."

P: "Let me try to clarify. Imagine the core central soul cloaked in layers of vibration. Imagine an onion being peeled. Or clothes being discarded. In our dimension/level of reality, we still have many layers of personality to shed. We may choose to return to experience more, to make our vibrations more complex—like weaving an intricate tapestry. Eventually, we 'move'—we shift—to other realms or dimensions, more clarified and closer to perfect harmony and unity. We only know a little about this process. Remember the nested Russian dolls?"

Me: "[This exists] beyond the dolls?"

TC: [Laughing gently] "That is the trouble with analogies. And language. Everything is here. We are embedded in Consciousness. We are Consciousness. There is no 'beyond.'"

Me: "So ... You want us to know we are all connected, there is no separation, and under everything is love, compassion, joy, ecstasy ..."

TC: [Nodding] "Something like that."

Me: "Why do you want us to know this?"

TC: "To make your lives easier."

P: "More than that, to help you fulfill your potential. To recognize you have the gift—the amazing gift—of eventually becoming—no, returning—to The One That Is All."

Me: "I'm picturing the Ein Sof (the Limitless One) above the top of the Tree of Life."

TC: "A heuristic device that falls short because it is an image of separation. Separations. But it will do as a metaphor for the gradual experience of separation from Unity to duality to—triplicity—and on and on, until you *forget who you are. Who you truly are. And [until you] remember again. And forget. ..."*

Me: "Whew. ... I think that's enough for now."

TC: "We agree."

Me: "Thank you so much. I look forward to our next conversation."

TC: "As do we."

40 minutes. I felt very spacey after this. Sent a copy to Nigel and Gary.

I told them we would talk more, but I needed to wait a few days. I had a busy week ahead.

I was working with Gary on the music project to raise the vibration of people and the planet that we had dreamt about, but it was not going smoothly. We were having serious problems working together.

Although we had co-authored nine books in our Powerful Places Guidebooks series and co-authored other books as well, and we thought we knew how to work together, the composition project was a new endeavor.

Gary wasn't sure he wanted to do it. At his age, after not composing for 30 years, he wasn't even sure he *could* do it. But more importantly, he had told me repeatedly that he had left behind the driven composer self he had been, and he didn't want to bring him back. That composer self was ruthless and single-minded.

I had blithely minimized his concerns. After all, we had produced many books together—we would make it work! This was a project given to us by Spirit. We had an obligation to do it, no matter how challenging it was.

But Gary was right to have misgivings. He had never composed in collaboration with someone else. His composer self was ruthless, demanding, arrogant, and driven. While I slowly explored various concepts and collected ideas and quotations, listening to inner guidance, waiting for inspiration, he pressured me to be more focused and hurry up—to get something DONE!

Meanwhile, he had to master a complicated new music software program called Sibelius. Learning it required enormous focus and sustained effort. He began composing pieces in dreamtime, just as he had during his 30 years as a professional composer. His sleep was interrupted. My sleep was interrupted.

Gary began composing short pieces and demanding that I tell him if they worked with the libretto—which I couldn't, since I hadn't completed the libretto. While I waited patiently for inspiration and guidance, he waited impatiently for content.

The fault lines in our relationship (every relationship has them, smaller or larger, papered-over, mended, or festering) were beginning to show. It was not a pretty sight. Our shared dream was becoming a nightmare.

I held onto the initial vision. I knew we had to get through our relational issues in order to create a musical event that would lift the vibration of the people who participated in it. But first, we had to lift our own.

Saturday, 4 May 2014

I began my morning with my Brigid meditation. (I lit a candle for Goddess/Saint Brigid on the 4th of every month. Other women lit candles on other days.)

Then I shifted gears and called on The Collective and Plotinus.

    Me: "I said I'd talk with you today. It's good to be back with you!"

    [My eyes fill with tears.]

    TC: "We also look forward to these exchanges."

    Me: "I have only a few questions."

    TC: "We await."

    Me: "Are any of you—or a part of you—reincarnated now?"

    TC: *[Pause as they consult each other. I sensed a communal headshake.]* "No."

    Me: "Why [not]?"

TC: "No reason. No reason, no urging to incarnate now. Perhaps later. Or sooner."

Me: "Can you tell [me] now who you are?"

TC: "Some of us you know: Plotinus, Hypatia, Marsilio."

Me: "Thoth?"

TC: "He drops in and out."

Me: "Are there others?"

TC: "Not at this moment, but there can be. [Smiling] Why? Are we not enough to answer your questions?"

Me: "No—no—I'm delighted. Just wondering."

TC: [Nodding]

Me: "Is there anything you can tell me to help raise my vitality?" [I am feeling very tired.]

TC: [Pause] "We are not doctors. But we advise more play, more relaxation, more laughter. You are entirely too serious. If you keep your nose to the grindstone, you will wear it out [off]."

Me: "OK. Does talking with you tire me out?"

TC: [Nodding] "Of course, a bit. We have to approach/match each other's energy levels. Levels as in frequency."

Me: "Do you ever get tired?"

TC: "No, never. Well—not as far as we have experienced. Tiredness is a function of the body-form, not the spirit."

Me: "Sometimes people say they are tired in spirit, or soul-weary."

TC: "Yes, that is an expression you use, but it is not accurate."

Me: "Thank you. ... What language do you speak?"

TC: [Laughing] "That's like asking humans what language do you speak! Humans speak many. But we don't speak many. And we don't speak. We communicate without sound."

Me: "But you use words."

TC: "It's impossible to explain to you. It might sound like music, if it had sound. It's more—conceptual. Immediate. Like talking to yourself. But that's not accurate, because you use words and grammar [when talking to yourself]."

Me: "It's like a Vulcan mind-meld from Star Trek?"

TC: [Laughter] "That's as good a description as any. Why does it matter?"

Me: "I want to understand your world—your dimension."

TC: [Sigh] "Well, newbies here still use words until they realize they don't need to."

Me: "Can you communicate with nonhuman beings?"

TC: "Of course. Thoth, for example."

Me: "From other planets?"

TC: "Of course. Think of it as a built-in universal translation app. But you need to understand we don't talk about the same things you do on Earth."

Me: "You don't?"

TC: "No, obviously not. We don't ask what's for dinner. Or, who's going shopping. Or say, 'I like your dress.'"

Me: "Of course not. ... What do you talk about?"

TC: "We share concepts."

Me: "Uh ... OK. ... Can you tell me how soul or spirit and body are linked?"

TC: [Pause, nodding] "Excellent question but difficult to answer."

H: "We are limited in our understanding, but it appears to us there is a link—an energetic cord—that connects the physical [form] to the spiritual."

Me: "So a fetus links with a spirit?"

H. "No. The fetus is only a physical form until the spirit—or soul—links with it."

Me: "How does the DNA, family history, etc. then link with the soul? Or does the soul carry that history?"

H: "Good question. [Pause] The pure soul has no history, familial or otherwise. But as we go through incarnations, there is a residue left on the soul that encapsulates its previous experiences—an energetic marker. When the spirit embodies—it doesn't actually, of course; rather, it comes into relationship through attachment/linkage to the fetus."

Me: "But doesn't the fetus have DNA and genetic family history?"

H: "Of course. They link together."

Me: "So we are reborn into a fetus with a certain genetic history in a certain family tree—and we bring our spirit and its past-life residues with us?"

TC: [Nodding] "Something like that."

Me: "Do we choose which fetus?"

TC: [Laughing] "Of course!"

Me: "On what grounds?"

TC: "To—hopefully—experience other emotions, experiences, etc. to help us fulfill our potential."

Me: "Hopefully?"

TC: "Of course. The best [laid] plans of mice and men ... Remember, there is free will, randomness—nothing is predetermined."

Me: "Nothing?"

TC: "Not that we know."

Me: "What about astrology?"

TC: "That's information, not predetermined."

H: "Well, I beg to differ. There is a grand overarching scheme of things—but it's like your Newtonian versus quantum distinction. It doesn't pay attention at the micro level."

P: "I'm not sure I agree."

Me: "You can disagree with each other?"

TC: "Of course! We don't know everything."

Me: "My friend Ariel told me that if your soul doesn't have the experience it needed/wanted in this life, it can/will return again."

TC: [Nodding] "Of course. If it chooses to do so for its development."

Me: "I think I see. … Sometimes life experiences seem very hard. Very tough."

TC: [Nodding] "That is how you learn and how all those you come in contact with learn."

[I had a mental image of a butterfly flapping its wings in Japan and impacting the weather in Spain.]

Me: "Do gods/deities reincarnate?"

TC: "Not exactly. They can choose to appear on Earth, but they don't have the same potential to develop—unfortunately for them."

Me: "They don't have potential?"

TC: "No. Instead, they have superpowers. It's a trade-off."

Me: [Smiling] "I see. Do the gods hear my prayers?"

TC: "That depends on many things. Your intensity, fervor, commitment, needs—and if they want to listen."

Me: "Oh."

TC: [Smiling] "Better to pray for help from your guides."

Me: "Or—The One True Being?"

TC: [Shaking head] "The Unity is so far removed—and yet, it's always here at every moment since there is no separation."

P: "But focus on remembering you are it—it is you. Then no prayers are needed. All is as it should be."

Me: "Prayers [express] that human longing for things to be different."

P: "Exactly."

Me: "Thank you. I'm stopping now. I look forward to another conversation soon."

TC: "As do we."

40 minutes, more or less. I sent a copy to Nigel, Tessa, and Marchiene.

Saturday, 11 May 2024

Evening meditation.

Me: "Hello, Collective! Thank you for being here."

TC: "We are always here."

Me: "Can I ask a few questions?"

TC: [Nodding]

Me: "Our friend Nigel has lots of questions for you."

TC: "We know."

Me: "Is there a productive way to work with them?"

TC: "Productive?"

Me: "I mean … I think some you've already answered."

TC: [Nodding]

Me: "And some seem—well, for example, 'Define purpose.'"

TC: "Yes, we see what you mean. 'Purpose' has many meanings."

Me: "Purpose of life? Of existence?"

TC: "He asks many questions."

Me: "Yes."

TC: "He must ask himself why he asks so many questions. Especially when we have already answered some of them. Does he not listen? Or do we not give him the answers he wants to hear?"

Me: "I think ... I don't know."

TC: "Choose some and we will answer. Or try to."

Me: "OK. Until I say otherwise, these will be from Nigel. What is the purpose of life?"

TC: [Sigh] "Human life? An amoeba's?"

Me: "I don't know. Maybe, human life?"

TC: "To fulfill its potential. Potential is not the same as purpose. Your friend always looks ahead instead of behind."

Me: "Who or what created the universe?"

TC: "Very difficult to answer. Created ... universe ... Again, language is an impediment. Does he mean what the telescopes on your satellites report back? They are limited in what they see. Created ... That assumes something came into being that wasn't before and that something 'did' it. Everything simply is and has been and will be and evolves. ..." [Evolve isn't quite the right word.]

Me: "Why do species become extinct?"

TC: "Why not?"

Me: "Hmmm. If they didn't, there wouldn't be space for new species to evolve."

TC: [Nodding] "That's good. You are learning. Everything is in flux. One outcome is things, beings, species come and go. It is the nature of things."

Me: "Why does death exist?"

TC: *"See what we just replied."*

Me: *"Why did God/Supreme Being make so many mistakes in inventing life on Earth?"*

TC: *[Sigh] "Supreme Being. Inventing. Mistakes. So many mistaken assumptions. What is a mistake? Something that doesn't work out the way you think it should. Nigel has a very narrow view. Where would we be without mistakes? There is no perfection."*

Me: *"Is there what we call the devil?"*

TC: *[Pause] "There are forces that seem antipathetic to you and the way you would order the world."*

[I sense a mental huddle.]

H: *"Evil refers to human activities that seem cruel or destructive, like my brutal death."*

Me: *"Exactly."*

H: *"It is activity generated by humans who forget they are also part of one greater—Consciousness. We have addressed this question before."*

Me: *"Yes … How do you communicate with other life forms—or do you?"*

TC: *"Of course we do. We have told you we are in communication with beings/life forms from different planets."*

Me: *"How do you communicate?"*

TC: *"It's a sort of conceptual telepathy … the closer you are to Source, the easier it is to communicate with other beings—and the less need [there is] to communicate.*

Me: *"Can you say more about the 'how'?*

[I get a mental image of an octopus shifting color and shape rapidly.]

TC: *[Responding as if they see what I see—or maybe they sent me the image mentally] "Yes, that's one way. It is vibrational."*

H: *"Words are vibrations. Vibrations create form."*

Me: "Can you help Nigel on his science project?"

TC: [Laughing gently] "That all depends on him. He will need to spend time learning to communicate with us directly. And then [laughing gently again] he will probably no longer have much interest in his current science project."

Me: "What is love?"

TC: "Connection. Oneness."

H: "Compassion. Lack of separation."

P: "There are different kinds of love—you remember that, of course: brotherly, parental, romantic, 'love of God'…"

Me: "Can we prove Newton didn't have the whole picture?"

TC: "Of course! We already have! He wasn't a quantum physicist."

H: "However, his alchemical experiments indicate he was well aware his work on physicality was insufficient."

Me: "Nigel has a lot of questions on Mind, Consciousness, etc."

TC: [Sigh] "Language again. He doesn't know what the words mean, so how can we talk about them?"

P: "We can say that Consciousness permeates everything and animates everything—but that doesn't answer anything."

TC: "Tell Nigel he needs to realize that the universe is poetry, not a laboratory experiment."

Me: "Ah. … And we experience poetry differently from, say, a nonfiction history text."

TC: "Even your history texts are, in fact, poetry—but we digress."

Me: "[I have a] totally different question to ask."

TC: [Nodding]

Me: "Our friend John works with a spirit group in another realm that he calls the Druid Council. We told him about you today, and he wondered if you are the same as his group, just presenting yourselves differently?"

TC: "No, we are not the same."

H: "I beg to differ—at some level, of course—"

TC: "Of course. At some level we are the same. Like a branching tree diagram. The higher up you go to the One True Source, the more similar we are. But at the level at which you and he speak, we are separate groups of entities—once-human, transhuman, occasionally deities, angels—who coalesce for a specific time to communicate as one."

Me: "What else would you like to tell me now?"

TC: "We commend you on beginning to play again."

[Nodding with approval]

Me: "Anything else?"

TC: "Yes. Lighten up. Don't take it all so seriously. Enjoy yourself. Life! Enjoy being alive. The mystery of it. The incredible opportunity."

Me: "Thank you. I will take these words to heart."

TC: "They are words not just for you but for all of you living on this Planet Earth."

P: "Or anywhere else!"

TC: [Laughing] "Indeed."

Me: "Thank you again. Until the next time."

30 minutes.

Saturday, 18 May 2024

I'd been very busy working on the music project, originally named *Hallelujah Hurrah* but now renamed *Celebration!**.

I had sketched out the libretto and we had settled on the performing forces: An MC reads the narrative script; a chorus leads the audience in singing rounds and chants; a percussionist strikes the gong; and a string orchestra/quartet/pianist performs the music. An MP3 recording of nature sounds plays in the background.

The MC leads the audience from stillness into gratitude, from gratitude into an awareness of how everything (plants, minerals, oceans, hummingbirds, humans) is made of the same elements, is related and interconnected, and, finally, that we are all One. The audience participates by reflecting on their experiences and by singing and reading responsively. The libretto includes a mixture of poetry, narrative, quotations, quantum physics, a Native American prayer, and interfaith readings.

I selected phrases for Gary to set to music.

Gary and I continued to struggle to collaborate better. I was tired and stressed from our interactions.

Gary tried to find a way to compose music without becoming his old ruthless, driven, "take no prisoners" composer self. It was a self he had banished 30 years ago when he took early retirement and stopped composing, just before we were married. It was a self I had never seen. He had banished it—but now it was back in full expression, running his life. Running our life.

Was it possible for him to compose music and not be that self? He didn't know how to. They seemed inextricably linked. Desperate, he reached out to Elizabeth Diamond Rose and asked for help.

How ironic. A project intended to raise the vibration of people and the planet was lowering our vibration. Or rather, *it* wasn't lowering our vibration: *we* were.

That evening, we had a WhatsApp video call with our friend Bernadette. I decided to tell her about channeling Plotinus and The Collective, knowing that she had a long history of non-corporeal contacts. She was eager to learn all she could about my experience. She gave me some questions to ask them the next time we had a conversation.

I was beginning to tell people about Plotinus and The Collective, but I was still very reticent. I didn't want people to think I was crazy or strange. Nor did I want them to raise doubts about the validity of my experience. It helped when I realized that some people—like Bernadette and Nigel—were intrigued and excited by my experience rather than put off by it.

Sunday, 19 May 2024

Morning meditation.

Me: "Hello!"

TC: "Hello."

Me: [Wondering if I should ask for evidence again.]

TC: "You are conflicted."

Me: Yes."

TC: "You want to believe."

Me: "I do—"

TC: "Yet doubt creeps in."

Me: [Sigh]

TC: "We understand. The proof is in the transmission and its value to you and others."

Me: "It is. Valuable. Of value. … I have a question. Why me?"

TC: "Why not you?"

Me: "I mean … for decades, I've been given/had [occasional] contact with [spiritual] beings. Why?"

TC: "There are two 'whys.' Because you are receptive. Because they [and you] want to be of service."

Me: "Our friend Bernadette asked [last night] what you all do in your dimension."

TC: "Ah. Well, what we don't do is eat, sleep, go shopping. [Smiling]"

Me: "How do you pass your time each day?"

TC: "Remember, time for us is very different. We flow back and forth."

Me: "Back and forth? You can influence the past?"

TC: "No, not exactly. But we flow from now into the future and back. Just a short distance."

H: "Distance and time shift [their] nature in our dimension. It's been quite interesting for me to experience it."

Me: "Can you say more?"

H: "Difficult indeed to describe [the] experience in words, like describing the taste of an orange. Tart, sweet, juicy—it's not the taste itself but a description. ..."

Me: "Hmmm. Do you—or someone—compose music there?"

TC: "Not exactly."

Me: "I'm wondering about Gary's 'aspect of himself' composing in your realm."

TC: "Ah yes. Well, we 'entertain' ourselves by creating forms—but we are in a different dimension—so it's a different process. No actual paintbrushes or pianos."

Me: "Do you listen to music?"

TC: [Nodding] "All the time. We are surrounded by exquisite vibrations, both visual and audible."

Me: "So you can see and hear?"

TC: "Of course. Sort of. We don't have eyes or ears, so the experience is—visceral."

H: "Although, of course, we don't have viscera either."

Me: "Where does the music come from?"

TC: [Pause] "Another, higher dimension."

P: "It's quite Platonic, really. Or similar to your Tree of Life symbol. As we/everything rises up in vibration, it becomes simpler, more—profound. More—basic."

Me: "Like ideal forms? Platonic solids?"

P: [Nodding] "Something like that. The underlying structure of the universe."

Me: "Sounds like it could be a computer program set in motion and generating more complex ... things."

TC: [Nodding] "As above so below."

Me: "You mean this is all a computer simulation?"

TC: "Not at all! Only that basic laws are at play at all levels."

Me: "Are they the same laws everywhere?"

TC: "We don't know. Remember, we are like the nesting Russian dolls."

Me: "So it *could* be a computer simulation."

TC: [Pause] "We don't believe so. It is much too complex."

H: "And 'it' is Consciousness creating everything and in everything. There is no separation. That's what I've learned."

Me: "But—"

H: "Let me continue. Consciousness is in everything. Is everything. There is no separation. A computer simulation would be outside of its creation."

Me: "Oh. ... So ... what do you do in a typical day? And why?"

TC: "Words. Time. Day. It's not meaningful. We exist and interact with each other, experiencing the exquisite music and beauty of Beingness. We interact with humans and other beings, for the promotion of the highest good."

Me: "Highest good?"

TC: "Development of the fullest potential of all that is."

Me: "Of your free choice?"

TC: "Of course. Some of us interact with you and others who are open and willing to be of service. Some of us choose to reincarnate and experience more of the infinite variety of life."

Me: "On Planet Earth."

TC: "And elsewhere."

Me: "When you reincarnate, is part of you in the other dimension still?"

TC: [Nodding] "Just as part of you as well is in this dimension of what you call the afterlife."

Me: "Ah. I think I understand."

TC: "The you you think *is* you is only a fragment of who you truly are."

Me: "Can I contact myself in the afterlife?"

TC: "You could, but it would be confusing."

Me: "Oh. ... So, where does music come from?"

TC: [Pause] "It doesn't come from anywhere. It, like everything, is always here."

Me: "Well, Gary's compositions?"

TC: "They flow through like language, like words, like we are talking to you."

Me: "Flow from where?"

TC: Your/his experience is they (music, ideas) come to him. They are always here and available. The expressions ... the sounds ... their combinations are infinite. It's a selection process that he is engaged in."

Me: "Like an artist? Or a writer?"

TC: [Nodding] "Infinite possibilities. Some more pleasing than others and more pleasing to one person than another. All is possible."

Me: "I'm getting tired."

TC: "Of course."

Me: "Thank you for this visit. [Pause] I still want to know, why me?"

TC: "You chose this before you came to Earth. And you forgot. We have been reminding you until you were ready to step into your fullness."

Me: "Chose what?"

TC:" To have an easy relationship with the other realms. Some of you call this being psychic. Whatever. You chose this—and you forgot. For many reasons. Trauma. Your family. Society. But now you are remembering."

Me: "Why did I choose this?"

TC: "To be of service. Enough now for today, we think."

Me: "Yes … Thank you. I agree. Thank you, beloved friends."

TC: "You are welcome."

30 minutes.

Sunday, 26 May 2024

Gary and I talked about some of these questions while we drank coffee at Gipsy, and Plotinus came through again. He spoke through me, saying something like:

PS: "I am always here with you. Remember the One. Remember, what happens, happens; and what follows, follows. Remember the One. Remember to always act from a higher perspective. The ethical life is the only life well lived. Thank you."

Me: [I am trying to write this down.] "I can't remember all you said."

P: "It doesn't matter. Remember, you [all of you] are so very loved."

Me: "You sound like Suzanne Giesemann!"

P: "Because she is speaking Truth."

Me: "Thank you."

Friday, 31 May 2024

Gary and I continued to go through a very rough time. The stress of Gary's old composer-self being nasty, demanding, and rude, my reactivity to this unpleasant person I was living with—I triggered myself into remembering a very bad time in our relationship. I brought it up to him, asking for clarity and reassurance. That didn't go well.

Why couldn't I just get over it, I wondered. Most of the time I thought I had, but then the memory would come back, like a festering sore. I hoped that if I could just get clear about it, I would no longer think about it. Or, maybe, I just needed to let it go. My trying to talk about it just set us into another cycle of miscommunication and mutual defensiveness.

Saturday, 1 June 2024

Meditating at my altar.

Me: "Hello again! I need help with [Gary and my] relationship issues."

P: "We are no longer human."

Me: "I know that, but—"

P: "To forgive is divine."

Me: "How can I feel [secure]?"

P: "You must feel [secure] within yourself."

H: "And stand strong. Stand up for your beliefs."

Me: "I realize that now. I haven't always done so."

P: "It is understandable."

Me: "But going forward—"

P: "Going forward, act with kindness and self-integrity."

Me: "I will. But what about the past?"

P: "I told you, what is done is done, what happens, happens. What good is it to dwell on past actions which cannot be recalled—as in, undone?"

Me: "You are right."

P: "No good comes of it. The actor cannot undo the action. The only good is to change the behavior in the present and for the future."

Me: "You are right."

P: "Do not dwell on the past. It is past. Learn the lessons inherent in the actions and go forward—with joy and trust in the future."

Me: "Sometimes that's hard."

P: "Of course."

H: "Act with integrity. Be clean. Stand by your values. All will be well."

Me: "You promise?"

H: [Gentle laugh] "I cannot promise, but I can make a calculated assessment. I stood up for my values and I was murdered. It happens. Fortunately, that is not your situation."

Me: "What happens, happens."

H: "I would have been murdered anyway. My very presence was an insult, a provocation, to those of a radically different persuasion."

Me: "Thank you. I have a lot to think about."

P: "Has he shown sincere apology?"

Me: "Yes, finally."

P: "You believed him."

Me: "Yes, finally. Before, I wasn't sure if he meant it or was just saying it."

P: "So there is definite progress."

Me: "Yes."

P: "Focus on that, not on the past."

Me: "I will. Thank you. … Any advice about my cough?" [I have a bothersome cough but no other symptoms.]

P: [Laugh] "Not [my] specialty, but warm water with honey and lemon might help."

Me: "Thank you."

P: "Does he love you?"

Me: "Yes."

P: [Nodding] "So there you have it. Well done."

15 minutes.

Tuesday, 4 June 2024

I woke up in the middle of the night gasping and choking, unable to breathe. I instinctively jumped out of bed and ran into the living room, struggling to breathe. I literally thought I would die.

My airway was stuck shut with gunky stuff that I tried violently to cough loose. After convulsively hacking for what seemed like minutes but couldn't have been that long, I was able to breathe again. Had I swallowed something in my sleep? I had never had anything like this happen, not even years ago when I had bronchitis.

I went back to bed, but soon I bolted out of bed again, choking, struggling to breathe, and ran into the living room, emitting a high-pitched whooping sound as I gasped for air. I told myself I had to relax—that panicking wouldn't help—but it was very hard to relax when I couldn't breathe. I coughed and hacked until I got my airway open.

Instead of going back to bed, I sat on the sofa, trembling, afraid to lie down. I sucked a throat lozenge to numb my throat and tried to breathe slowly and carefully. The coughing paroxysm happened one more time. I waited anxiously for the nearest clinic to open. Soon Gary was awake and waiting with me.

At 8 am, we called a taxi and hurried to Urgent Care. The doctor listened to my story and my lungs, and he asked if I'd been around children. Not that I remembered. Did I have any other symptoms? Sore throat, runny nose, fever? No. A mild cough for a few days, but that was it. He treated me for bronchitis because he heard something in my lungs, and he told me to return in a few days if I wasn't better.

I wasn't. I tried hot drinks, throat lozenges, over-the-counter mucus busters, but nothing helped very much. I made an inhaler of essential oils, including copaiba, which I had read was good for spasmodic coughing. I was exhausted and scared, waking up gasping two or three times a night with an eruption of terrifying coughing. I tried to sleep in our bed, but within a few hours, I would wake up choking. I ended up spending the night propped up on the sofa. Each time an attack happened, I was afraid I wouldn't be able to breathe again. Ever.

We went back to the doctor. This time, he decided I had whooping cough, also known as pertussis. He stuck a long swab up my nostrils and took a nasal sample to culture. He prescribed an inhaler, a powerful mucus dissolver, and antibiotics.

Whooping cough? That was something kids got! Then I remembered I had been riding Girona public buses, and they were filled with school kids. That must have been where I caught it.

The doctor told us there was an epidemic of whooping cough in Spain and in the US because children had missed vaccinations because of Covid and also because of rising anti-vaccine sentiment. I was the unlucky recipient of someone's highly infectious airborne bacteria.

I Googled whooping cough and learned that I might crack a rib or two from the force of coughing, but I probably wouldn't die of it. However, it was more dangerous for babies, young children, and the elderly. That included me.

I took the powerful antibiotic the doctor said would kill the bacteria in a few days, but that was only mildly reassuring because there was no guarantee that would relieve the symptoms. And the symptoms were horrible. They call pertussis "the 100-day cough" because that's how long it usually lasts.

I wrote to a friend of mine who had had whooping cough years ago as a middle-aged adult, and she recounted her traumatic experience. She said it had taken six months before the cough had disappeared completely.

A few days later, I visited my private doctor, who put me on corticosteroids and monitored my progress daily via email. She told me that even though the bacteria was destroyed by the antibiotic, which was obviously a good thing, the damage to my airways would take a long time to heal.

I asked Elizabeth Diamond Rose and Stephanie to send healing. They got right on it. I felt reassured that I was doing everything I could: Western medicine and energy healing from a distance.

It took me weeks to get over the worst of it. Gary's support and constant care helped enormously. I would have been terrified if I had been alone, afraid I would suffocate to death and nobody would even know. I spent nights propped up on the couch, trying not to go into a paroxysm of coughing. Whenever Gary heard me gasping and struggling to breathe, he would jump out of bed, run into the living room, and stroke my back to help me relax. He'd sit beside me and hold my hand. He was scared, too, but tried not to show it. During the day, I rested and tried not to cough.

Gary was there without fail, helping me, loving me, taking care of everything necessary to keep the household running—shopping, cooking, cleaning up. As dreadful as my having whooping cough was, it enabled Gary to demonstrate how much he loved me. I could see it in everything he did. I had never felt so loved by him before.

I occasionally checked in with Plotinus/The Collective for advice, but I didn't do any regular meditation or my usual healing practice. I needed all my focus just to stay in my body.

I asked Plotinus for advice regarding whooping cough, and he again suggested drinking hot water, lemon, and honey. That turned out to be the best way for me to soothe my throat and lessen the intensity of the cough. As soon as I started to choke, Gary would start the kettle heating.

Plotinus advised, "Rest, rest, and more rest." Repeatedly. Thanks, Plotinus!

Very gradually, I began to recover.

Thursday, 25 July 2024

I was extremely grateful to celebrate our 30th wedding anniversary, which coincides with the Day of Santiago*, a regional holiday in Spain.

I woke up thinking of The Collective and the name "Alfred." I thought Alfred might be a doctor, which would be appropriate. Could it be the late famous Dr. Livingstone? But when I asked The Collective, I was told "Not."

Elizabeth Diamond Rose suggested I check in with my spirit guide(s) for advice about feeling better and about the X39 photon patches she had suggested we try. I decided to ask The Collective.

I also Googled "Alfred," trying to find a doctor with that name. No doctor showed up. Alfred the Great, the 9th-century Anglo-Saxon king known for his wisdom, law-making, emphasis on education, and warrior strength, seemed the most likely match. Puzzling.

Morning Meditation. I felt Plotinus arrive.

> Me: "It's good to be back."
>
> P: "We are glad to see you again. Of course, we always 'saw' you and watched over you."
>
> Me: "Thank you. Do you have any healing advice for me?"
>
> P: "Take it easy. Take it slowly. Don't hurry. Rest, rest, and more rest."
>
> Me: "Is there a doctor among The Collective?"

TC: "Paracelsus."

[Paracelsus was a renowned Swiss physician, alchemist, and philosopher who lived from 1493 to 1541.]

Me: "Does he have recommendations about food, diet, etc.?"

TC: [Pause] "We will locate him and ask."

[Pause. I sense another energy join the group. It is Paracelsus.]

Para: "Eat according to the seasons. Balanced, variety. Not too much or too little."

Me: "Seasons as in WildFit*?" [A food-freedom program that recommends cycling what you eat based on historic seasonal food availability.]

Para: "You could say that. However, now it is summer. Later it will be fall."

Me: "What about my high cholesterol that [showed up on my recent bloodwork and] spooked my doctor?"

Para: "I don't understand that terminology."

Me: "Keeping my heart healthy."

Para: "Eat well a variety. Enjoy the foods around you. Don't worry about your food."

Me: "What about the [photon] patches [that Elizabeth Diamond Rose recommended]? Are they good for me?"

Para: "I don't understand these things. However, Light [photons] is always good. You must ask your inner wisdom and trust its response. You don't need me as a go-between. You know, your body knows best."

Me: "Thank you. … Who is Alfred?"

TC: [Pause, looking at each other. Alfred joins the group; they make space for him.]

Al: "I am a wise warrior, come to give you strength and counsel."

Me: "Are you Alfred the Great, the Anglo-Saxon king?"

Al: [Nods]

Me: [Seeking evidence] "Can you tell me something [about yourself] I don't know?"

Al: "I fought well but was wounded at the Battle of [Loughton? Lightbridge?]"

[I looked that up later but couldn't find such a battle. A battle in London, yes, but not the other places. Which didn't mean that he wasn't wounded there 1100 years ago, but I didn't find it on Google.]

Me: "Thank you for joining The Collective."

TC: "We have your best interests always at heart."

Me: "What can I do creatively?" [I am eager to start being creative again!]

TC: "Rest still. You'll know when the time is ready to begin a new adventure."

Me: "How can I get stronger sooner?"

TC: "Rest, rest, and more rest."

Para: "And eat well and properly!"

Me: "Is there more advice?"

TC: "Yes. Do not stress about the world or your family. It does no good. Send prayers and blessings. And let it all go."

Me: "Thank you."

TC: "We will go now so as not to tire you."

Me: "Thank you. Oh—wait! What about my right eye's weird vision thing [that happened] last Monday?"

[Four days ago, blind spots had suddenly appeared in my right vision. It felt like I was looking through Swiss cheese. They disappeared after 15 minutes. I was worried, so we had gone to the ER. The doctor told me it was probably a visual migraine, something I had never had before.]

TC: "Nothing to worry about. A message from beyond that things are not what they seem, are not what they appear. We see through a glass darkly but then face to face."

Me: "Thank you. Goodbye until next we meet."

TC: "We are always here, watching over you, Beloved."

Tuesday, 30 July 2024

I was feeling tired and stuck. Time to ask for guidance! And time to be grateful that they were here, eager to help.

Me: "I want to ask a few targeted questions. … I'm glad to be here with you."

P and TC: "We are glad to be here with you, too."

Me: "I have some questions to ask."

TC: "Of course."

Me: "Are you [The Collective] my spirit guides?"

TC: "Of course. What else could we be?"

Me: "But you are different from Helen and my other spirit guides that I meet in the forest clearing I go to [in my expanded consciousness] during meditation."

P: "Of course. We have different purposes. We are more information-oriented, less general and emotional support."

Me: "Do you know each other?"

P: "Of course. We all 'know' each other. We are not separate in the way you are in physical form."

Me: "But you maintain your separate personalities?"

P: [Nodding] "Of course. A personality is a terrible thing to lose! [Smiling]

But we rise above the story that limits who we were, while we still maintain our unique 'flavors' or 'chords'—resonances."

Me: "I think I understand. ... What advice can you give me about the X39 photon patches? I wonder if they are just a gimmick. Do you still recommend them for me?"

P: [Nodding, with Paracelsus next to him]

Para: "Very curious items. I do not understand them. But I think they will help balance your humors [a classical paradigm of how the body functions] and improve your health."

Me: "So I should use them?"

[Nods]

Me: "And Gary? [Should he use them?]"

P and Para: [Conferring] "That we are not sure—we cannot answer for him."

Me: "OK, thank you. Another question. What about my taking R.J. Stewart's newly expanded Miracle Tree course? I took the earlier version years ago. I'm attracted to it."

P: "There is nothing new for you there. You want to connect more with angels—you don't need that course."

H: "Good day, Elyn."

Me: "Hello, Hypatia!"

H: "It [the Miracle Tree/Kabbalist Tree of Life] is another construct, one of many to organize the world. Since you have already worked with it, and it didn't take you far [Unclear. Maybe, 'didn't "take" for you'], why do it again?"

Me: "Maybe this time I'll really get it [as deeply as] some of the other students."

H and P: "It's not your path."

P: "You didn't get it because it's not your path. Very much an intellectual construct."

Me: "OK. Thank you."

P: "Of course, you can take the course, no harm."

Me: "I long for a teacher, guidance, new and deeper experiences."

P: [Smiling] "We are not enough?"

Me: [Smiling] "I get it. Of course you are. Why work through intermediaries, constructs, when I can talk with you directly?"

P: "Exactly."

Me: "What about my diet? I'm so confused."

P: "No, you aren't. You know you do best with what you call Spring [low carbohydrate, lots of vegetables, protein]. You just prefer to eat otherwise."

Me: "OK. Point taken. ... I'm feeling so stuck, bored. I want to do something new and important and creative, but I can't get going."

P, H, Para: [In chorus] "Rest, rest and more rest! Not just physical but in all fields—mental, emotional. Rest, recover. It is good you are feeling stuck. [That shows that] your energy is returning."

Me: "Can I make it return faster?"

P: "Rest, rest, and more rest. And change your diet to what you call Spring."

Me: "You told me before to do Summer!" [Summer in Wildfit* includes sweet vegetables and some fruit.]

P: "I thought you could, but you [immediately] did Fall." [Fall in Wildfit is lots of sweet fruit, carbs, beans, even grains.]

Me: "Point taken. OK. Thank you. I just want to feel more energetic, to have a project—to not be so hot! It's so hot in Girona in the summer!"

P and H: [Laughing] "You fight against your reality, which makes you more tired. Surrender."

Me: "OK. Thank you. I think I'll stop now. Oh—another question. When should I start the X39 photon patches?"

Para: *"Any day is good. You don't need to wait, but first shift your diet to Spring so as not to confuse your body."*

Me: *"Thank you. Goodbye."*

I realized my attraction to taking R.J.'s course was my longing to be part of a spiritual community again. I wasn't only interested in R.J.'s teachings, which were always good, although that was part of it. I wanted to have shared spiritual experiences. I missed that.

Thursday, 1 August 2024

I was taking Sarah Thomas's seven-part Shift Network video course, "Daoist Doorways into the Wu," a highly esoteric approach to working with crystals and stones. Crystals and minerals intrigued me, but up until this course, I had relied on what I read about their different attributes (protection, healing, calming, etc.) rather than having my own experience.

That evening, Gary and I watched Lesson 2. Sarah suggested asking your spirit guides and helpers for support in intuitively choosing stones for a practice we were about to do.

I thought, "Sure, I can do that." I asked The Collective for guidance. They said they didn't know much about crystals, but they'd bring someone who did. Who might that be? Pythagoras.

Pythagoras? *Really?* He was a very important 6th-century BCE* Greek philosopher and mathematician. His work had an enormous influence on music and geometry, among other disciplines. However, I didn't think he knew anything about crystals and stones. But Pythagoras it was.

During the practice, I "saw" Pythagoras place a golden fluorite crystal on my belly and a large, watermelon-colored point on my heart chakra, the point facing up. Then I promptly forgot what had happened.

Later that evening, Gary and I were talking about mediumship, contacting the Other Side(s), and the importance of evidence. I said I still might wonder whether my conversations with Plotinus and The Collective were the products of my imagination or my subconscious, except that several times I had been given irrefutable evidence that these inner contacts were real.

I suddenly remembered Pythagoras had assisted me during the class practice. Was there any evidence that it really was him? I Googled using the search string "Pythagoras and crystals." One of the first references that popped up was an article in *History Today* from 1956 ("Pythagoras: Artist, Statesman, Philosopher - Part II"):

"… In boyhood, as his father's apprentice, he was drawn to mathematical inquiries by observation of the crystals used by gem engravers. Sir William Ridgeway once pointed out that: '… combining his knowledge of crystallography, gained from his father's trade [he was a trader], with that of Egyptian geometry, Pythagoras conceived the world as built up of a series of material bodies imitating geometric solids. Quartz crystal would give him a perfect pyramid and double pyramid; iron pyrite is found in cubes massed together; the dodecahedron is found in nature in the common garnet; and the beryl is a cylindrical hexagon.'"

I was stunned. The Collective *did* know who to bring in as my guide to work with crystals and minerals! This was another piece of irrefutable evidence—a "gold nugget," as Susan Giesemann would say—that these contacts were real. There was no way I had known any of this about Pythagoras.

Saturday, 10 August 2024

Gary and I watched another one of Sarah Thomas's "Doorways into the Wu" classes on crystals and minerals. Some of the participants were having impressive interactions with their crystals; I, alas, still found my stones non-communicative. Apparently, I could talk with Plotinus but not with my polished obsidian disk or my rose-quartz point.

Although Gary and I were getting along much better than ever, I felt very sad. I often wanted to curl up into a fetal position and weep. It was time to ask for more insights from The Collective.

Me: "Hello Collective!"

TC: "Hello!"

Me: "I need help getting through these days."

TC: "We know. We are always here, supporting you."

Me: "What's going on? Why am I cycling in and out of despair?"

TC: "You are processing old stuff. You are taking out the garbage, so to speak."

Me: "Tell me more."

TC: "Over a lifetime, detritus accumulates. Emotional 'waste.' If it isn't cleared out, it rots and ferments—like a compost heap."

Me: "I thought I'd gotten over all this stuff."

TC: "You got over it by covering it up. It's like an ant hill that's hardened on the outside but full of tunnels and craters and buzzing ants inside. Knock the top off, and they come out running!"

Me: "I get it. But how do I get through all this now?"

TC: "Just breathe. Remember to breathe. And breathe into the pain, the sorrow, the sadness, the anger. It *will release*."

Me: "Ariel talks about sending it to the Light."

TC: [Nodding] "Much better image than 'getting rid of it.'"

Me: "Ironic that shining a fresh light on the past—seeing it through new eyes, seeing my part in it, my acceptance, [seeing myself] not only as a victim—all this 'light' just makes it hurt *more*!"

TC: "Yes, because you're uncovering it. It's all been lurking in the dark, dusty corners of—we will call it—your psyche. Light shows the [scurrying] ants in the broken-open ant hill."

Me: "So all these painful thoughts are like ants scurrying around?"

TC: [Nodding] "You could say so."

Me: "So how do I get rid of them? Call in an exterminator?"

TC: [Chuckling] "Not exactly. Notice your language: 'Get rid of.' They served a purpose. You did what you did. It helped you get through difficult times. Now it's time to do it differently and release all that injury into the Light."

Me: "'Where there is injury, pardon.'" [Quoting a line from the Saint Francis Prayer]

TC: "That's a start. Pardon yourself. Pardon others. We are—you are—only human. From this side, it looks very different."

Me: "Tell me!"

TC: "It looks ... trivial. No: less important. Like flakes of stuff, not substantial. Experiences that you have learned from and continue to learn from. Once the learning is done, they will be released to the Light—and there's learning in this review and release process as well."

P: "You are fortunate to have a loyal companion on your journey."

Me: "Yes, but he's part of the problem! The things [that happened]—"

P: "Ah, Little One, he's only human, too, and has had his lessons to learn. I can assure you he doesn't feel good about some of his actions."

Me: "For sure?"

P: "For sure."

Me: "How do I know I won't be hurt again?"

P: "It's like pain and suffering. [Sometimes pain is unavoidable] suffering is optional."

Me: "Oh."

P: "And he is truly a changed person. You know that when you interact with him. Changed but still the same. He's cleaned—is cleaning out—his midden heap, his garbage dump of emotions and behavior, of past issues that have driven him to feel like he had no way out, no way not to do what he did to survive."

Me: "But he was wrong!"

TC: "It doesn't matter. Wrong is irrelevant."

Me: "He hurt me!"

TC: "He did what he did, and you were hurt. Reasonably so. He has apologized."

Me: "How can I be sure it won't happen again?"

TC: "Nothing is sure in life. You must trust him and truly forgive him."

Me: "I thought I had, but the recycling/revisiting of my pain means I haven't, huh?"

TC: "Nodding."

Me: [Sigh]

TC: "Remember—he's only human. Well, not literally, since he and you are of course much more than human. Remember: he has his unique lessons to learn, [his] unique opportunity for growth, and so do you. You've come together to give each other those opportunities. It's not by chance. None of it is by chance."

Me: [Sigh] "That really helps."

TC: Yes. So clean out your garbage dump. Truly *forgive* yourself *for when you didn't treat yourself very well.* Know you are always loved—and that humans just do the best they can, and sometimes that doesn't feel good enough. But so it is."

Me: [Sigh]

P: [Smiling] "And then someday you'll be on the Other Side, with us, giving advice and support to another struggling human."

Me: "Feels better on your side, I bet."

H: "Better? There are advantages. Clarity, disengagement, no suffering—but there are losses as well. The struggle in life is worthwhile. I miss the breeze in my hair, running my fingers through a babbling brook, the loving praise from my father. [She gives a kind of 'mental shake' to herself.] But there is also much wonder on this side and much beauty. Indescribable. And great love."

Me: *"Thank you. I feel loved and I feel supported. Thank you."*

TC: *"Our pleasure. We are always here for you."*

30 minutes.

Later that day I had a Zoom session with Elizabeth Diamond Rose. Using her unique combination of energy healing, channeling, and astrology, she helped to clarify what was going on. She said that because I was at my emotionally safest ever, I could now revisit and release my old, wounded stuff. I could let the old traumas surface, traumas that went back a lifetime. And she gave me techniques for helping to clear the energy from my body.

When I reread the conversation I had had with The Collective, I was reminded of lessons I had learned from Jake Eagle, a wise and gifted counselor with whom we had worked for years. He taught about personal responsibility and that nobody "does" something to you. He wasn't talking about physical violence but about words or actions that one partner does and the other uses to hurt themselves. Someone does something, and you respond from your personal history, which includes past wounds and traumas. Taking full responsibility for your emotions and responses was the way to freedom. His SAGE process teaches how to change the language we use to reduce reactivity and increase clarity in our daily interactions.

My cry "But he hurt me!" was an example of me not taking responsibility for my behavior and reaction. Gary had done/said things that I used to hurt myself with. He had done what he did, and I did what I did with it. During the last few weeks, I had shifted from blaming him for things that had happened in the past to recognizing my part in those interactions—but then I had slid back into an old pattern of victimhood and blame. Which got me nowhere. Which got us nowhere. Recognizing that pattern helped me begin to feel better and even more determined to "clear out my garbage dump."

Saturday, 17 August 2024

We had completed the libretto, the music, and the audience brochure for *Celebration!*. Gary had composed 20+ pieces, some long, some short, some instrumental, most with choral parts. Even though we had reached the goal—completing the music and libretto—the goal had moved. Now we had to find out if it "worked."

Gary created the music as MP3s and printed out the MC script and audience brochure. We invited a small group of friends to come to our home and participate in a trial performance. I was going to be the MC. Depending on the audience's response, we would tweak the program. The performance would take about 60 – 75 minutes.

I was nervous about the event. Would they like it? Would it do what we wanted—raise their vibration, make people feel part of a larger whole?

I went into meditation and contacted Plotinus.

> Me: "Welcome, Plotinus. I felt you 'come in' earlier while I was watching Suzanne's Monthly Connection recording. Thank you for waiting."
>
> P: "Welcome, Elyn."
>
> Me: [Thinking about Nigel and tomorrow's run-through of Celebration! but without saying anything.]
>
> P: "It doesn't matter how well it goes."
>
> Me: [Surprised] "It doesn't?"
>
> P: "No. You have done what is needed—bringing it through. What happens next is out of your hands."
>
> Me: "But we want it—the performance—to be a success!"
>
> P: "The project is so much more than the performance. It's your own development, you and your spouse's, as you've learned to work together in love and harmony."
>
> Me: "Oh."
>
> P: "All of this is creating thought-forms that exist in your world and spread. Thought forms of love and Unity and Oneness. That's what matters."
>
> Me: "But doesn't it matter—or rather, how can it matter if Celebration! isn't performed?"

P: "It will be. But it's like the sound of a tree falling in the forest—it falls and makes a sound whether anyone human hears it. The sound waves happen. The land feels it fall. The birds hear it. The quantity of performances doesn't matter."

Me: [Hesitant] "OK. …"

P: "Or if you prefer this image, it's like ink in water. A tiny drop colors the pond. It spreads and expands and amplifies."

Me: "OK."

P: "Remember, every act you do is like that. Every thought you think is like that. So act with kindness and love."

Me: "I get it. I will remember. Is there more you want to share?"

P: "Not today. Except—be well, my child."

Me: "Thank you!"

Sunday, 18 August 2024

We did the run-through of *Celebration!* with our friends. They liked it. A lot. One person had come in with arms crossed in resistance and declared, "I don't know what I'm doing here." After the performance, he looked much more relaxed. He reported, "I felt held in the arms of tranquility!"

What a relief—and what an affirmation. The struggle had been worth it. Not only for the project but also for our relationship.

Monday, 19 August 2024

Plotinus showed up. I told him I was still pondering signing up for R.J.'s new "The Miracle Tree" course that would start on the 23rd, even though my finger-dowsing (kinesiology*) response was neutral: not in my interest, and not *not* in my interest.

> Plotinus was quite clear: "No. We are your teachers now. You want to keep being a student, to have [human] teachers, but enough. No more."
>
> Me: "I thought, maybe this *time* I'd get it."
>
> P: "There is no 'it' to get. It's here always. It's you. There's nothing to get. End of story."

In other words: "Stop being a student, claim your authority." They (Plotinus and The Collective) were there to help as guides, not teachers. It was hard to break my lifelong habit of thinking of myself as a student, but it was time.

I'd been feeling Plotinus' presence much more often those days. He and The Collective were available when I needed them.

Wednesday, 21 August 2024

> Me: "Dear Plotinus, tell me [again] why you said, 'No more R.J. courses on Kabbalah.'"
>
> P: [Consulting The Collective] "You have just made an important connection in your music project Celebration! with the five elements and alchemy [about which you already know a little]. This is a different way of organizing the world and more fruitful for you."
>
> Me: "Please tell me more."
>
> P: "The mixture of hot cold wet dry is more 'embodied.'"
>
> Me: "But it's not organized like [the Tree of Life sephirot*] around contrasting concepts like kindness/discipline—[the elements aren't about] qualities/values."

P: *"Of course not, but you already understand that balance. The balancing forces of the sephirot. Why do you think you need another course?"*

Me: *"I've felt that other people 'got' it more deeply, experienced it more profoundly, contacted the higher levels, the angels, more better."* [I smile at my intentionally poor grammar.]

P: [Sigh] *"Your perfectionism and refusal to step into your own power show up again. You contact us, remember? So why do you want to revisit which archangel is associated with which sephira? That's such human stuff. Very limited."*

Me: *"I think I get it."*

P: [Nodding] *"You are already in contact with the other realms. You already understand how to live better by balancing opposites. What more do you want?"*

Me: *"I get it. I get it!"*

P: *"You have me and Hypatia and Pythagoras—and others—at your disposal. Do you really need to memorize the names of different angels on the head of a pin?"*

Me: *"You are right."*

P: *"It's regressive for you. It is fine for others to play mind games and solve secret puzzles. You don't need that. You are already in contact with the Other Realms. I won't say 'higher'—just other. As, for example, your writing* Celebration! *and how the words flowed through you."*

Me: *"I get it. Boy, you're intense. Adamant."*

P: *"We are frustrated—well, if we were human we would be—at your continual refusal to claim your own authority."*

Me: *"OK! But I also think I want to take the course in order to have community."*

P: [Sternly] *"Are you friends with any of the people from the previous courses? Did you have community before?"*

Me: *"Not really. At the beginning, in live classes in Boulder, Colorado, maybe. Some of those people became friends. But I remember during R.J.'s* teacher training in England, I felt excluded. The British students were all connected, but I wasn't. Of all my fellow students, only Ronit in Israel [continues to be] a friend, and that's in part because we are Jewish." [To be accurate, my ancestors were Jewish, but I was raised as a Unitarian-Universalist.]

P: "Exactly. Find your community where you are and be grateful."

Me: "Thank you. Much to think about."

P: "Not really. You know it all already."

Me: [Smiling] "OK, OK, I get the message!"

P: "We leave you now."

Me: "Thank you."

Monday, 26 August 2024

Gary and I had finished the libretto and music for *Celebration!*, but there was much more work to do to get it performed. Every time we disagreed about how to proceed, Gary wanted to give up on the project.

That evening, we had a huge quarrel over how to promote it. Gary threatened to delete all the *Celebration!* files from his hard drive. He said he didn't want to have anything to do with *Celebration!* if it caused us to argue, so the solution was to get rid of it. Delete it. End of problem.

I knew that *Celebration!* was a project we had been given by Spirit, and we had to complete it. I also knew that the fault lines in our relationship would just show up somewhere else. It wasn't *Celebration!* causing the problems, it was us.

Desperate not to lose all that we had done, I replied vehemently that *Celebration!* wasn't just *his* work, it was also *mine*. He didn't have the right to delete it without my permission. And I wasn't going to give it.

I told him (once again) that this was another opportunity to deal with our stuff. The project gave us lots of opportunities, whether we liked it or not.

Eventually, he calmed down and promised not to destroy the project we had worked so hard to create. He also said he didn't want to work on it for a while. Fine. We wouldn't.

Sunday, 1 September 2024

Sitting at my altar.

Me: "Hello, Plotinus! It's good to be back in this space."

P: "Hello! We have been waiting for you."

Me: "I know. I feel you are always close and I'm very grateful."

P: [Non-physical hand wave and smile]

Me: "I have a question."

P: [Nodding]

Me: "About my dreams."

P: "Oh?"

Me: "I keep having travel dreams."

P: [Nodding]

Me: "But they usually include getting lost or being unprepared or not knowing where I'm going."

P: "Yes."

Me: "What's that mean?"

P: "It is about life, the journey of life. We are *unprepared*, we do *take the wrong road* [NB: I typed 'round road' instead of 'wrong road', and that may have been correct—*I felt like I was going in circles.*], we don't know where we are going."

Me: "So—it's just about realizing that's how it is? Nothing specific about my journey, my future? I'd begun to worry the dreams were saying I'm not prepared for where I'm going, [or that] I'm lost …"

P: [Nodding] "It's the human condition. So much you don't know. The important thing is that you are traveling! You may miss a turn, you may end up somewhere else, but you are on the path."

Me: "'The path is made by walking'?" [A line from 'Caminante, No Hay Camino,'* a poem by Antonio Machado)

P: [Pause] "Partly. Sort of. Yes—and No. There is a plan, there is guidance, there is a goal, but you don't know what it is."

Me: "So how can I get there?"

P: "What is important is the journey and how you make it. With curiosity? Kindness? Compassion? Determination? Persistence? Or with anger, refusal, resentment, stopping the journey—"

Me: "I dreamt I wasn't prepared. Last night, I hadn't even checked out of my hotel room and packed my suitcase."

P: "That's good. You don't need all that baggage. Leave it behind."

Me: "But I'd have to pay for another night in the hotel."

P: "Only in your dream! [Laughing]"

Me: "And I've dreamt twice of a room that resolves to the number 9: 243 and 414."

P: "The number of completion. You are completing a cycle of reaction and response and moving into a new way of being in relationship."

Me: "That's good."

P: [Nodding] "It is indeed. You are making progress."

Me: "Even if I feel I'm taking the wrong path or totally unprepared?"

P: "We are always unprepared. It's the human condition. Get over it."

Me: "Different question: I'm tired a lot. Can you tell me what that's about?"

P: "It takes energy to close a cycle and begin a new one. Be gentle with yourself. Rest, recuperate. Rest some more. Eat well—eat better than you are eating."

Me: "Oh. …" [They knew what I was eating. No keeping secrets!]

P: "You know what to do, you just don't want to."

Me: "Fewer carbs."

P: "Much fewer."

Me: "No gluten, sugar, dairy."

P: "A little cheese is acceptable."

Me: "Meat?"

P: "Eat lightly, eat fresh, eat well. More vegetables!"

Me: [Sigh]

P: "Aim for that, but don't be rigid."

Me: "OK. And then I'll have more energy?"

P: [Nodding] "Eventually."

Me: "Take the Royal Jelly capsules?"

P: "If that helps you, yes."

Me: "Different question. [When I was sending healing energy to Tessa this morning and 'felt' something negative from a past life of hers] I 'heard' you advise me against trying to clear Tessa's past-life trauma. Why?"

P: "You are inexperienced in these matters. They can be dangerous for the uninitiated. The trauma entity/energy can jump not only into her current life but also into you. So do not venture into these realms of healing the past and trauma unless you know more."

Me: "Ask Elizabeth Diamond Rose for [advice]?"

P: "A wise move."

[I understood from this that it was not for me to do the clearing work, nor to ask Elizabeth Diamond Rose to do it for Tessa. That was for Tessa, if she chooses. The 'ask Elizabeth Diamond Rose' meant: Talk to Elizabeth Diamond Rose about the process in general and learn more.]

Me: "How does that happen, that a past life influences this life?"

P: "How? Everything is energy and waveforms. They continue resonating for—millennia—forever, though undetectable eventually. One can shift the frequencies. That leads to healing. But one must be very careful not to pick up the unwanted frequencies during the healing. You don't know enough to do this."

Me: "OK. I won't."

P: "Good. Anything else?"

Me: "Thank you. I have deep gratitude for my ongoing access to you and your presence in my life."

P: "About time! [Smiling] I've always been here."

Me: "Always?"

P: "Well, time is relative. I'm here now with you and that should be sufficient."

Me: "Thank you. Goodbye for now."

Sunday, 29 Sept. 2024

In bed, talking with Gary, I observed that everything we were doing spread out like ripples.

A week ago, I suddenly had enough energy after Elizabeth Diamond Rose's distant healing work to write an article about channeling Plotinus. I was reticent to go public, but Plotinus had been pushing me for several days to write about channeling him and The Collective.

I wrote it in one draft and sent it to Judie Fein, one of the two editors at the award-winning YourLifeIsATrip.com travel-writing website. She approved it immediately. The next day, I sent it to Ellen Barone, the other editor, along with photos we took of the Gipsy coffee nook at Palau Fugit. Ellen scheduled it to be published five days later.

[https://www.yourlifeisatrip.com/home/traveling-to-other-dimensions]

I was nervous about "coming out of the esoteric closet," but Plotinus assured me it was time. He also said, *"Well done, well done! And you have more work to do!"*

The article came out; we promoted it with Mailchimp (an app that Gary uses to send notifications to our mailing list); and soon I began receiving lots of encouraging responses.

Right after it was published, I had an extended Messenger exchange with my long-time friend and fellow Camino de Santiago pilgrim, Kathy Gower. She said she was in contact with spirit guides and helpers but felt her unworthiness to ask for help.

I told her, "Worthiness has nothing to do with it! They are *eagerly* waiting to help!"

That shocked her and opened her heart, mind, and eyes. It was a very important and timely exchange.

Positive comments flowed in, including from a high school classmate who had forwarded the link to our class of '64 group. That had made me nervous, but his response to me (and to a skeptical classmate) was reassuring. He wrote that he knew I was credible and wasn't making this up. Other replies were equally supportive. My going public was an opportunity for other people to have their own experiences affirmed.

Yesterday, I had planned to watch Stephen Berkley's award-winning documentary, "Life with Ghosts." Stephen had sent me a free link, but I discovered it had expired.

We had met Stephen during a Zoom course that Cheryl Page was teaching. Cheryl had invited the three of us (Stephen, Gary, and me) to join one of her classes. Stephen learned about my channeling Plotinus and said he'd like to interview us for his YouTube podcast, "Life with Ghosts – Let's Chat!" Great! Another way for me to tell people about The Collective.

Stephen was a copyright lawyer who began exploring communication with the deceased seven years ago. He decided to make a documentary because of the experiences his mother had had. The film (https://www.lifewithghosts.com/) documents individuals who participate in a test project to connect with their departed loved ones using Induced After-Death Communication (IADC).

I watched his podcasts with Cheryl Page and Suzanne Giesemann. Well done! Stephen wrote me about scheduling the interview, but then he didn't respond to my subsequent emails.

I got caught up in other projects and didn't watch the documentary with the link he had provided and it expired. Yesterday, I emailed him and asked for the free link again, and this time he responded immediately. "Life with Ghosts" is a fascinating documentary about an assisted communication process to help those dealing with extensive, long-term grief after the loss of a loved one.

I wrote Stephen a fan letter and included a link to my just-published YourLifeIsATrip.com article on Plotinus. In my message, I said that we had experienced both perspectives described in the documentary—first, the pathologizing materialism, and now, living with ghosts.

He got back immediately to schedule an interview with us. I was both excited and trepidatious. Stephen had indicated that one of the things that attracted him to our story about *Celebration!* and Plotinus was that I wasn't a trained medium—and that we had PhDs. That gave us credibility in his mind.

The credibility granted by our PhDs (mine from Princeton University, Gary's from Michigan State University) and academic credentials (Gary is Distinguished Professor Emeritus of Music Theory and Composition) was amusing to us. Lots of people with PhDs are flaky, misled, misleading, or deceitful. But I was grateful for whatever gave my unlikely channeling experience more veracity. It meant we would be taken seriously by more people.

Earlier that same week, Gary had been in communication with Joe, an amateur composer friend of a friend. He sent Gary information about a software program that generates excellent voice-quality singing voices. It was just what we needed to create a version of *Celebration!* to put up on YouTube. If the software worked, we wouldn't have to wait for a live performance to get *Celebration!* out into the world.

Lying in bed talking with Gary, I drew lines between the dots: everything was working out. It all felt guided. Not preordained, not predetermined, but guided and supported.

Gary commented on how they (the guides on the Other Side) carefully chose the most believable helping hands on this side to bring their messages to the public: Suzanne Giesemann (retired navy commander, now a medium); Eben Alexander (neurosurgeon at Harvard, a near-death experiencer); Cheryl Page (cancer researcher turned medium); us (Elyn, a writer, Phd, MDiv; Gary, PhD, award-winning composer, retired Distinguished Professor)—etc. People who most people would consider credible—not just some random "woogy woogy" ungrounded weirdo/flakes.

And they also chose us because we all said "Yes." We were willing to do the work and to be of service to Spirit.

Monday, 30 September 2024

I woke up early to talk to Plotinus.

Me: "Hello, Plotinus! So good to be back with you!"

P: "Indeed."

Me: "You know my question: what next?"

P: "Write the book."

Me: "Which book? *Adventures of Everyday Mystics*?"

P: "I don't care what you call it, as long as I'm in it."

Me: "A separate book?"

P: "For you to decide."

Me: "I don't think we have talked enough for a single book."

P: [Chuckle] "Then either we talk more, or you combine it."

Me: "OK. I'm very grateful you visit with me. It's very reassuring to me."

P: [Nodding] "Thank you."

H: "And what about the rest of us?"

Me: "All of you! So different and so wise."

The Collective: [Nodding]

[Pause]

Me: "Are we chosen [by you]?"

TC: "Obviously. A tautology."

Me: "OK, so why?"

H: "Why you, or why do we choose?"

Me: "Both."

[Consulting]

H: "You have the requisite skills. Writing, analytic thought processes. Openness. Fearlessness."

Me: "Hah! Hardly fearless! I was very nervous about the YourLifeIsATrip.com article."

H: "Fearless because you did it anyway."

Me: "Thank you."

H: "And why we are doing this, interacting increasingly frequently with your realm of existence: because it is necessary. The time has come."

Me: "Necessary because?"

H: "You as a species are headed for extinction, driven by greed and anger and fear."

P: "Living in separation from each other and the One."

H: "Ignorant, ignorant people!"

Me: "So, how does my article or Celebration! help?"

H: [A bit annoyed] "It's obvious how Celebration! helps. Don't ask wasteful questions."

Me: "Sorry."

P: [Taking over] "The task is to enable human beings to realize their true nature of connectedness and love. It is easily forgotten in the turmoil and distraction of their raising, their being born into and living in this world of materiality and differentiation."

Me: "Who directs you to do this work with humans?"

TC: [Looking at each other] "Nobody directs us. We sense the need. As The Collective, we are part of the greater collective field of energy—[Universal] Consciousness. We know what is needed."

Me: "Thank you. How do you know who to work with? Do you follow our bios?"

TC: [Laughing] "No need. We sense your energy fields. It's all embedded there—your wounds, your gifts, your skills, your day-to-day triumphs and disappointments."

Me: "That's impressive ... or rather, I can't get my head around how you can know, since there are billions of us!"

TC: "It's not for you to know. ... Your view is by nature limited. ... Think of a Polynesian navigator who knows how to read the vast ocean and sky for signs of a distant island—and navigates unerringly to the destination."

Me: "Oh, I wish I could!"

TC: "With more training and determination, you will also learn to read the signs to reach your destination."

Me: "Which is?"

TC: "Fullness and completeness in all its manifestations."

H: "And service."

TC: "Of course. That's the expression of it all."

Me: "Thank you. I'm grateful—and I know Gary is—for the opportunity. And for all the support."

TC: "You are welcome. Just continue to do your part."

Me: "With gratitude and pleasure. So, the next 'more to do' is a book project. [I need to begin by] Looking at messages I've received from you, putting them in a context, perhaps alternating with research, interspersing messages with research on mediumship, worldview, NDEs*?"

TC: [Nodding]

Me: "Or: *Adventures of Everyday Mystics* with [channeling] Plotinus as an appendix? That no longer feels right."

TC: [Nodding]

Me: [Sigh] "Lots of work to do! I'm so glad you'll be with me—or I couldn't do this."

TC: "We are always with you. … Any more questions?"

Me: [Laughing] "Who'll win the US election?" [Donald Trump, Republican, and Kamala Harris, Democrat, bitterly competing to become president of the US in November.]

TC: [Serious] "One thing is to win, another is to govern."

Me: "That's ominous."

TC: "It should be."

Me: "Oh my."

TC: "You see how important the work you are doing is. So much anger and hatred are fed by separation."

Me: "Is there a cosmic battle between the Forces of Good and Evil?"

TC: [Sigh] "Too simplistic by far. Perhaps, better framed, the forces of connection and separation, of unity and—not diversity—but rather isolation. Notice it's not 'versus,' it's 'and.'"

Me: "So, it's not a battle like in The Dark is Rising [an award-winning Young Adult series by Susan Cooper]?"

TC: "It's a natural ebb and flow of natural forces built into the universe of manifestation. A teaching moment, if you will."

Me: "So, don't fight against it?"

TC: "Correct. Don't fight against it, but—in your terminology—bring the Light to it. The Light of love and connection. That energy shifts the balance."

H: "*The* imbalance."

TC: "Now Hypatia, we have agreed to disagree about that."

H: "She [Elyn] doesn't know that."

TC: "Point taken."

Me: "You guys disagree?"

TC: "Of course! We are still not ... dissolved, melded—returned—to the One. We maintain something of our personalities and, obviously, our engagement with the world."

Me: "I see. ... I'm getting tired. ... Thank you and goodbye for now."

TC: "Goodbye! But we are never gone, remember. We are always here with you. Just get quiet and still—and listen."

30+ minutes.

I sent the channeled conversation to Tessa, Nigel, and Gary. I immediately got this reply from Tessa:

"I think this is fabulous! You are clearly the right person to do this, and I think you are ready, although I appreciate what a big task it will be. This, combined with *Celebration!*, will be a powerful force for good and for opening the energy of the planet. And, boy, do we need it now! If there is anything I can do to support you as you take this on, just let me know. A lovely message to read as the new week starts. Lots of love, Tessa"

Gary told me he was in awe of the information—and the challenge of doing this important work. He said, "We are going to need LOTS of help!"

And we were getting help with *Celebration!*. First, how unlikely was it that our mutual friend contacted Joe, Joe got back with us a few days later, and it turned out he was a skilled (enough) composer and used software that generates choral voices with words. With this, we could put up a version of *Celebration!* on YouTube. We wouldn't have to wait to record a live performance.

Gary said we would need help for all we were doing—well, there it was! There was Tessa, offering to be of support. And Stephen was going to interview us, which would promote *Celebration!*. And our Catalan artist friend Carles was getting ready to send the *Celebration!* files to his contacts. We had help on both sides of "the veil."

Friday, 4 October 2024

Interesting and somewhat disturbing exchange on WhatsApp with my relatively new friend, Cynthia Ketting. I'd sent her a link to my Plotinus article, but I hadn't heard back. I wrote her on WhatsApp to ask if she'd gotten the link, read it, didn't like it, didn't want to talk about it, or—?

Cynthia had a long history of going on spiritual retreats, doing Centering Prayer, and exploring the more mystical aspects of Catholicism. She had seemed open-minded about different kinds of spiritual experiences during our previous conversations.

Cynthia replied: "I did read the article. It was very interesting, and I believe you had the experience. Channeling spirits is not something I feel at all comfortable with, however. A good friend [the one who will visit Medjugorje, the site in Bosnia-Herzegovina of a recurrent apparition of the Virgin Mary] used to work with an exorcist in the Boston area ten years ago or so. I am familiar with some of her experiences and don't feel comfortable opening the door to any spirits! Perhaps you are very skilled at discerning spirits. I know I'm not!"

Me: "I look forward to talking with you more about this, if you are comfortable doing so. You have such a broad range of experience, different from mine. Coffee next week at your fave place in the Devesa Park?"

A bit later, another message from Cynthia: "All I know is, many of the people she was exposed to (she is a psychologist as well) blindly dabbled in things like channeling, and what started out seeming benign got out of hand quickly with physical, mental and other manifestations. ... Not common, I imagine, but it happens. Be careful."

Me: "I remember you mentioned your [visiting] friend also visits Medjugorje. If you think it's appropriate, I'd love to meet her and hear about her experiences. I won't mention Plotinus."

Cynthia: "Her trip is jam-packed. ... I'll let you know. To be honest, she'd probably sense your new friend."

Me: "I'll tell him to stay away!"

The conversation was an eye-opener. Over the centuries, the Virgin Mary was often reported to appear, especially to children. Seeing an apparition of Mary at Medjugorje was OK, but channeling was dangerous. The first was approved of by the Church but channeling wasn't. Catholic beliefs include both holy apparitions and conniving demons. Cynthia's friend had assisted in exorcisms, so she knew that non-physical beings were real. As a good Catholic, she also knew that direct spiritual contact with beings from the Other Side was something the Church discouraged, and any claims to do so were rigorously investigated.

I didn't doubt that there is nasty stuff out there in the other dimensions, but I knew that Suzanne and Cheryl and Karen and David (to name a few reputable channelers) focused on connecting with the Light and Highest Good, not on anything else. I knew that Elizabeth Diamond Rose had had encounters with some pretty unpleasant shadow energies, but she also had plenty of experiences with beings of Light and Love.

There was good and power and beauty—witness Plotinus and The Collective—on the Other Side, eager to communicate. Maybe what you contacted, or what contacted you, was influenced by how balanced you were, your vibrational level, and what you attracted. And your motivation. Were you ego-driven? Greed-focused? Or was your motivation to serve others and bring more Light and Love into the world?

Was I being gullible? Misguided? Used? Was I ripe for a stealth takeover from some nefarious spiritual being? I always asked that only beings of Love and Light approach me, and I sensed I was protected. I felt into my experience with Plotinus, Hypatia, and The Collective. They wanted to help humanity, including me. They gave me excellent advice. They always respected my boundaries. They withdrew if I asked them to; they didn't speak through me if I said "No."

I reached out to Plotinus. What I "heard" was, *"There is nothing to fear. We are with you."*

Saturday, 5 October 2024

My 78th birthday!

During my morning meditation, all my spirit guides showed up to celebrate my birthday. I was so grateful for their support, encouragement, and concern.

I asked Plotinus again about Cynthia's comments, and I got the clear message that, of course, there are all kinds of beings out there. Just as on this earthly plane, there are some sketchy neighborhoods that you want to avoid. Especially at night. Plotinus also reminded me that Light attracts Light. There was nothing to fear if your vibration was high and clear.

I remembered Suzanne's YouTube talk, "Did I pick up a negative entity?", and her conclusion. She realized that her energy was off balance, and it could be cleared. And she did so.

The view of the Catholic Church (and many other religious groups) was Good versus Evil, priests in charge, be afraid of sin and the devil. Was it any wonder that some people opened up to negative energies? Or maybe these were expressions of their own inner shadows?

After a thorough review of my experiences, I decided I would continue my contact with Plotinus and The Collective. I was not afraid I was being tricked by something evil that wanted to "take me over." Besides, I had plenty of evidence that they were real, albeit departed, people, with positive motives, not shadowy, murky beings in disguise.

I thought about Cynthia's comment that she didn't think she'd be good at discerning good from bad spirits. There were some simple ways. Ask them who they are. I'd been taught by various teachers that if you asked, they have to reveal who (or what) they are. Ask for evidence. Sense how they feel. Sense how you feel. Do they ask you to do things that harm others or yourself? If so, watch out. On all the tests, Plotinus and The Collective came out as filled with Light and Love—and good advice.

Conversation with Plotinus and The Collective.

> Me: "So good to talk with you. So full of gratitude on my birthday that you are here, guiding me."
>
> P: "You are welcome. We are eager to make our knowledge known in the world."
>
> Me: "I had a briefly unsettling conversation with Cynthia about 'Beware of being possessed!'"
>
> P: "Do you feel possessed?"
>
> Me: "Absolutely not!"
>
> P: "Correct. We have no interest in 'possessing' you—only in informing you, engaging you, supporting you."
>
> Me: "But there are beings that would?"
>
> H: "My turn! Let me speak. [Pause] There are all kinds in Heaven and Earth. The mob that tore me apart in my Alexandria life were possessed. But not by demons. By fear and hate. Those are the real demons."
>
> Me: "Cynthia talked about exorcism, beings taking over."
>
> P: "She speaks from a limited perspective."
>
> H: [Impatient] "Of course, it can happen, but only by mutual agreement."
>
> P: [Nodding] "Well said."
>
> H: [Gathering steam] "Just as with the mob that dismembered me and

scraped off my flesh with mussel shells. They, too, agreed to be taken over. Humans are the worst. The worst. No need for spirit possession when you have power and greed and the hidden fears within to possess you."

Me: "So I have nothing to fear?"

P: "'But fear itself,' to quote, I think, Winston Churchill." [Correction: it was Franklin D. Roosevelt.]

H: "It's all about power and control—and then the loss of individual control in the sway of the collective."

Me: "Was Hitler possessed?"

P: "By power and greed and ego."

Me: "And Trump?"

P: "Such an interesting case. His soul agreed to come to Earth as the target [who would spread] so much hate and racism and misogyny and fear … a powerful soul indeed—hard to withstand such energies [the hatred and fear directed back at him as a target]."

[I realized later there was another side to what the soul of Hitler or Trump experienced: adulation, power, ego gratification, and more power.]

H: "You don't have to like a powerful soul—just recognize it's acting out its destiny."

Me: "And 'the Burning Times' [witch hunts]?"

The Collective: "Ah yes. Another example of human frailties and acting out of fear, greed, hate, power."

Me: "I'm hearing a lot of repetition here."

TC: "Yes, you humans have your individual souls but there's also a—collective zeitgeist that also needs to—"

H: [Breaking in] "Has the opportunity, the possibility—"

TC: "To advance. That's what you Lightworkers are doing: raising the collective vibration of humanity."

H: "May you do it soon enough."

Me: "You care?"

TC: [Nods] "Of course. We were all human once. Well—most of us. The ones you've met."

Me: "Are gods/goddesses once human?"

TC: "Some were, others weren't. Some will be, others won't."

Me: "They can change 'species'?"

TC: [Nodding]

Me: "Like our friend's spirit contact, Athena?"

TC: [Nodding] "More like—the soul vibration—everything has a unique soul vibration—can 'incarnate'—like Zeus, coming to Earth as a swan to rape Leda."

H: "Or Jesus coming as Jesus."

Me: [Quizzical. I don't understand.]

H: "Christ Consciousness coming as Jesus."

P: "Or Shiva or Krishna or … Thor or Thoth …"

Me: "It sounds very fluid."

P: "It is."

Me: "And none of these are evil entities taking possession of a human."

P: "Correct."

TC: "Sometimes there are agreements—conscious or otherwise—that enable a negative or lower-energy being to co-inhabit a human."

Me: "Possession."

TC: "Of sorts. Mutually beneficial, agreed upon, until it isn't. It never is in good balance for long."

P: "But it's easy to avoid. Just say NO."

Me: "Check out the entity?"

P: *[Nodding]*

H: "They can't 'enter' without permission. Do due diligence. Ask who they are. Ask if they are who they say they are. What are their motives? [What are] yours?"

Me: "I was so startled when Plotinus came through—not afraid but shocked. I needed him to respect my boundaries and give me evidence."

P: "That was very wise. It's important to test new acquaintances on your plane of manifestation—getting to know people [better]—as well as acquaintances from our dimension."

Me: "[Do you need to be careful] in your dimension?"

TC: "We attract—like you do—according to our vibration. High frequency to high frequency. There are others here, but they cannot harm us. We simply repel them [repel versus attract, like a magnet] with our energy."

Me: "Gary's guides talk about the Church and its authority determining what's acceptable."

TC: "Of course! Institutionalized terror is OK if they are doing it."

Me: "Hence the destruction of the Cathars, the Gnostics."

TC: "Indeed."

Me: "It's important to trust oneself."

TC: "Absolutely."

H: "And to do due diligence."

Me: "Are there cosmic laws about this?"

TC: *[Nodding]* "Indeed."

Me: "Such as?"

TC: "Asking if they are who they say they are—and if they aren't, they HAVE to leave."

Me: "Gary and the [one we refer to as the] 'hitchhiker.'"

[Back story: Some years ago, during a time when Gary was afraid of death, he was contacted in meditation by the spirit of a departed composer. Gary naively invited the spirit to experience life through him, in exchange for him promising to pave the way for Gary in the afterlife. It was not a good idea. It started gradually in his dreams, but soon Gary had to fend off the compulsive urge to compose. It was a struggle of wills. Then Gary became mysteriously weaker and weaker, until he could hardly walk. He was diagnosed with profound anemia, so profound he could have died from it, but there was no discoverable cause. Gary started getting iron infusions, which helped, but he was still weak. It occurred to me that perhaps the 'hitchhiker' had something to do with his loss of vital energy. We used various techniques to expel/release the energy form, and Gary recovered. Coincidence? Maybe. One could argue that the 'hitchhiker' wouldn't want to kill off its host, but Gary had refused to give in to the urge to compose.]

TC: "[That example of] the 'hitchhiker' is complicated because Gary gave permission. Many times, that's the entry key—you know that—you say 'Yes,' and they can enter."

[I am reminded of Susan Cooper's series, *The Dark is Rising*, where giving permission enables a nefarious being to enter a specific place.]

Me: "And then you can say NO, and they leave?"

TC: "More complicated because of the initial YES. Outside help is often required for release."

Me: "What about curses? You didn't say YES, but someone curses you. That can be real, right?"

TC: "Yes. Free will enables powerful humans to [searching for word]—"

H: "Misuse—"

TC: "Misuse their power on others for evil—what you call evil—purposes."

H: "It's all part of life experience."

Me: "What about Tessa [who has a painful, progressive genetic disorder]?"

TC: "A complicated case. It's moving forward her spiritual growth and Nigel's."

Me: "But at such a cost!"

TC: "It's a challenging narrative—story—they have chosen to play in this life."

Me: "It's not fair!"

TC: "Fairness has nothing to do with the story they are acting out. Personal growth through suffering, deepening love greater than superficial attachment and gratification ... all that is part of it."

Me: "I don't think I could survive."

TC: "Your challenges have been different."

Me: [Nodding] "A heavy conversation."

TC: [Nodding]

Me: "I remember you—Plotinus—said originally, we incarnate to have experiences and evolve."

P: "Yes. And we evolve faster from the difficult than the easy."

H: "My brutal end was painful."

Me: "How did it help you evolve?"

H: "By rising above pain and suffering into forgiveness."

Me: "Wow. That's heavy."

H: [Nodding]

Me: "I am tired. I need to stop. I want to end on an upbeat note of gratitude for all of you. Your presence in my life has transformed it."

TC: "You are welcome."

P: "My child ... you are welcome."

H: "Dear friend, you are welcome."

Me: "Thank you."

Tuesday, 8 October 2024

Pilgrimage-related stuff kept showing up. In my dreams, I was walking pilgrimage roads, or trying to find where they began, or helping other people to walk them. The Camino de Santiago (also known as the Camino Francés, a 1000-year-old pilgrimage road that stretches 500 miles across northern Spain) was the topic of my PhD dissertation and my first published book *Following the Milky Way – A Pilgrimage across Spain*. Gary and I had walked various Caminos together in Spain, Cornwall, Ireland, and France—but why was I dreaming about pilgrimage now? At our ages, it was unlikely we would ever walk a pilgrimage road again.

I had just received in the mail two Ireland-to-Wales Pilgrimage Trail Credentials. These were documents designed to be stamped along the pilgrimage way to verify the journey. I'd ordered them, so that was no surprise. But why had I ordered them? Was it curiosity? Hope? Nostalgia?

Walking by the Catholic diocese bookstore near the Girona Town Hall, my attention was snagged by a coffee mug with a picture of Santiago (St. James the Greater, the first martyred apostle) in the window display. The slogan beside the staff-carrying, scallop-shell emblazoned pilgrim saint was, "The kilometers don't count if I'm not walking at your side."

I knew what the Church wanted the slogan to mean: Walking the Camino de Santiago without Christian intention wasn't a pilgrimage. But for me it meant something else. He (Santiago) had been walking beside me since the first time I walked the Camino in 1982.

I went into the bookstore and bought the mug and a plasticized map of the Camino Francés. I did not know why. Nostalgia for the Camino's importance in my life? But why now?

Sitting at Gipsy in Palau Fugit a little later that morning, I asked Plotinus.

> Me: "Why [am I getting] all this Camino de Santiago stuff?"
>
> P: "Because you are embarking on a new Camino."
>
> Me: "What kind of Camino?"

P: *"That is for you to discover."*

Me: *"A new writing project? Your book? Everyday Mystics? Or?"*

P: *"It's much more than that. It's the Camino of your life. [This was an ambiguous statement—it's the Camino of my life, or it's the path of my life, or ...] I will always walk beside you."*

Me: *"Not Santiago? [Thinking of the coffee cup] Or are you Santiago?"*

P: *[Sounding slightly miffed] "I am Plotinus. You know that."*

Me: *"But why all this Camino stuff and Santiago?"*

P: *"A convenient way to get your attention. And, as you said, he always walks beside you. Always. As do I."*

[A new voice began communicating.]

Santiago/St. James the Greater: *"I've always been here but we haven't communicated."*

Me: *"Why?"*

Sant: *"Because you weren't ready."*

Me: *[I thought, that's probably true.] "Are you part of The Collective?"*

Sant: *"Sometimes."*

[I felt him withdraw. I changed the topic to politics, which are so dire right now.]

TC: *"Rise above it, observe the human story from a distance."*

I remember Suzanne's expression, "Isn't that interesting!" Instead of getting upset or outraged, get some distance on the situation by observing it with detachment. "Isn't that interesting that humans behave this way."

Note: I told Gary some time ago that I had had an unexpected visit with Santiago during one of my conversations with my guides. At that time, Santiago affirmed he had been guiding me since I began studying the Camino in Summer 1981. I wondered: Maybe—just maybe?—he had been guiding me even before then, orchestrating my spending the summer of 1981 in Sahagún de

Campos in Spain, a very small town located on the Camino, so that I would discover that people were once again walking the medieval pilgrimage road.

Santiago was not a talkative contact like Plotinus and The Collective. I hadn't been ready to communicate with him before. Maybe that would change now.

Odd to talk about spirit beings as talkative. Maybe "communicative" would be more accurate. After all, only Plotinus (and occasionally The Collective) spoke aloud through me. Hypatia had never made any effort to do so, and The Collective only a few times. Even without vocalized sound, I could always tell who was communicating: The vibration or frequency of their silent interactions was as distinctive as if they spoke.

Thursday, 10 October 2024

I was feeling a bit nervous about what the "pilgrimage of my life" phrase meant.

Yesterday we were in Girona's Trueta Hospital ER for 5+ hours because of Gary's spiking blood pressure. We contacted Stephanie to send Pranic Healing, but there was a 10-hour time difference between us and Australia. In the past, Stephanie had been able to get Gary's blood pressure down almost immediately.

Was this "pilgrimage of my life" something to do with Gary's (or my) health challenges? Plotinus had reassured me there was nothing to fear and that curiosity was a better attitude. I was working on it, but it was hard.

Or maybe the pilgrimage was a pilgrimage into the Imaginal Realm—and back. If so, my companions on the journey included Gary, Plotinus, Hypatia, and The Collective.

Friday, 11 October 2024

I woke up channeling a new book project for Gary: *Spirituality 101*, a collection of practical, easy-to-understand information on broadly spiritual topics—including pilgrimage, dowsing, breathwork, labyrinth walking, chanting, sacred movement—topics that shared the "glue" of taking people beyond the limitations of the materialist world. Later, after many conversations and Google searches, we changed the tentative working title to *Conscious Living—a Tasting Menu*.

Sunday, 13 October 2024

We had coffee at Tessa and Nigel's and met their visiting friends, Tim and Gema, who were interested in so-called spiritual topics. We had a wide-ranging conversation about synchronicities, channeling, minerals, gemstones, and much more. Gema had a lot of fear around some of these topics because she lacked knowledge. I realized that I had information that Gema needed to hear.

I told her how to cleanse gems and minerals and how to charge them. I told her that yes, there were entities out there that might want to come in and weren't the best (Gema told a story about a friend's friend who had let some kind of negative energy inside her and it was not nice)—but you don't have to be afraid. You set the intention. You surround yourself with Light. You ask for only the best/highest vibrational beings to come near. You learn simple clearing techniques, including regular chakra balancing.

I told her that usually when something negative happens, there is some kind of exchange, conscious or otherwise, that has been agreed upon—like someone wants something and the entity wants something, so they agree to help each other out. We told the not-before-told-publicly story of Gary's non-corporeal "hitchhiker," and the agreement they had that he would help smooth the way for Gary when Gary passed on, and, in exchange, the "hitchhiker" would be back in this world and able to compose again. And how that hadn't been good for Gary.

I kept having the feeling that these were stories she needed to hear and that I was speaking Truth.

Gema told us about a crystal she had been drawn to, but she was not sure it was a good stone. She was afraid she might take in bad energy, so she didn't buy it. And she regretted it. Lack of information can lead to fear.

The night before, I had dreamt about a row of gemstones for sale. The one I wanted to buy—but didn't—was a polished upright pink, translucent stone with gold veins in it. The stone Gema was talking about was semi-translucent, like pink quartz, with white and/or brown veins. Hmmm. Was I dreaming about her stone last night? How curious.

Tim and Gema told us about numerous synchronicities that had occurred the week before. They had been struggling with the decision to euthanize Minnie, their very old, very loved, and very ailing dog, and whether to be with Minnie when it happened. The woman sitting next to them in a café/bakery turned out to be a lawyer who also worked with animal rights. After their conversation, they decided to be with their dog during the euthanasia.

As Tim was describing this experience, I spontaneously went into an altered awareness and sensed an oval, fluffy energy behind his shoulders/head, filled with love. I realized it was departed Minnie, showing affection—an energetic hug saying everything was fine. I was startled. First I channeled Plotinus and The Collective, and now a pet!

Tim left the room, and I told Gema what I had seen. I said I wasn't sure I should say anything, but she said I should. I also asked whether Minnie was white and small/medium in size. It turned out she was a Jack Russell terrier, mostly white. That was the evidence I needed. I told Tim, and he was comforted. Seeing how much better Tim felt, I understood why Suzanne Giesemann emphasizes the healing capacity of mediumship.

Oh my! Now I was channeling pets. I kept sensing something energetically around Gema, too, but I felt no urgency to tell her, so I didn't.

We talked about the energy of places and spaces, and what could be done to clear them if they felt "off."

We got ready to leave. Nigel and Tessa said we wouldn't be able to meet the following Sunday because they would be gone.

Where were they going? Hostal Spa Empúries.

Hostal Empúries? That was one of my favorite places, a boutique hotel with an excellent restaurant, located in an isolated area beside a beachfront boardwalk overlooking the Mediterranean.

I told them I was envious. The previous week I'd checked online about staying there—I wanted to spend a few days by the sea—but it was too expensive. I'd even investigated the transportation options, but taking the bus felt daunting and the taxi was costly.

They suggested we join them. Tessa had found a reasonable room rate from Sunday to Tuesday, and they would rent a car to get all of us there and back. What a delightful synchronicity.

I was buzzed. Channeling a dead pet. Channeling/speaking Truth to Gema to give her information she needed. Last night's dream of a pink stone with golden veins. Hostal Empúries. YES! I was in the flow—even if sometimes it felt like I was riding the rapids in a very small canoe.

With promises to make reservations with the hotel, we said goodbye and walked home. I needed to talk with Plotinus about all this, but first I needed to get grounded. So we sat on a bench outside the nearby Archaeology Museum. Later, back home, I found a polished piece of hematite in my crystal/mineral collection and held it in my hand. I also put my string of hematite beads around my neck. Thunk! I could feel myself coming back into myself.

Monday, 14 October 2024

We recorded the podcast interview with Stephen Berkley for his YouTube channel "Life with Ghosts – Let's Chat." I felt anxious about going public. I'd had positive responses to my article on YourLifeIsATrip.com, but this was an interview on a YouTube channel. I would be seen, not just read.

I was really coming out of the esoteric closet. No longer flying under the radar. I much preferred to be unobtrusive, unseen, but I knew we had to do this for Plotinus and Hypatia and The Collective.

Stephen was interested in us because we hadn't been searching to reconnect with a loved one, and because we had PhDs. He liked interviewing academic/professional types because we were taught to be analytical and rigorous. He made a point of referring to us as Dr. Aviva and Dr. White throughout the interview.

He homed in on Plotinus and what channeling him was like. He wanted to know if Plotinus would "come through" during the interview and tell him something evidentiary that he could check out. I said I couldn't do that kind of thing—I'm not a professional medium.

He wanted to know why Plotinus was coming through now and to me. I answered, "Because it is important now for people to rise above division, to recognize we are all One."

Stephen had trouble relating to the "all One" concept, so we talked about *Celebration!* and the importance of gratitude.

He asked, "Why did Plotinus contact you?"

I replied, "Because I'm open. And I said 'Yes.' And because we can help get Plotinus's message out to the public."

He wanted to know how it felt when Plotinus first came through me. He said he would have called an ambulance and checked himself into the psych ward if that had happened to him. And so on.

Afterward, I felt that I had been less than eloquent when talking about Plotinus's messages—I just wasn't prepared. I was still too much in the "I just channeled a dead man!" stage to be prepared with a list of Plotinus (and Hypatia) quotes and a coherent storyline.

However, I did talk about how important it is to *know* that there is life after death and that consciousness continues. I repeated that several times. And about the role of evil in the world: That we incarnate to learn and grow, and we learn faster from bad experiences than from good ones. And that our perspective about evil is very limited. Evil enables some people who encounter it to respond with goodness. I guess I did an acceptable job.

I asked Plotinus afterward, and he replied, *"It was good enough. It could have been better."*

I'm sure it could have been, but I wasn't prepared to quote Plotinus word for word. I should have been. I felt disappointed in my presentation, so I decided to send Stephen a brief email with some of Plotinus' own words, along with an intro to *Celebration!*. Hopefully, he would include that in the edited version. (He didn't.)

That evening we had dinner with John and Sally, a San Francisco lawyer and his therapist wife. We had met them by chance years ago during their annual visit to Girona. They had read my article about channeling Plotinus and were very curious.

John challenged what I said—not disbelieving me, but pushing for more evidence. His view was that Plotinus liked to talk: He was an important guy, he said, with his own Wikipedia page. He wondered how Plotinus knew about Iamblichus. Were they alive at the same time? Good question. John seemed to suggest I should not trust Plotinus because "he's a guy." Huh?

Sally was curious about the details. Did I actually *talk* to them? I told them that yes, I had conversations with Plotinus, Hypatia, and The Collective, though often without spoken words. Was I conscious during these exchanges? Yes. It wasn't like something took me over and I went into deep trance, nothing like what I'd seen in ethnographic documentaries or modern horror movies about temporary spirit possession.

Between the interview with Stephen and the dinner conversation, Plotinus was thoroughly out of the closet. As was I. I had a moment before going to sleep when I wondered if I should ask Stephen not to post the interview, but then I got my courage back.

Thursday, 17 October 2024

Tessa had started wondering whether the spirits of previous inhabitants in their house might be trying to get into her body. I reassured her but also suggested the house did need clearing. Gary was having more blood pressure spikes, and I may have had one as well. So much was happening.

I checked with Plotinus, who replied, *"All is well, all will be well. There is nothing to fear."*

Thank you, Plotinus. And thank you, Stephanie, for sending Pranic Healing to both of us.

Sunday - Tuesday, 20 - 22 October 2024

We had a delightful escape with Tessa and Nigel to the Costa Brava coast and Hostal Spa Empúries. Excellent food, company, alone time, downtime, relaxing. Ahhhh. I/we needed that.

Thursday, 24 October 2024

I had been feeling so busy, so overwhelmed. At least Gary's blood pressure seemed stable, thank goodness, but we had had to deal with a financial crisis. Our investment broker for 30 years at Wells Fargo suddenly stopped working with us because of new company rules restricting accounts with US citizens residing outside of the US. Suddenly, we couldn't access any of our financial resources. We needed to transfer money to pay our Girona rent and utilities bills ASAP.

We tried to find a replacement broker, but it wasn't easy. Several we approached informed us they also had to follow new, more restrictive rules. Finally, our Wells Fargo broker recommended someone who could and would work with us. What a relief!

Plotinus came through and had me sit down with him on a bench. He made me promise to talk at length later.

Later that afternoon:

Me: "You are ready to speak to me?"

P: "With *you*. Of course. I told you so earlier, come sit with me and let's talk."

Me: "It's been too long, except for snatches of time when I'd reach out to you."

P: "Indeed it is too long."

Me: "I worried if you'd still be here."

TC: "We are always here. You have but to ask."

Me: "I am so relieved."

P: [Clearing throat—as if he had one—as if to say, 'ahem'!] "So now, let's talk."

Me: "What do you want to tell me?"

P: "It's a dangerous time on Earth. You must do all you can to alleviate suffering, to restore harmony."

Me: "As with Celebration!?"

P: "A good beginning. You must spread the word about the Other [Realms], release people from their traumatically narrow visions of the material—only material—world."

Me: "I see that. The Conscious Living book project?"

P: "A good one. Yes. We will help Gary."

Me: "The Plotinus Speaks book project?"

P: "Yes, but we need more conversations to express the reality of the Other Realms.

Me: "I can ask you questions from The Spirits' Book [an extensive series of interviews with channelers, conducted in the 19th century by the French educator Allan Kardec]."

P: "It was a noble effort."

Me: "How do you know what's going on [here on Earth after you die]?"

P: "We watch, we listen."

H: "And we observe."

Me: "Hello, Hypatia! Elizabeth Diamond Rose says I should ask you about the color magenta. I've been very attracted to it recently."

H: "I know little of colors, preferring the purity of white. But it is true [that] all colors have their ... namesakes ... their attributes. Your friend Elizabeth Diamond Rose is finely attuned to all these subtleties."

Me: "Do they really matter?"

H: "Only to some. And to some they matter a great deal, [for they are] fine-tuned to the vibrational differences between one green and another, the subtle differences in pitch, if you will, to use a musical analogy. There are the pure main cardinal colors—red, green, black, blue, yellow, for example—and then there are the myriad varieties. Some like them pure, others like them more ... subtle."

Me: "And you?"

H: "I like white. [Chuckling] Quite appropriate, now, on the Other Side."

Me: "What color are you?"

H: "No color at all, a mere wisp—a barely perceivable vibrational pattern floating in the air."

Me: "But I saw you—and Plotinus—"

H: "We can put on form—the garb of form—like you put on clothes."

Me: "How?"

H: "Hard to explain to someone in your dimensional space, but a bit like having a frequency dial."

Me: "Hmmm."

P: "Enough of this. Shall we talk about other topics?"

Me: "Yes, please. What?"

P: "Ask me."

Me: "Are all souls on the Other Side good?"

TC: "Of course not. Though what you understand by 'good' is very limited."

P: "Souls in your plane live lives of different degrees of morality and ethics. When they cross over, the actions of the personality stay with them for a while. Some of them are very inharmonious."

Me: "Are they dangerous?"

P: "Not to us, but to themselves and to you, they can be."

Me: "So not all spirit contacts are good to make?"

P: "You know that. You've often given the example of walking at night in a bad neighborhood of [New York or Chicago] [In other words: you must be careful]."

Me: "Do they—these spirits—live with you or are they segregated?"

P: "A good question from your perspective, but not too meaningful here. We have no danger from them. They may whip about and snarl, but they can't harm us. They can disturb for a moment our harmonious environment, but that is all. Like a fly buzzing."

Me: "But for us? Do they interact with us?"

TC: "Sometimes, in some places."

Me: "Do I—am I at risk?"

P: "Some of them are attracted to the Light, but they can do no harm if you do not invite them—if you are not attracted to the dark."

H: "Dark also seeks dark."

Me: "Suzanne Giesemann spoke about seeing 'cocooned' souls, protected from the other souls, with guards, until they had healed or been re-educated."

P: "We all have free will, and that includes the freedom to make bad choices and harm others."

Me: "So what about the cocoons?"

TC: "There are many varieties of souls coming to the Other Side. Some are eager to change their trajectory. You understand, when we say 'soul,' this is not the deep or true soul, it's the personality distortion that we are describing. So they may agree to be cocooned as Suzanne describes—to be re-educated."

H: "Others like to cause trouble and it will take many more lives/incarnations before they are willing to submit to purification."

Me: "What about Hitler?"

[Silence]

P: [Slowly] "His soul took on a big task to be burdened for a long time with so many deaths … so much hatred."

Me: "Like Trump?"

P: [Nodding] "Very strong to withstand so much hatred sent to him. Maybe that's why his mind is beginning to fail."

Me: "Will he be cocooned on the Other Side?"

P: "Hard to know. Perhaps his soul will be eager to be purified."

Me: "Who makes these decisions?"

H: "We all have free will. Each of us does. We can create cocoons and guards, if that is what we desire."

Me: "Cynthia Ketting warned me about 'letting you in'—that you might be evil in disguise [trying to possess me]."

TC: [Laughing] "Do you imagine so?"

Me: "No."

TC: "She is a product of her unfortunate upbringing, which actually feeds by fear the very thing she fears."

Me: "Well, I'm relieved."

H: "Really?"

Me: "No, I wasn't worried."

H: [Smiles] "The mob that dismembered me, do you think their souls were evil?"

Me: "Mostly not. Mostly unconscious and then ashamed, I suppose."

H: "Correct. The ones who organized it and did not participate—they were more culpable."

Me: "Did they ask to be purified?"

H: "I never asked. I could find out, but I have no interest in the past. Only in now, and perhaps the future."

Me: "Any advice for me? I feel so overwhelmed these days."

P: "Choose your activities wisely. Determine what is in your highest benefit. Do that first."

Me: "Thank you. It is so good to be back with you!"

P and TC: "Likewise."

Me: "Oh—a question—why did Gary and I feel so weak and tired walking on the coastal boardwalk past the ruins of Empúries [on] Tuesday?"

P: "Much had happened there. You were sensitive to the energies of the past."

Me: "The ruined temples?"

P: "Only a small part of the issue. More, the battles of armies for conquest."

Me: "Why us, then? [Why did we feel it?]"

P: "You are both becoming more sensitive."

Me: "It's not very pleasant!"

P: "Call on me for help and I—"

H: "WE—"

P: "Will make it easier."

Me: "How?"

[P sent an image which I understood as smoothing the frequencies.]

Me: "I'm tired. Thank you."

P: "Blessings on you."

H: "Yes—bless you. Keep doing the good work."

Me: "Goodbye for now."

P: "Oh—and keep doing your daily practice. I'm able to tune to you easier then [when you have been doing it regularly]."

Me: "I will. Blessings all!"

Elizabeth Diamond Rose's comments re this information:

"Always ask anything you need to know! Re Hypatia—I knew her color was white, but the question was more designed to get you to engage with her rather than just wait for her to talk to you. It's interesting how they talk. I observe that whilst they will answer questions to quieten the ego mind, they really only want to download their information. I guess that's the habit of a teacher lecturer.

"So maybe it will be quicker and easier to just receive the downloads, then digest it and process it afterwards. Because every time you ask questions that are human, you get the same kind of repetitive answers. Or maybe like Neale Donald Walsh, it will be much more about a dictation-style book at first."

Monday, 28 October 2024

During my morning meditation, I "heard," *"You have work to do! The Plotinus book. The* Conscious Living *book."*

I talked with Plotinus a little later.

Me: "Hi, Plotinus. I need advice."

P: "I am here."

Me: "Is it in my highest interest to take Caitlín Matthews' course on 'The Golden Verses of Pythagoras'* as commented upon by Hierocles?"

P: "You can do so, of course. It's a rehash of my own teachings, so why not go to the source? However, if it is easier, more disciplined, do her course."

Me: "What do you think of 'The Golden Verses'?"

P: "Good enough, I suppose, though my work is more original and better."

Me: "Thank you."

H: "I knew of this man. His reputation was good."

[Note: I think he lived after Hypatia, but maybe they overlapped. Or she knew him in the Other Dimension. Or she's wrong. Or confusing him with another. There was another Hierocles who lived a century before Hypatia.]

Me: "Thank you. … Elizabeth Diamond Rose says it's better to ask you what you want to tell me than to ask you questions."

TC: "Elizabeth Diamond Rose is wrong. Partially. Both are acceptable, though yielding different results."

Me: "Is one better?"

TC: "They serve different purposes: ours versus yours."

Me: "I'd like to serve yours."

P: "All right then. These are dangerous times in your world. On the one hand, it doesn't matter what happens—the world goes on, souls learn lessons. On the other—"

H: "On the other [hand], we want to help, to lessen the destructive tendencies."

Me: "Why?"

H: "A very good question. Why should we care? We are not there."

P: "Call it nostalgia."

H: "Or an effort to soften the blows."

P: "We are still human enough to want to intervene, to give advice."

Me: "But aren't we here to learn lessons?"

H: "You can learn to avoid burning yourself with fire by singeing your fingers—or by burning to a crisp!"

Me: "Oh. So ... what do you want to tell me?"

P: "These are dangerous times, with much hatred and violence unleashed. Remember who you are: part of the One Great Source. Connected to each other across time and space."

H: "What you do to others you do to yourself."

[I 'see' what physicists call 'quantum entanglement' or Einstein called 'spooky action at a distance.']

P: "Remember who you truly are. The Light within. Connected to everyone and everything. Act with loving kindness. Know there is more than this petty material world you fight over. Rise above greed and complicity. Be true to your True Self. Awaken to the Truth, the Light within."

Me: "How?"

P: "Slow down. Meditate. Act with kindness and condolence, compassion. Begin with yourself. Like ripples, the energy will spread out around you, encompassing you and those you interact with, with a more harmonious vibration. Your Celebration! is an example."

Me: "We are trying to get it performed."

P: "Even bringing it here to your planet is a positive act."

Me: "What more can I do?"

P: "Pray, meditate. Raise your vibration. Be pure and true in your interactions, with love and compassion. Do not judge lest you be judged."

Me: "Sounds biblical."

TC: "There is wisdom amidst the dross."

Me: "It's a lot to take in. I'm tired."

P and TC: "Rest now."

Me: "Thank you all."

Monday, 4 November 2024

We had an unexpected call from expat American friends in Portugal, Lyn and Bob Sheedy. They wanted to talk about spirituality and complained that there was nobody where they lived with whom they could talk about these topics. Lyn is an animal communicator; she trained to communicate with living and departed dogs and cats (and other animals, I supposed). If she mentioned her expertise to anyone they met in Portugal, their eyes glazed over, or they glanced away nervously. She'd learned not to mention it.

I agreed that it was very hard to find spiritual community where they were—it was hard almost anywhere! Unless you lived in a Hindu ashram or a Catholic (or Buddhist) monastery. Thank goodness for the Internet, which enabled us to connect with like-minded people all over the world.

I told Lyn that finding people we connected with spiritually was like constructing a Venn Diagram of partially intersecting circles: we overlapped in different ways with different people, and some more so than others. I told them about my "coming out of the esoteric closet" and the interview on "Life with Ghosts – Let's Chat," #021. I thought it would be available soon, but I didn't know when.

While we were talking, they went to YouTube and found the interview. It had been up since Oct. 24. Perfect timing, since Plotinus' message of unity and oneness needed to get out NOW, the day before the US elections. [https://www.youtube.com/watch?v=YqyoQ6I-gjE&list=PL-yaVPdhBZF-ISgeZak-LZfT62Kjj368QS]

I marveled at this trail of breadcrumbs (AKA synchronicities). Plotinus nudged Lyn to call me out of the blue; we had a conversation about the difficulty of talking about our spiritual interests with others; I told them about coming out of the closet with the YourLifeIsATrip.com article and Stephen's interview on "Life with Ghosts – Let's Chat!"; they went to check out his YouTube channel; and the interview was already up. I had thought Stephen would tell us, but he hadn't, and I hadn't thought to check.

Gary immediately sent a Mailchimp announcement to our mailing list. The night before the elections. Plotinus *really* wanted to get the message out

ASAP, so he had nudged our friends to call us. At least, that was one possible way to connect the dots.

Friday, November 8, 2024

Lots had happened. We had what I called "the Spirit wind" blowing behind us to get us back to work on promoting *Celebration!*. Elizabeth Diamond Rose had called and encouraged us to get it performed as soon as possible. Our efforts to get someone (for example, a large US church music department) interested in it had gotten no response. A few of Gary's old students expressed interest, but, Gary said, any live performance would require a year or two lead time and funding, which we couldn't provide.

Gary delved into the software Joe had recommended that generated life-like choral voices, but it was impossibly complicated. He was disappointed. What to do? We needed to get *Celebration!* out there as soon as possible. We wanted to record a live performance and post it on Gary's YouTube, but we weren't making any progress.

Expediency won out over aesthetics. We decided to post a version that would have a computer-generated orchestra and percussion, no chorus, and no audience. It would be a poor substitute for a live performance, but it was the quickest, best solution we could come up with. Gary's compositions would play as MP3s and our friend Lori, who has an excellent voice, was eager to participate. Gary, who also has an excellent voice, and Lori would sing the lyrics. I would be the MC and read the script.

However, during the first recording, their singing didn't work well with the computerized music, and my soft, gentle voice was not commanding enough. A few days later, we re-recorded *Celebration!* with Lori as MC, and with Gary and me softly singing along with the music. That recording worked well enough to post on YouTube.

Gary realized that YouTube posts required some kind of visual component. Rather than just selecting a single image, he started searching for hours for public-domain photos to illustrate the themes in the libretto: gratitude, the five elements, connection, relationship, Indra's Net, "We are made of the stuff of stars."

We were back to working on *Celebration!* full-time all the time, and I was very tired of it. I wondered: Were we inspired, or were we compulsive? Gary and I always prided ourselves on getting things done. We worked hard when we had a project. We worked nearly non-stop until we finished it. And, since we worked at home, that meant that Gary would often get up in the middle of the night with an idea or to finish something, and I would sometimes work through mealtimes.

As we have gotten older, we couldn't work as long or as steadily, but we did as much as we could. Were we focused, inspired, or compulsive? Creative ideas flowed through us and we felt driven to express them. That was both focused and inspired. However, we were obviously compulsive when we kept on working when we were making mistakes and were too tired to think clearly, or when we were driven to finish even though we were exhausted physically and mentally. That was happening a lot. The cause was worthwhile—making *Celebration!* available to the public as soon as possible—but we were definitely compulsive.

Sunday, 10 November 2024

I visited with Plotinus during my meditation in the afternoon.

Me: "Hello, Plotinus!"

P: "Greetings, Beloved Elyn."

Me: "I have a new name for you: Holy Wisdom."

P: "For me alone?"

Me: "Well, you and The Collective."

P: "I accept that naming, then, on behalf of all of us."

Me: "I am very tired and stressed from trying to record Celebration!"

P: [Nodding]

Me: "Can you help?"

P: "Indeed. Read my Enneads. Follow my practices. They will lead you to a more balanced and humane life."

Me: "Meditation?"

P: "For example."

Me: "What more?"

P: "Cultivating an attitude of detached compassion."

Me: "Like yesterday with my friend Marjorie [who was upset about her husband]?"

P: "Yes. You did very well."

Me: "Thank you. You knew? You saw?"

P: "We watch over you and see more than you imagine."

Me: "Isn't that intrusive?"

P: "We hope not. That's not our intention. We just see more, from a higher perspective."

Me: "Into the future?"

P: "Only a short distance. We are not that much higher above you on our vibrational plane."

Me: "Did you nudge Elizabeth Diamond Rose to call us to urge us to record Celebration!?"

P: "Well, it's not quite like that. We [Plotinus said 'we,' not 'I'] set up a vibrational field to encourage certain possibilities—certain vibratory resonances—to come into play."

Me: "Why am I suddenly thinking of the Hypogeum in Malta?" [I saw it last night in a stupid, inaccurate 'The UnXplained' episode.]

P: "It functioned on similar principles in your dimension, making it more likely for certain things to occur."

Me: "Hmmm. Now I'm thinking of Trump." [He won the election.]

P: "He is an example of extreme focus and intention. It works wonders in your world."

Me: "But he's dreadful!"

P: "I am not judging him, his character, his actions."

Me: "Why not? You are big on morality!"

P: "Indeed. Take care of your own actions, act properly, circumspectly, honestly. Do not concern yourself with others' actions."

Me: "But what about the PLANET?"

P: "I understand your concern about the immediate—and short-term—fall-out to the Earth, but She will right it herself."

Me: "If humans become extinct, what happens to the Spirit Realm?"

P: "It will [continue to] be populated from other planets and stars. Not only humans inhabit our realm."

Me: "Oh. ... A tangential question, about our friend's relationship with the goddess Athena."

P: [Nodding]

Me: "Is she real?"

P: "Ah. What is real anyway? Am I real?"

Me: "I think so. You gave me evidence."

P: "Then perhaps I am."

Me: "You are not just my subconscious speaking."

P: "Indeed not [sounding slightly offended]! I am who I am. And who I say I am."

P: "But is Athena?"

P: "Why do you care?"

Me: "I don't want my friend misled or in trouble."

P: "He has his challenges to face as you have yours."

Me: "I get it. None of my business."

P: "On a particular point, no. Are the gods real, in general? Of course they are! Manifestations of frequency, vibration, and energy, as are we all, but beginning from a different beginning point that was not materia physica to start with. They learn to materialize, but it wasn't their—isn't their—'natural' state of being."

Me: "OK. [Pause] I'm very tired."

P: "You must learn to manage your energy better. I know these are intense times for you, but you need to practice austerity."

Me: "Austerity?"

P: [Nodding] "In your engagements. In how you spend your time. [Avoid] Meaningless activities, time- and energy-wasting engagements."

Me: "But Marjorie needed support!"

P: "To get her through one more turn of the wheel. Until the next one. You help her keep spinning the wheel."

Me: "Oh."

P: "Out of compassion, but it spins, nonetheless. Choose where to spend your energy—and with whom. And relax. Read my recommendations and we'll talk about them next time."

Me: "OK. Thank you. Good night."

P: "Good night, Dear."

Months earlier, I had purchased a copy of *The Enneads*. Given Plotinus's channeled directive, I started to read it. It was very heavy going. Fortunately, Marchiene had recommended Lex Hixon's book, *Coming Home – The Experience of Enlightenment in Sacred Traditions*. Chapter Five is "There is Only the One – Plotinus and the Metaphysics of Spiritual Quest." I read it once. I read it again. It was still pretty dense. After all, I wasn't a philosopher—I was an anthropologist and a writer. I found it easier to learn from what Plotinus said, rather than from what he wrote.

Friday, 15 November 2024

I thought I would talk with Plotinus, but, instead, a powerful being draped in a white flowing Grecian robe, hair covered with a veil, showed up in my inner vision.

Goddess: "Who am I?"

Me: "I don't know! [Thinking] Fierce, powerful, all-knowing, feminine—femaleness—personified ... Athena/Minerva?"

G: "That will do for now."

[Pause as I take this in.]

G: "You had asked Plotinus if I was real. I have come to show you I am."

[Longer pause as I pondered why the goddess had appeared. I had asked Plotinus about Athena, but was there another reason she showed up? I had just finished a Shift Network online witchcraft course (my first ever), taught by Phyllis Curott, founder of the Temple of Ara. I had taken it out of curiosity. I'd never studied witchcraft. I wasn't attracted to herbal concoctions or spellcasting. But Phyllis combines shamanism and modern witchcraft, and honors gods and goddesses, although the Goddess in her many guises is central. Phyllis's version of witchcraft is very grounded and well-researched. It appealed to my anthropological background.]

Me: "Why am I drawn to Phyllis Curott's work?"

G: "She speaks Truth. You have been constrained within an armor of your own making—and society's—but now you can begin to break free."

Me: "Was I a witch before [in previous lives]?"

G: "No. A priestess often, but not a witch."

Me: "I saw myself burned at the stake."

G: "As a priestess, a pagan, not a witch, though they may not have called you that."

Me: "Is this my new path?"

G: "Your next adventure. Bringing grounding to your mental concepts. Embodying them."

Me: "Like in Celebration!."

G: [Nodding]

Me: [Looking for evidence] "You don't have Athena's shield or sword." [Correction: A spear, not a sword, is one of Athena's attributes.]

G: "I don't carry them everywhere. They are for the ignorant, the uninformed, who need objects to identify my power. You didn't. I applaud you."

Me: "How can I strengthen my relationship with the Goddess—with you?"

G: "Intentionality. Repetition. Practice. Habit. Daily call on me. I will come."

Me: "What about Plotinus? And Hypatia?"

G: "They are not much interested in gods and goddesses."

Me: "Will they desert me [if I spend time with you]?"

[Suddenly, familiar voices/vibrations join the conversation.]

P: "Never! Enjoy your diversion—and call on me as often as you like."

H: "It's about balance—between heart and head, male and female, active and receptive."

G: "Thank you, Hypatia. You should know."

H: [Nodding] "A difficult balance indeed, and one I didn't always manage to maintain."

Me: "So, it's time for 'body.'"

H and P: "Something like that."

Me: "And receptivity."

H and P: [Nodding]

Me: "A different path to go down: witchcraft!"

G: "She calls it that, but it is natural magic, a truer understanding of the world you live in. And since you live there, it is important to be fully there."

Me: "Thank you. I will get a statue of you, but without a shield and spear!"

G: "A difficult task. [Sigh] We become so stereotyped in your world. You humans like—rely on—repetition, easily identifiable markers of identity."

Me: "I'll do my best. I've seen you. I'll look for a statue that looks like you. Whatever name it has."

G: [Nodding]

Me: "Thank you, Plotinus and Hypatia—I did not want to lose you as my guides. You are so wise."

P: "I will think of it as your pilgrimage to Delphi—or joining a Mystery School from my time. An initiation, which I can't give you. Blessings I bestow."

Me: "Thank you. Goodbye, all, for now. Phyllis's Temple of Ara calls me."

Afterthoughts: I felt the numinous presence of the goddess. I couldn't identify her by attributes or symbols because she didn't have any, but the name "Athena" came to me. At first, I wondered if the name was a 'thought fragment' left over from asking Plotinus about her, but she/Athena affirmed I could call her that. Which didn't, of course, mean that's who she was. Or maybe it did. It was an ambiguous statement.

Suddenly, I was reminded of when and how my meandering journey down the esoteric path started. I was living in Ames, Iowa, home to Iowa State University (ISU). During "Women's Week 1990" at ISU, the acclaimed witch Starhawk was the keynote speaker. After her lecture, she and a few members of a local coven led the large audience in a spiral dance in the Memorial Union ballroom.

While the women beat their drums, hundreds of us repeated a simple chant while we traced a fast-moving, spiraling path around the room. The drumming and singing got more rapid, our steps got faster—and suddenly I heard the most exquisite flute music I'd ever heard. It floated over the drumming and chanting. It was pure and beautiful and clear.

After the dance was over, I asked the people next to me, "Who played that incredible flute music?"

They were puzzled. They looked at each other and agreed: Nobody else had heard the flute. I asked the drummers from the coven. No. Nobody had heard it. But I *knew* I had heard the flute music. I knew it just as certainly as I knew that I was alive and breathing.

That experience shattered my materialist mindset like a lightning bolt. It demonstrated to me beyond any doubt that there was much, much more going on in reality than my materialist "if you can't see or measure it, it doesn't exist" worldview had ever imagined. I'd read about something called "the music of the spheres." Was that what I had heard? I didn't know, but I knew I had been gifted with a paradigm-breaking experience.

I said "Yes" to the mystery and began, ever so timidly, to try to search for the source of the flute player and the exquisite music. I explored energy healing modalities, Sufi practices, Kabbalah, geomancy, dowsing, Western esotericism, shamanism, Active Dreamwork, and sacred geometry. I followed a circuitous trail of breadcrumbs, or what looked like a trail, through the forest of possibilities.

I thought about my just-completed conversation with Athena about witchcraft. Perhaps I had just spiraled back on a higher level of the ever-evolving spiral dance. Skeptical as I might be about witchcraft, I knew that magic was real. I had experienced it in the Memorial Union ballroom many years ago.

Saturday, 16 November 2024

We ran into our Catalan artist friend Carles walking home from shopping. I had recently shared with him my channeling experiences. He pulled out his iPhone and showed us photos of a small, rock-crystal icosahedron (20-sided Platonic solid) engraved with Greek letters. It was displayed in the Puglia Archaeology Museum, near where he was developing an art project. He wondered if Pythagoras—or Plotinus—would know something about it.

As I looked at the icosahedron, I grew extremely dizzy. Carles kept talking while I leaned against a nearby wall for support, trying not to show how light-headed I felt.

Carles said that online information suggested the object was probably used for divination; it would have been tossed like a die. My intuition was that it was not meant to be seen by the public. It was not meant to be on display in a museum. I "got" that the engraved Greek letters were some kind of 3-D Magic Square* (a Magic Sphere?), and that the piece was powerful in itself, rather than something to be used to tell the future. I told Carles.

Carles nodded affirmatively. He, too, felt the object shouldn't be on display and was powerful, perhaps magical.

I continued to feel light-headed even after we got home. Whew. Not sure what that was about. I needed to ask Plotinus about it.

In meditation, Plotinus told me he didn't know much about the object because he was not interested in that sort of thing. Pythagoras, on the other hand, knew a lot about it—and he said it was not a divination tool or toy but, rather, a magical item. I understood that somehow it gave power to a place or decision. And, also, I "got" something about a 3-D Magic Sphere.

I had no idea what that meant. All I knew was that looking at the photo of that object, I had received an energetic hit. It was unsettling. Later, Carles told me he, too, found it disorienting to look at.

Monday, 18 November 2024

I sat down to meditate, and Plotinus showed up.

Me: "Hello, dear Plotinus. You want to talk with me?"

P: "Indeed, I feel a certain urgency."

Me: "What do you need to—want to—tell me?"

P: "Take care of yourself. Don't overdo. Remember to enjoy life."

Me: "Eric Edmeades [the founder of Wildfit] says, 'Success is how much you enjoy your life daily!'"

P: "And you?"

Me: "Not really. Not exactly. Too much work and pressure, I've forgotten how to play, to relax. It's hard to do, with Celebration! still being created."

P: [Nodding] "All the more reason. Make a list of pleasurable pursuits to bring more balance to your life."

Me: [Sigh] "I am very serious."

H: "Indeed. And so was I. Much to do in the world and so little time to do it in."

Me: "Did you enjoy your life?"

H: [Nodding] "Oh yes. The pursuit of knowledge was for me the ultimate pleasure!"

Me: "So, pleasure doesn't have to be vacuous."

H: "Of course not."

P: "But play—play is something else. For itself, not for its results. Play like a child. Remember?"

Me: "I don't. [I was always serious—especially after my brother Tommy died [in an accident when he was almost 7 and I was almost 5]. I remember playing hide and seek, going for walks alone in the woods. The hills were covered with tiny bluebells. I think pilgrimage comes closest."

H: "But wasn't that [physically] grueling?"

Me: [Nodding] "Yes, but simple. Just walk. Be in nature. Nothing else to do."

[Pause]

P: [Briskly] "I don't recommend pilgrimage for you now. But I do recommend relaxation."

Me: "Making incense cones?" [I had been making them but stopped after I had whooping cough because smoke irritated my lungs.]

P: [Nods]

H: "Go for walks nearby. Visit a museum."

Me: "After Celebration! is launched."

P: "I recommend you do not wait—at least not more than a few days."

Me: "I'd like to return to Hostal Empúries and just relax."

P: [Nodding] "That's the idea. Soon."

Me: "I promise."

P: [Shaking metaphorical finger] "And don't do things you don't want to do—like reading books for the book clubs! Or visiting with Donna!"

Me: "Yes, I know! Change of topic. From your perspective, what about Trump, etc.?"

P: "We have lived through many upheavals, tyrants, would-be replacement tyrants ... everything passes."

H: [Nodding] "Even the turmoil in Alexandria—a mere blip in time. The Alexandria I knew—the library before, all gone. Long gone. Everything changes."

Me: "'She [the Goddess] changes everything She touches—and everything She touches changes.'"

P: "Your new guide Phyllis's wise words." [Actually, they are the lyrics of a popular chant that Phyllis used in a recent teaching.]

Me: "You approve of her?"

P: "I approve of your ongoing growth. Do you learn more deeply, experience more profoundly?"

H: "Are you more connected and compassionate?"

Me: "I have just begun."

P and H: "These are the signposts. Everything changes—but we must work for it to change for the better. By working on ourselves."

Me: "Thank you both."

Tuesday, 26 November 2024

Just after we posted *Celebration!* on YouTube at https://youtu.be/eCIjtfoBJ98, I "heard," "You've done a great job. And your work has just begun."

Oh no! Not more work! I was so tired! Spirit *had* to find a way for us to work in a more equilibrated way. We had labored nonstop to choose photos for the YouTube version. It was not an easy process. We had invited several groups of people to view evolving versions on Gary's computer and give us feedback. We had revised the photos to be more inclusive. We had revised them again. Finally, we had posted *Celebration!* on YouTube. We were exhausted. It was like running a marathon, except the finish line kept moving further away the closer we got.

There was more to do. There was *always* more to do.

Gary opened Mailchimp, the listserv mailing app he had used for our YouTube interview announcement a month ago, but this time something in the program had changed and it didn't work. He tried desperately but couldn't solve the problems. I suggested he let it go for a while, till he was more rested, but he refused. He worked late into the night and woke up early. I suggested maybe someone else could help, but again, he refused.

Our relationship issues came up again. His historic pattern of compulsiveness and withdrawal, getting exhausted and stressed—becoming oblivious to me and to the world around him—was in full force once again. My historic pattern of feeling abandoned, unseen, ignored—unconsciously becoming irritated and resentful—sprang into full blossom in reaction.

When I tried to talk to him about it (which usually didn't happen until I was angry), he felt attacked and threatened and just wanted to escape. Which led to an even worse scenario. It was discouraging and alienating.

During the next week, I received occasional input from Plotinus, telling me/us to go PLAY! It was hard to do, but we made reservations at Hostal Empúries for the following Sunday through Tuesday. Hopefully, away from *Celebration!* we could rediscover our balance.

I kept repeating my mantra, "We can't do a project based on gratitude, connection, and Oneness if we aren't experiencing it ourselves!"

Monday, 9 December 2024

We stayed at Hostal Empúries, trying to recover from stress and the strains that stressed our relationship.

After a day watching the Mediterranean changing colors, the moon rising over the glittering sea, and walking along the coastal path to the nearby Greek and Roman ruins of Empúries, we began to unwind.

Monday evening, I gave Gary an Angelic Reiki healing in the hotel's secluded library. We sat next to each other on comfortable, slightly worn, leather armchairs. The room was gently lit with the golden glow of antique floor lamps. We both moved deeply into meditation.

Gary's guides—and Plotinus!—came through to him more powerfully than they had ever done. He felt their presence. He was speechless and stunned. Although he didn't channel anyone, he knew they were there in a way he had never experienced.

Tuesday, 10 December 2024

We had been going through a lot of emotional intensity. After the Angelic Reiki session, we could tell that something major had shifted in a good way. We began to recover our equilibrium, both individually and as a couple.

Wednesday, 11 December 2024

We were back home, and I was doing my morning meditation, when I heard a loud message in my "inner" hearing: *"Talk with Plotinus!"* So I did.

Me: [Teary-eyed] "Hello Plotinus!"

P: "Welcome, Beloved Child."

Me: [Crying] "I am so weepy! So tired! Emotionally drained."

P: "I have been—"

H: "We have been—"

P: "Telling you to rest and play."

Me: "I don't know how to play. … Why is this such a hard time?"

P: [Pause] "You have more growing up to do. It isn't easy."

H: "But we are here supporting you."

Me: "What do you mean, [I have more] growing up to do? I'm 78!"

H: "Indeed. But you have old patterns to let go of, release."

P: "Patterns of blame and resentment, of anger and disappointment."

Me: "What—I'm not allowed to feel disappointment or anger?"

P: [Soothing] "Of course you are. Feel them—and release them. Let them go. They do not serve you."

H: "Relationships are very difficult. More difficult than astronomy or mathematics."

P: "Or philosophy!"

H and P: "That's why we never married!"

Me: "So how can you give me advice [about relationships]?"

P: [Laughing gently] "From our higher perspective. We see the larger picture."

H: "Your disappointments matter, but in proportion. Be proportionate."

P: "Emotions flow where attention is directed. Focus on the positive, the pleasurable, not the disappointments. Let go."

Me: "I'm very tired."

P: "We keep telling you to rest and play."

Me: "I don't know how to play."

P: "Yes, you've said that several times."

H: "What gives you pleasure?"

Me: "Making fiber art. A good book. Baking, which I can't do now [because I'm not eating grains or sweeteners]."

H: "Focus on what gives you pleasure and do that. Play can come later."

Me: "I'm so grateful you are here! [Crying] Sometimes I've been feeling so alone!"

P and H: "We are always here."

Me: "Are you my new primary guides?"

P: "We have been watching over you for a very long time."

Me: "And now Gary, too?"

P: [Nodding] "He, too. We are here to support you both."

Me: "I keep getting dreams about pilgrimage. Why?" [Note choice of words: not having but getting.]

P: "Because that is the true nature of life. A journey to a goal."

Me: "What goal?"

P: "Self awareness. Self mastery. Self knowledge."

H: "And like a pilgrimage, it's an adventure, with unknown encounters, challenges, rewards."

Me: "Getting lost—"

P: "And found."

Me: "Losing the way—"

P: "And recovering it."

Me: "Never giving up."

P and H: [Nodding]

Me: "As long as you are with me, I can do this."

P and H: "We are always with you."

Me: "What about Santiago? Elen of the Ways?" [Those are other guides who have shown up periodically.]

P: "They are avatars of the Guide. The Guide on the journey."

Me: "Are they with me?"

P: [Nodding] "Sometimes."

H: "Often. As needed."

Me: "What about the rest of The Collective?"

H: "They are here when they can be of help. But right now, we are here with you always."

Me: "I like the balance of male and female [among my guides]."

P and H: [Nodding]

H: "It's not by accident."

Me: *"Gary has changed in wonderful ways. Sending me Angelic Reiki. Being more caring and attentive. I appreciate it. I admire his ability to do so—and I fear his relapse into obliviousness."*

P: *[Nodding] "That's where your work is."*

H: *"Your woundedness."*

P: *[Nodding] "You need to honor your truth, express your feelings, and release them."*

H: *"Fear serves no purpose."*

Me: *"It protects me from disappointment."*

P: *"No, it sets you up for disappointment."*

Me: *"Oh. So, what do I do?"*

P: *"Relax, rest, recuperate. Release your old fears."*

H: *[Nodding] "So it's annoying when—you are annoyed when he's so preoccupied, yes?"*

Me: *[Nodding] "It feels awful. Inconsiderate. Not loving."*

P: *"He does what he does, and you do with it what you do. Just as he does with your complaints what HE does."*

Me: *"A match made in Heaven."*

H: *"Well, not exactly."*

Me: *"Only I can change my reactions, right?"*

P and H: *[Nodding]*

Me: *"OK. I hear you. I'll try not to take it personally."*

P *[Clapping non-physical hands] "That's perfect!"*

Me: *"I've got a lot to think about."*

P and H: *"We are always here, supporting both of you to 'grow up' and be as fully human as you can be this time around."*

Me: "Thank you. It's wonderful Plotinus is showing up for Gary in his meditations."

P: "Of course! He has reached a place where he can see me and interact with me more."

Me: "And you, Hypatia?"

H: "I'm not engaged with him in that way. Of course, there is an energy overlap since I am with you."

Me: "Thank you both. I feel better."

P and H: [Nodding]

Me: "Goodbye for now!"

After this session with Plotinus and Hypatia, Gary and I sat down at my altar to send Angelic Reiki to a friend. But first, we had an extremely positive conversation about our recent dysfunctional interactions.

Gary explained that his obsessiveness about Mailchimp was because he was desperate. He felt he had to solve the problem, had to keep going until he did, only it was too complicated, and he couldn't. It required all his concentration, so he was withdrawn and preoccupied.

I explained that I was so habituated to his pattern that I didn't notice his withdrawal and preoccupation until suddenly it got to a point where I felt overwhelmed by it. And then I reacted by stomping around or responding angrily and telling him how I felt about his behavior.

To which he reacted by feeling afraid (as if my anger was going to hurt him), desperate, and hopeless because he couldn't do it any better or any differently. Then he would decide that he should just leave me—walk out the door—because he was so scared and trapped and saw no other solution.

I experienced his behavior as withdrawal, culminating in punishing me for having confronted him about his behavior (Gary saying, "The only solution is for me to leave!"). He experienced it as the only way out of an untenable situation.

We had reacted to what we experienced the other person doing to us rather than to what they were feeling.

As we talked, I heard his feelings of desperation, and I responded from my heart, rather than feeling abandoned and angry at his withdrawal. He heard what I needed. I heard what he needed. What a breakthrough!

I never could have imagined that channeling departed souls would lead to personal transformation and improve my relationship with Gary. After 30 years of marriage and several couple's therapists, without whom our marriage wouldn't have survived—we were finally learning to release and shift our patterns at an even deeper level.

Thank you, Plotinus and Hypatia!

We agreed to remember the following principles: "Elyn will talk about how it feels to her." "Gary will talk about how it feels to Gary." And we will ask each other: "How does it feel to you?"

Me: "I felt abandoned … hurt … disconnected from you."

Gary: "I felt desperate. I was 99% done-in before you got angry, and then I was afraid, and I just couldn't do anything anymore. I wanted to escape."

Hearing each other's feelings, we responded with love, not anger and pain.

We needed both the help from Spirit and from Jake Eagle's SAGE process—skills we needed to not just occasionally remember but to use frequently. Jake had taught us that people do things, and we use these things to trigger our historical wounds and traumas. They are just doing what they do—and we do with it what we do. Now we added to that the importance of asking about feelings and responding with feelings. When we did that, we came from the heart, not from hurt.

And the heart is always full of love. Gary was determined to be a better partner—and so was I.

Thursday - Tuesday, 12 - 24 December 2024

The next two weeks were a blur. Several events stood out. First, Gary frequently began quoting Hypatia's observation, "What we do to each other, we do to ourselves." What a perfect lesson to learn from *Celebration!*. This statement grounded the abstract concept "We are all One" in the day-to-day of living. It even provided an action plan.

Second, we were getting along much better. After all these years, we had finally had another major breakthrough.

Third, I started making fiber art again. I hadn't made fiber art for many years; I'd been too busy writing. I told myself that Plotinus and The Collective had told me to play, so play I would!

I was inspired by reading Sharon Blackie's book *If Women Rose Rooted* for the SoulReading book club I was in. I wanted to give something back to the wounded Earth. I wanted to honor the Earth Mother and acknowledge the brutalized Goddess of the Land. What to do? Some kind of fiber art project, I decided. A contemporary art quilt to hang on the wall.

I had taken a photo of a shop logo on a building in nearby Banyoles: a Celtic-style Tree of Life in which the roots entwined with the branches. That was the design upon which I would base my contemporary art quilt.

Gary photoshopped the photo to remove the parallax, and we had it enlarged and printed at a nearby copy center. I traced the pattern onto black silk, cut it out, and appliqued it to a silvery-white silk background. I quilted it with batting and a backing fabric, and I framed it with two black silk borders, one narrow, one wide. The finished art quilt was nearly one meter wide and one meter high.

Oh, the joy of making sacred fiber art. It was nothing like writing books or the libretto for *Celebration!*. It was wordless, visual, and deliciously tactile. It also made me wonder again about the source of creativity.

When I first began making fiber art, over 20 years ago, I would "download" a mental image and begin to create it. I made large, three-dimensional free-standing figures I called Fiberalchemies. At the time, I didn't think much about the process. But now I realized that the inspiration for my fiber art, like the ideas for my novels and the concepts for Gary's compositions, came from the Imaginal Realm(s). It was my task to manifest them, to turn them into something physical. This was both a challenge and a gift.

I was happy. Maybe I was a little compulsive, but Gary found that amusing. He wasn't triggered the way I was when he was compulsive.

Wednesday, 25 December 2024

I was happy making fiber art, but I also wanted to cry. A lot. Often. Memories of long-ago events would rise to the surface and I would weep. Stuff I thought I had dealt with long ago, like my brother Tommy's tragic death when he was nearly 7 and I was nearly 5. Or the times I hadn't stood up for myself. Or … The list was long.

I did what I had learned to do: I sat down at my altar to talk with Plotinus.

Me: *"Please visit with me, Plotinus!"*

P: *"I'm always here."*

Me: *"I feel so sad these days—weepy, sad. [Even though I am happier.] Why?"*

P: *[Pause]* *"You are coming to terms with your past. You are feeling the pain and grief of—many things."*

Me: *"Reading* If Women Rose Rooted *started that."*

P: *"It made you aware of much you have suppressed."*

Me: *"It's worse now!"*

P: *"It will be for a while. Remember the image you got this morning of the ship on stormy waters?"*

[In morning meditation, I asked to be given or shown an image of what I need to know today—a technique taught by Cheryl Page—and this morning, the visual was of a storm-tossed ship.]

Me: *[Nodding]*

P: *"It's like that, until the Winds of Remembrance blow themselves out."*

Me: *"I long for calm seas!"*

P: "They will return."

Me: "Soon?"

P: "What is time?"

Me: [Sighing] "Things are better now than ever with Gary, so why am I sad?"

P: "You are releasing old emotions you stored up. You are always good in a crisis. Now you are letting down—I prefer to say 'releasing.'"

Me: [Nodding] "But it hurts! I don't want to feel sad about Tommy's death and how I was abandoned [emotionally by my parents], about stuff between Gary and me in the past. Why can't I just move on?"

P: "You are moving on. You are feeling your grief and sadness and releasing it. No more projecting onto Gary."

Me: "We are relating better than ever, so why this grief NOW?"

P: "Because it's safe."

H: "That was *my* line, Plotinus!"

Me: "Hello, Hypatia!"

H: "Just remember, I eschewed relationships, so I have no advice. But I do know you are so very loved."

Me: [Crying]

H: "Remember, we are here always!"

Me: "I'm crying from loneliness, abandonment, broken promises—"

H: "It's safe now to release and then move forward, shining your light more brightly than ever."

Me: [Sniffling] "I feel so vulnerable, open to other people's emotions."

H: [Nodding] "You are going through a transformation, and it will be like that for a while."

Me: "Why?"

H: "So you can be of ever-greater service to the world."

Me: [Nodding] "Good to know there's a purpose."

P and H: [Nodding]

Me: "OK. ... Different topic. Plotinus, why do I keep dreaming about zikr*?" [A Sufi practice that temporarily alters consciousness. Years ago, Gary and I would occasionally do zikr.]

P: "Your friend Marchiene was correct. It is related to my work. The Sufis took in my philosophy and developed their own techniques, based on mine, for Union with the Divine—with the One."

Me: "I didn't know that. Did you do zikr?"

P: "Not exactly. I used breathing techniques, concentration, and some body movement to try to reach an altered state. I was only effective in achieving Union a few times, though I maintained a lighter state much more frequently. You will discover how much I influenced later thinkers. They may claim it's their own thoughts, but they were heavily influenced by me."

Me: "I'll be interested in learning more about that."

P: "Yes, but learning is less important than doing."

Me: "Would you change what you taught or wrote?"

P: [Nodding] "Yes, it's [expanded reality, life after life] even more indescribably perfect than I could imagine. Now, I'm not 'Alone with the Alone'—I have companions, including Hypatia, of course. But I am closer—without the constraints of physical form, I am closer to the One."

Me: "Do you still do the practices?"

P: "Of course! Differently without a body, of course, but part of my ongoing training and evolution."

Me: "Will you reincarnate?"

P: [Shaking his head] "At this time, I would say no, not likely. I'm being of service here and learning and experiencing more all the time. My trajectory is 'upward,' not 'back down' to Earth."

Me: "How can I make these times less trying for myself?"

P: "Remember who you truly are. Not your story, your soul."

H: "And remember, we are always watching and supporting you."

Me: "Thank you so much. That means so much to me."

P and H: [Smiling]

P: "Good! Now, let's get on with it!"

Saturday, December 28, 2024

I awoke with an existential/psychological/philosophical crisis about the nature of time: What is it? How can we move forward in time if only the present moment exists? Suddenly, the idea of everything all happening at once made more sense: We are "walking through" time that has already occurred. But then, what happens to free will? Our metaphors of time use space; we move forward or backward in time. How could that be possible?

I felt paralyzed: How can I even speak? How can I move? There's nothing there time-wise to be moving into! Gradually, the weird feeling faded, and I got out of bed.

In my morning meditation, I asked, "What do I need to know?" I was given the image of an old-fashioned circular alarm clock and the message, "You think it's telling time when it's only marking out even units through space." Oh my!

Maybe Plotinus was putting ideas into my head. Or maybe it was Hypatia. After all, she was the mathematician/astronomer in the group. Either way, it was time to have a session with them.

Me: "Welcome, Plotinus! I think you have wisdom to share with me about time."

P: "Not so much me as Anaxagoras."

Me: "Who?"

P: "Another ancient Greek. He knows more about the subject than I."

[Later, I looked him up: Anaxagoras was a 5th-century BCE, pre-Socratic Greek philosopher.]

Me: "OK."

[Pause. I felt the presence of another energy.]

Anaxagoras: "Hello, dear Elyn."

Me: "Hello, revered Anaxagoras."

A: "Thank you, but that sobriquet is not necessary."

Me: "What can you tell me about time?"

A: "It is a fascinating and difficult subject. Impossible to study outside of itself."

[I saw the image of a fish in water.]

Me: "Well, what can *you* say?"

A: "Our existence is predicated on movement, and movement requires a trajectory. Hence time."

Me: "But—isn't that space? We move in space."

A: "Yes, but movement requires something to move through, and through its movement moves. Hence, time."

Me: "Uh ... Can we move backwards as well?"

A: "Theoretically, but that requires precise positioning and repetition of precise action, or else it is a new action, a moving forward disguised as a moving backward."

Me: "How can we foretell the future?"

A: "You can't. You can approximate with intuition and contemplation, selecting from the likely vectors, but there is always the possibility of the unexpected."

Me: "Is time forward-moving or cyclical? Many societies view it as cyclical."

A: "That is an imprecise way of understanding. It is spiral. Days, seasons, events repeat, but never exactly. Nothing ever repeats itself. Except for certain scholars, who will remain unnamed. [Chuckling at an inside joke]"

Me: "So, I awoke this morning very unsettled. How can I move forward in time when there's nothing there to move into?"

A: "Ah, yes, the conundrum of the expanding universe—a spatial conundrum as well."

H: "However, if you recognize it's all Consciousness and everything is illusory—or at least partial—it becomes much easier."

Me: "Hello, Hypatia! I wondered if you would show up."

H: "Well, I do have some expertise in this area."

A: "Well-earned and well-deserved indeed!"

H: "Thank you."

Me: "So … Back to time. And Consciousness. Are we at the membrane of the present pushing into—what?"

H: "Metaphors are limited and limiting. Why do you struggle with the idea that there is only the present and the 'wake' that flows behind it?"

Me: "What am I 'pushing' into?"

H and A: "Pure creative potential."

Me: "Oh."

H: "Some things are automatic—like breathing. You don't have to think about it to do it. In fact, you can't think about it and do it without fail, 24/7."

Me: "So … it's just how it is?"

H: "It's how your manifested reality is configured."

Me: "And what about yours?"

A: "Without bodies we exist in a different form of reality."

Me: "What is time like there?"

[Laughter]

P: "Very malleable."

H: "We move back and forth easily in time."

A: "We are not constricted by space."

Me: "I'm confused."

H: "Because you cannot imagine not having a body."

Me: "Yes I can—when I meditate deeply."

H: [Nodding] "And [when you meditate] where, or there, where is time? It isn't. And space?"

Me: "Malleable, when I meditate. I can be in Egypt, or the clearing in the woods in the astral realm."

H: "Humans are limited in their perception of time and space. Space in the human realm is—physical. Concrete. You move through it; you move on it. Moving through the invisible atmosphere that surrounds you like water, filled with invisible energies—magnetic, microwaves, electronic broadcasts—you are not aware of them, but they are there."

Me: "What's that got to do with time?"

A: "It is invisible but present as an action."

Me: "Forward, backward, moving through time ..."

A: [Nodding]

P: "Remember—it's all the projection of the One. The Absolute Ultimate Consciousness that is beyond movement and Time. Inconceivable for us limited humans, approachable for a moment—or an eternity."

H: "We cannot grasp the true nature of reality. It's like asking a dust mote to invent a computer."

Me: "Oh ... So ... What's the point of it all?"

H: "Recognize the Mystery."

A: "Agreed. And acknowledge human limitations. And delight in the Great Mystery of it all—so far beyond thought!"

Me: "OK, I'll try."

P: "It does give perspective."

H: "Indeed."

Me: "Is it better on the Other Side?"

P: "Not better but different. Much more freedom of movement in time."

H: "But less concrete. No bodies."

A: "It's beautiful beyond description, but no one is writing poetry about it."

Me: "OK. ... Well, thank you all. Until next time!"

P: "You see what we are saying—now you are using time as an event!"

Me: [Laughing]: "OK!"

Re-reading this conversation, I realized that I needed to ask Plotinus more questions. For example, *why* he wanted me to think about time.

I also thought of more examples of time as an event or action: Waiting for the right time; the show will start when it's the right time (as in, a flower blooms when it is ready); let's get there on time—or we got there too late.

Later, I saw Caitlín Matthews' Substack (Caitlín Matthews - a Hallowquest Sanctuary) post, titled "The Mystery of Time Standing Still." She referred to the difference between the calendar and the movement of the sun, and the 12 days of Christmas as a time out.

"The Twelve Days of Christmas are a time when extraordinary things can emerge. The reason that they can do this is due to a recurring difficulty that every calendar maker since the world's beginning has encountered. However you try to divide the circulations of the sun into neat orderly packages that will work for your culture, these calculations fail utterly to be driven into tidy sheep-pens. The earth wobbles and a slippage of dates will keep occurring.

Most calendars have—if not annually— then regularly in the fall of years, a period called 'the intercalary days' when the odd bits of what are left over from those orderly calculations can be dealt with. Nearly every culture has decided to make these left-over bits of the year serve as a special festival for their gods.

"The mystery of time standing still calls out to us urgently after five millennia, to come into focus in our own moment of stillness which for us can, as for Oengus [Celtic god], encompass the entirety of the world."

Thank you, Caitlín.

When we FaceTimed with Marchiene, I asked her what she thought about time. She said she liked to think of time as a river that she could float down or get out of and sit on the bank and watch it go by. Lovely metaphor!

Monday, 30 December 2024

I decided to ask more "whys" of Plotinus.

Me: "What do I need to know today, Plotinus?"

P: "You are [everyone is] so very loved."

Me: "Thank you! I feel a little off balance. Strange dreams ... new moon ..."

P: "Do a chakra clearing."

Me: "OK. I need to ask more 'why' questions. So, like, why Anaxagoras?"

P: "He wanted to contribute."

Me: "But he said nothing about time."

P: "That in itself was a contribution. Perhaps to say you are thinking about the topic all wrong."

Me: "Oh. ... So ... time isn't real?"

P: "It's certainly not what it seems to be on your plane of existence."

Me: "And on yours?"

P: "Much more fluid—more like Marchiene's image of a river, flowing wide, flowing narrow, changing in rate of flow."

Me: "Huh."

P: "We can't really describe it to you since you are caught up in the stream of flow."

Me: "Hmm. Hypatia, can you help?"

H: "There are more useful things to contemplate, like synchronicity."

Me: "Doesn't that rely on time?"

H: "It occurs in time but is motivated outside of time, bringing together a confluence of events. Intention is all."

Me: "Whose *intention*?"

H: "Not yours, for sure!"

Me: "So, yours?"

H: [Nodding] "Spirit guides, those who see the larger picture—like puzzle pieces fitting things—people, events—together for the highest good."

Me: "Like my recent exchanges/encounters with my friends Evelyn and Ronit?"

H: [Nodding] "Indeed. You were able to be of service to the highest good for each of them."

Me: "I was very glad to do so."

H: "Just as Nuri was for you [encouraging your coming to Girona]. And Elizabeth Diamond Rose. And many others."

Me: "Oh. … Why did Anaxagoras want to talk to me?"

P: "To share his knowledge about the nature of reality so you would understand better."

Me: "[His concept of] Nous [Mind]? And everything existing as part of the whole of Mind/Consciousness?" [I had learned about those concepts later, but I didn't think he had talked about them with me.]

P: [Nodding]: "That sums it up."

Me: "But what about time?"

P: "Perhaps it's irrelevant or the wrong question. Also, it was another bit of evidence about the reality of our realm, of continuity [of consciousness] after death, affirmed again by your [renewed] contact with Evelyn and her experiences with her departed husband."

[Evelyn Begody has published a fascinating memoir, Living with My Dead Husband – A Navajo Woman's Year of Grief.]

Me: "Sigh. I hope Gary will return to me if he dies first."

P: [Nodding] "Never fear. He will always be with you."

[Pause]

Me: "I'm concerned about my health. Not anything big, no symptoms, but my high cholesterol, for example, and my [high] blood pressure."

P: "I can bring in Paracelsus—but like all of us, his knowledge is limited by his earthly paradigm.

Me: "So you aren't all-knowing."

P: "Of course not! We may learn more here, but what we learn is so—different—it doesn't have much application in your world."

Me: "Well, bring him in anyway."

[Pause]

[Paracelsus doesn't come. The Greek god of healing, Asclepius, shows up instead, in a flowing robe, looking like the statue in the museum at the nearby Ruins of Empúries.]

Me: "Wow! Greetings, Asclepius!"

Asc: [Bows]

Me: "Can you give me health advice about my high blood pressure and high cholesterol?"

Asc: [Answering slowly] "I don't know things from that perspective. I can only advise a sano [healthy] diet—vegetables, fruits, little meat, pure water … and crystals, minerals to lay upon your body or use as elixirs."

Me: "Which ones?"

Asc: [Thinking] "They have different names in your time. The golden sunstone on your altar will help, placed on your heart. A blue stone in your pocket—not lapis or azurite, a softer blue, rare but gentle blue. And elixirs will also help. And prayer, and meditation. … Let me know how that goes."

Me: "Thank you."

Asc: [Bows and withdraws]

Me: "Whew. Lots to think about! Thank you all!"

P and H: "Our pleasure to assist you. You have much work still to complete on your plane of existence. We wish you well—and healthy!"

Me: "Thank you. Goodbye."

Sunday, 5 January 2025

I was on a fiber-art-making roll. Some might call it a binge. I had finished "The Tree of Life" and immediately started another large wall hanging: an abstract Brigid's Cross, based on a sculpture I had photographed on the door of St. Brigid's Parish Church in Kildare, Ireland. I was having a wonderful time, even if I did tend to overdo it. I didn't want to stop. I was playing and having fun, just like Plotinus recommended. Making the art quilts provided focused, intense relaxation.

During meditation, I didn't talk with Plotinus, but he was there.

I suddenly found myself in an infinite, featureless space. I understood that there are innumerable quantum realities everywhere and that I can communicate with Plotinus and The Collective (and they with me) because we are (quantumly) close in frequency. As are, relatively speaking, the angels and archangels.

It becomes harder and harder to communicate beyond that because the frequency gap is so much bigger. And beyond it all is the Alone, just like Plotinus talked about. I felt infinitesimally small but not insignificant. Even the tiniest mote was a necessary part of the whole.

What was the purpose of it all? To grow through experience. All the events of my story were trivial in comparison to the larger picture, but they were also an integral part of it. The soul's task was to grow in knowledge and experience—and in Love and Light. We were all connected through Love. Not passionate love. Not parental love. Not even brotherly/sisterly love. It was different from all of those. It was both less individual and more personal. It encompassed everything. I understood that you could think of gravity as mutual attraction.

Gradually, the visionary experience faded.

Tuesday, 14 January 2025

Me: "Hello, Plotinus!"

P: "Hello, Dear One."

Me: "It's been a while since we've talked more than briefly."

P: [Nodding]

Me: "I know you are with me always."

P: [Nodding]

Me: "I think you have given me space to play and relax."

P: *[Nodding]*

Me: "But now it's time for serious stuff again."

P: *[No reply]*

Me: "Maybe I can do both?"

P: *[Nodding]*

Me: "I will try to learn to balance [work and play] better."

P: *[Nodding]*

Me: "A question. Elizabeth Diamond Rose spoke with someone named Sonisius today. Is he part of The Collective?"

H: "Not exactly."

Me: "Hi, Hypatia!"

H: "Hello, Dear One."

Me: "Who is he?"

H: "A vibratory form of interest, but not a past human."

Me: "A demi-god? An angel?"

H: *[Shaking head]* "Neither. A [particular] frequency, as his name suggests. There are many beings of all sorts in other dimensions."

Me: "But you know him?"

H: "He comes around at times and enters into our—conversations … our experiences."

Me: "What are they like?"

H: "Indescribable in your realm of existence—a kind of modulating of individual frequencies that creates vibrations—resonances—like a butterfly's wings or a hummingbird's."

Me: "For what purpose?"

H: "Pleasure. And personal refinement. We still need to purify, to remove the 'dross' from our energy fields."

Me: "Why?"

H: "As we evolve and move further into the Light, our Light needs to be—'clearer'—[with] less 'dust' or distortion."

Me: "So that ... what?"

P: "Eventually, we approach the One True Light, the Source of All Being. To do that, we have to leave imperfections behind."

Me: "Is that the goal?"

P: [Pause] "Eventually, for all beings, that is the goal: Reuniting with the One Source of All."

Me: "So what happens to all your [life] experiences [your personality]?"

P: "They become part of the larger tapestry, the Field of Consciousness. They enrich its textures, complexity."

Me: "It evolves?"

P: "'Evolve' is a weighted word with expectations. I would simply say it becomes more of its potential."

Me: "Oh. ... And Sonisius?"

P: "As Hypatia explained, he's not an ex-human or transhuman."

Me: "Is he a cosmic being?"

P: "You could say that because we are ALL cosmic beings. Just as you have myriad life forms on Planet Earth, there are myriad life forms in the other dimensions."

Me: "Elizabeth Diamond Rose is interested in him and his relationship with The Collective."

H: "As I said, we are familiar with him and he comes and goes."

Me: "But unlike the rest of you, he wasn't human."

H: "Correct. He's an alien. [Laughter]"

Me: "Are faeries and elves real?"

H: "Of course! They are different-dimension beings who 'show through' in your realm on occasion and more easily in certain places than others."

Me: "And plant divas? And the Spirit of a Place?"

H: "They are much more material, grounded—rooted—in your world. They don't exist outside of it."

Me: "But faeries do?"

H: "Oh yes! In their own worlds/kingdoms/realities. 'Out beyond the Western Isles …' Those ancient Irish knew a thing or two."

Me: "What about the Virgin Mary?"

H and P: [They look at each other. A long pause.]

H: "Well, there are myths and stories. And there are beings and spiritual beings … The Virgin Mary is a myth. But the Divine Feminine [with which she is identified] is a real energy, a true presence, although mostly lacking in your reality these days. Like the gods and goddesses of Olympus, human attention shifts. [This meant that the gods and goddesses of Olympus have faded from view, are rarely worshipped, and thus have 'lost' energy.] The Divine Feminine still comes through as an apparition—it depends on the culture—bringing her powerful energy to your planet. But too often, she is ignored or her message used for political ends."

Me: "What can I do?"

H: "Honor the Divine Feminine. Venerate her power in yourself. Honor your own innate feminine divinity. For a start."

Me: "Whew. I hear you. I'll try."

H: "Surround yourself with tokens—objects—of the Feminine. That helps keep her present in your mind."

Me: "Thank you. I'm tired now. Thank you. Until next time!"

P and H: "Au revoir! Adieu!"

I sent Elizabeth Diamond Rose a transcript of the conversation. She replied: "I love how they talk to you!!!" And she sent me the Wiki entry for Synesius, the correct spelling for the person she had meant. At the age of 20, he had gone with his brother Euoptius to Alexandria. There he became an enthusiastic Neoplatonist and a disciple of Hypatia.

I told Elizabeth Diamond Rose I would ask Hypatia for more information, given that she and Plotinus had not identified him as human.

Elizabeth Diamond Rose replied: "Feels like it will be the same answer. It often is, isn't it. They seem to be repeating the message of frequency over identity, which is the universal way and the new gig on Earth's new paradigm shift. I think they are easing you in and I love how careful they are with you. Not sure where they're taking you right now. But they know what they're doing. And not everything is for industry and work. Sometimes guides come just for us."

I went back into meditation and asked Hypatia about Synesius/Sonisius.

> H: "You had the name wrong. And yes, I knew him, but he was much less significant to me than I was to him."

Meantime, I continued to do more fiber art. I felt inspired. The third large wall hanging I made was in honor of my sometime-spirit-guide Elen of the Ways. The central image was a stylized reindeer based on a 9th-century Viking coin but with antlers based on a 7th-century BCE* Scythian reindeer pin. I was having a lot of fun.

Thursday, 30 January 2025

It had been a long time since I'd been focused enough to talk to Plotinus. I'd been preoccupied with fiber art projects for more than a month. I felt inspired—it gave me great satisfaction to create something with my hands—something tactile, something not made of words but of visual images. I enjoyed planning each piece, choosing/constructing the image, deciding how to create it, and shopping for the perfect fabric and threads in local shops or ordering on the Internet. I reveled in feeling the textiles in my hands and stitching the pieces together. Making the contemporary wall quilts was a kind of meditation. It was also compulsive, I realized, when I kept working even though I was so tired that I started to make mistakes.

After I finished the quilted art piece I called "Elen of the Ways in Her Reindeer Guise," I was available again for conversation. I sat in front of my meditation altar and asked Plotinus to visit.

Me: "Hello, Plotinus!"

P: "Hello, Beloved."

Me: "I've been so preoccupied, I haven't visited with you for a while, but I sense you are near."

P: "Always near, as are Hypatia and others in The Collective."

Me: "I need advice."

P: "Always. [Smiling]"

Me: "Health stuff, blood pressure. Does doing Angelic Reiki raise it?"

P: "I can't answer that. I'll ask someone who will know."

[Pause. I sense a familiar energy.]

Asclepius: "Hello, Elyn."

Me: "Thank you for coming! Can you answer my question?"

Asc: "Well, it needs translation. We have a different understanding of health and unwellness. [Pause] Bringing energy through your system indeed shifts the internal pressures and balances. It is a temporary thing and not bad."

Me: "Why does it happen?"

Asc: "Again, it is hard for me to translate my understanding of the body and yours. You see it as a physical manifestation. I see it as a composite composition of energies and—humors [classical theory that bodily fluids like blood, bile, etc. influence the temperament and health issues]—more like the Chinese medicine you work with. Putting additional energy into the system temporarily shifts it, like forcing high-speed water through a hose. Nothing to be concerned about."

Me: *"Unless the hose springs a leak!"*

Asc: *[Nodding] "For that reason, you need to take care, eat well, exercise, lead a healthy life."*

Me: *"Can I do more than I'm doing?"*

Asc: *"Yes. Eat more citrus. What you call vitamin C."*

Me: *And my cholesterol?"*

Asc: *[Laughing] "A made-up construct."*

Me: *"But it exists!"*

Asc: *"Yes, but it is not a culprit. It is your Western medicine's attempt to find cause, not correlations. They look at the wrong things and ignore the whole picture. You are not your cholesterol."*

Me: *"And HDL or LDL?"*

Asc: *[Smiling] "Nor those things either. Your modern medicine fails to grasp underlying concerns it cannot or does not measure."*

Me: *"Alina [my acupuncturist] says it's inflammation; Angelique says it's stress."*

Asc: *"More words, more words for imbalances. The best things to do are eat well exercise, relax, lead a healthy life with healthy relationships."*

Me: *"Thank you."*

Asc: *"My pleasure to be of service."*

Me: *"I think—I feel—I'm doing the right things and [have begun] including homeopathy."*

P: *"You are doing the right things."*

Me: *"I want to shed my old constricting skin like a snake sheds its skin—letting go of old patterns and habits of thought that no longer serve me."*

P: *"It is well."*

Me: *"Can you help?"*

P: [Kindly] *"A snake sheds its skin naturally. So can you. It is a natural process to let go of old wounds and habits. What is unnatural is holding on to what doesn't serve us. But we—you—humans do it anyway."*

Me: *"How to let go?"*

P: *"Remember—we are all one. We are all part of the One."*

Me: *"Old wounds … grief, anger, betrayal …"*

P: *"The latter is your interpretation. Let go of it. Release your interpretation, your projection. Send love and compassion. BE love and compassion."*

Me: [Nodding]

P: *"See yourself shedding, letting go, releasing. Even say the words: Repeat them as you release your too-constricting skin."*

Me: *"I will try. Thank you."*

P: *"Anything else?"*

Me: *"Thank you for being present in my life. By the way, where's Hypatia?"*

H: *"Here, as always."*

Me: *"How are you?"*

H: *"Here, we are always well. Not that the word has meaning here."*

Me: *"Do you have advice for me?"*

H: *"Yes. Occupy yourself with meaningful projects. Give thanks often. Be grateful. That will take you far toward shedding your skin that is too tight and uncomfortable."*

Me: *"You are right. Thank you. Goodbye, all."*

Sunday, 2 February 2025

Our friend Tessa was having a very difficult time. Her degenerative condition was causing great pain, and she was going to need to undergo a very invasive surgery. I asked Plotinus in meditation how to help her heal.

P: "Only Tessa can heal herself."

Me: "And my cholesterol and blood pressure? How do I heal that?" [My doctor was quite upset at my most recent bloodwork.]

P: "Only you can heal yourself. For the blood pressure, let go of your old story, your always being in a state of high alert. Relax. Don't worry about the cholesterol."

Later, I had a brief conversation with Plotinus about R.J. Stewart's new, expanded Tree of Life Part 2 course, which I was considering taking, even though he/they had made it clear that Part 1 was a waste of my time.

P: "You humans love your models."

Thursday, 13 February 2025

We listened to one of Suzanne Giesemann's YouTube videos. One of the questions she (via her channeled group Sanaya) answered was how to tell if the messages you received as a medium were real or your imagination. Suzanne stressed the importance of sensing how the messages felt, and that, with experience, you would learn to tell the difference between what was *really* coming to you from the Other Side and what was your ego subconsciously making up a story.

It was all too easy for a "baby" medium (a newbie) to unintentionally create a story instead of staying with the information they received from Spirit. That was one reason that asking for evidence was so important.

It was sobering to hear Suzanne say that, even after all the years she's been a highly acclaimed evidential medium, she would still occasionally have a moment of doubt about it all. "It's the ego kicking in," she said. "Just pat it on the back and send it on its way."

I thought back to my first encounter with Plotinus. I knew he wasn't a figment of my imagination because he had spontaneously spoken through me! When later I asked him why, he had said he wanted me to know he was real. It worked. Otherwise, I might indeed have wondered whether I had just made him up. Nonetheless, on various occasions, I asked him and some of the other beings from the Other Side to give me evidence. Each time I was able to confirm the evidence, it strengthened my belief—no, my *knowing*—that they weren't products of my subconscious or my imagination. They were real. They were much wiser than I am. And they were proof of the continuity of consciousness after physical death.

It was time to connect with Plotinus again.

Me: "Welcome, Plotinus."

P: "Welcome, Elyn. You have been preoccupied, not very approachable."

Me: "Except for small moments, like, 'You humans love your models!'"

P: [Smiling] "Yes. And now you are off on another tangent—that geometrical formulation you know as the Tree of Life."

Me: "Yes. Do you disapprove?"

P: "Neither approve nor disapprove. Only curious about the project. Is it a diversion from deeper work?"

Me: "Or a roadmap to deeper experience?"

P: [Sigh] "You humans love your models. They are not the territory. They are limited and incomplete—yes, inadequate—human attempts to codify the ineffable."

Me: "R.J. talks about [working with the Tree of Life leading to] breakthroughs, transformations of consciousness."

P: "Yes, yes, I know. It's kept people occupied for centuries, creating more and more correspondences."

Me: "Bread and circuses?"

P: [Laughing] "Indeed, quite so."

Me: "But is there nothing of value?"

P: "Maps are useful for charting the territory and even setting a path to reach your destination. But they are not the territory."

Me: "I want to explore the territory. I thought this would help."

P: "Yes, as did your [Daoist] crystal course and [everything] you study helps."

H: "Do you still not understand everything is flux? And in flux?"

Me: "I've had flashes of [awareness that] we are all coalesced energy forms—but that's not a 'place' you can live in on this planet. You have to resolve back to material density."

H: [Harrumph] "As long as you don't get stuck in, mired in the bog of physicality."

Me: "How do you all function there, where you are?"

H: "It is—we are—much 'lighter'—in both senses. That's what you should strive for—lightness of body, seeing Light in everything—expanding, nurturing the Light."

Me: "Thank you. R.J. cautions about false inner contacts."

P: "As well he should! But he is limited, unfamiliar with verifiable techniques that remove the guesswork."

H: [Sniffing] "And he's a bit … shall we say… doctrinaire?"

Me: "I agree."

P: "So why did you decide to study with him again?"

Me: "I 'asked my fingers' [muscle-tested using kinesiology*] and the answer was yes. To be in community, to have some guidance and discipline."

P: "We can't give you discipline, but we do try to give you guidance."

Me: "I appreciate that. I value your wisdom."

P: "We are a bit wiser than we were on Planet Earth, but we are still fallible. We have less 'distance' between us and Wisdom than we did on Earth, but we are still limited. We do the best we can."

The Reluctant Medium

Me: "So ... my anxiety [about world events, friends] ... suggestions?"

P: "'Not my energy,' as Suzanne advises."

Me: "But it is—we are all connected!"

P: "Does it serve you to be so empathetic, and anxious, for other people's suffering? You are less able to help them then."

Me: [Nodding]

P: "You are still shedding your [constricting] snakeskin. ... You are tender, fresh. ... Be wise. Be cautious. Be self-contained."

Me: "But I care!"

H: "That's fine and good and admirable, but not at your own expense. That serves no one. I agree with Plotinus: 'Not my energy.'"

Me: "What can I do to help in these chaotic times?"

TC: "Pray for the highest good as outcome. Send blessings. And more blessings. The world needs love and healing. Send blessings."

Me: "I will. Thank you. I need love and healing too."

P: "Indeed. Send blessings to yourself. And we send them to you as well as we can from our side."

Me: "You can?"

P: [Nodding] "Energetically we can engage your world. So, Blessings!"

Me: "Gratitude, gratitude. Thank you. Tired now."

P, H, and The Collective: "Till next time."

Saturday, 15 February 2025

Me: "I have a question for you, Plotinus."

P: "Yes?"

Me: "Why [am I channeling] all you Greeks?"

P: "Why not? Similar vibrations."

Me: "Did I have a past life in Greece? Or Alexandria?"

P: [Hesitating] "It's possible."

Me: "You don't know?"

P: "We don't know everything. Suffice to say, you have an affinity for us, and we for you."

H: "Oh, don't pussyfoot around so much, Plotinus. Of course she did."

Me: "What kind of past life?"

P: "We don't like to share details unless they are helpful."

Me: "I'm asking."

P: "I know."

Me: "Was I a Pythia [a priestess oracle at Delphi)?"

H: [Nodding] "Among others."

Me: "Tell me who/what! Elizabeth Diamond Rose indicated [in jest] that I may have been you, Hypatia."

H: [Nodding] "We are all part of each other."

Me: "Is there a name I can fact-check? Evidence?"

H: "There was a Jewess ... I think you may have a relationship with her. The woman who invented the bain-marie."

P: [Nodding] "After my time."

H: "Closer to mine. Brilliant. Misunderstood, but brilliant. Definitely a connection to you."

Me: "Can I have evidence?"

H: "A balance-weight."

[I see the image of two balance trays suspended, one on either side of a central piece.]

Me: "Thank you. I'll look her up."

P: "We come together through affinity. You've noticed, Hypatia was a student of a student of mine."

Me: "But I wasn't."

P: "I came to you because of the questions you were asking. I sensed you were open to hearing me and sharing my ancient but modern wisdom with the world. I was not wrong."

Me: "But I need to do more—a book, a chapter …"

P: "Indeed."

H: "Including [me] as well!"

Me: "Of course! … I'm tired. I think I'll stop now. Until the next time."

P: "There is always time."

H: "And no time. Until the next time out of time. Blessings, Dear One."

Me: "Thank you."

I did a Google search and learned that Maria the Jewess, the first actual alchemist, lived somewhere between 0–200 CE. However, her birth and death information are unreliable. Plotinus lived 204/5–270 CE and Hypatia lived c. 350/37–March 415 CE. Maria couldn't have lived after Plotinus' time and closer to Hypatia's. That part of what they told me was incorrect. Maybe time on the Other Side is more flexible, and precision less important.

But Plotinus and Hypatia did get the balance evidence correct. Maria the Jewess's most famous adage was, "'Join the male and the female, and you will find what is sought.' In other words, balance opposites to get the hoped-for result."

Tuesday, 18 February 2025

Things were going so much better between Gary and me. We were less reactive, more transparent, more loving in word and deed. Gary kept quoting Hypatia and saying, "What you do to someone else, you do to yourself!"

After a very difficult and tumultuous year, we finally seemed to be in a place of smooth sailing. When I asked, "What do I need to know today?" in my morning meditation, I saw a boat sailing on smooth water, or occasionally at anchor in a peaceful bay. Such a change from last year's stormy seas!

I had finished three fiber art projects and was thinking about starting another, a Green Man wall hanging, based on the medieval image of a face sprouting vines and leaves. I knew that Plotinus and The Collective were eager for me to start writing about them, but I wasn't sure how to begin. I'd been helping Gary on his *Conscious Living* project, but I knew I had to do more. So, where to start?

Me: "Welcome, Plotinus and Hypatia and The Collective!"

TC: "Welcome, Dear One. Why are you calling us all together? Not that we need to be called, since we are always all here."

Me: "I need advice—and wisdom—from all of you."

TC: [Nodding, each one of them, waiting.]

Me: "First, what project should I embark on next? Conscious Living? Adventures of Everyday Mystics, *with a chapter on Plotinus? A Green Man fiber art wall hanging? Or?*"

P: "Or something completely different?"

Me: "I'm open to suggestions of all sorts."

[Pause]

P: [As spokesperson] "It's not either/or."

Me: [Expectant, waiting]

P: "It's all and more."

Me: "Conscious Living, Adventures of Everyday Mystics, Plotinus, Green Man?"

P: "Well, the Green Man is merely diversionary. But the rest, yes. Support your partner's work. Rewrite some of the chapters in Conscious Living. Even out the tone. Begin to think about Adventures of Everyday Mystics and the interviews. Gently walk yourself back into the shallow water. Reread my wisdom in my writings and embed it in your book, along with interviews and a section on my channeled information. ... No, [the] latter [about me] is a separate book."

Me: "Hypatia? What about you?"

H: "[Write about] me and Maria the Jewess and other underserved, underrecognized women. The Pythia."

Me: "Another book?"

H: [Nodding] "An anthology introducing us. Remember, years ago, you began collecting names of powerful women from the past? You were creating questions and practices [for the reader to imagine herself as each of the women]."

Me: "Huh. I'd forgotten that. So many projects! How to prioritize?"

P: "Neither this nor that, neither here nor there, always centered."

Me: "Hmmm. Help Gary with Conscious Living. Begin making interview questions and framework for Adventures of Everyday Mystics. Continue talking with all of you. Perhaps a different book [about channeling Plotinus]. And now—a book of important women in the past?"

TC: "Nodding."

Me: "A lot to do! Will I live long enough?"

TC: [Consulting each other] "We are here to help you live as long and well enough. Have no fear. Have no fear. We are with you, beside you, behind you. Release, relax, recalibrate, remember who you truly are: a gift of the Divine Expression of Itself."

Me: [Nodding]

TC: "*Now, begin! You are so very loved.*"

Me: "[Suddenly realizing] And then—there's Elizabeth Diamond Rose's work! [The writing/editing projects I've agreed to do with her.]"

TC: [Nodding]: "*A footnote. Easily done.*"

Me: "OK. Thank you."

TC: [Nodding]

Me: "Much gratitude to all. Goodbye for now."

Thursday, 20 February 2025

During morning meditation with Gary, I had a surprise visit from Jesus. Yes, Jesus! Not someone I thought about very often, or even occasionally, given that I was raised in an agnostic, humanist household.

At the beginning of my meditation, I asked to be given or shown something I need to know today. Placed (figuratively) into my open hand was a miniature currach with a tiny mast and sail. A currach is the ancient, wood-framed, skin-covered boat that Irish saints used to sail the seas.

The message I received was, "Stormy waters, smooth sailing—all are part of the adventure! And it is an adventure. If there is no wind, the boat can't go anywhere. It needs the breeze. If there is too much wind, there is lots of upheaval and the chance of capsizing. But have courage and determination. And remember, it's an adventure."

I had just finished contemplating this message when a huge ethereal being appeared in my inner vision. He was floating in space, surrounded and glowing with light. He wore white flowing robes—I think he stepped out of a mandorla*, but I might have added that detail after the event. He was luminous. I tried to see his face, but I couldn't because it was glowing with light. Everything about him was radiant. Purple or pink light shimmered around his head.

Words cannot describe the impact of this being.

Stunned, I mentally asked, "Who are you? St. Germaine? Or—"

I "heard" the name Jesus. Jesus?

Then he said, "But [names don't matter]—we are all One in the Light."

I understood without spoken words that he had come to tell me that we (me, you, Gary, all of us) are watched over, supported, and protected. That there is nothing to fear.

I burst into tears. This was such an affirmation of what we are doing—not a reward, but an acknowledgment of support and encouragement.

I kept crying. I opened my eyes and couldn't speak. I closed them again, but the apparition was gone. It had lasted only a few moments, but it could have been an eternity.

I opened my eyes again. Gary was staring at me, concerned.

I gasped, "Uh—uh—" but I couldn't form words. Gary looked even more worried. I knew he was wondering if I was having a stroke, so I forced myself to speak a few words. But it took a while to "come back" enough to do so.

Tears streaming down my face, I tried to describe my astounding experience. Words could not do it justice, but I tried.

Gary was thrilled. He exclaimed, "They've got our backs!"

We both felt surrounded by divine encouragement, support, and reassurance.

I knew that this support was unconditional. You didn't have to earn it or be a good person. Jesus was (and other divine beings were) simply there, watching over us, supporting us, loving us. All of us.

As the day went on, I could close my eyes and still experience an echo-memory of the event. It was so powerful.

I had no doubt I had encountered Jesus, even if I hadn't asked him for evidence. The experience was all the evidence I needed.

I found a series of romanticized illustrations of the Ascended Masters on Mark Dodich's Astromark.org website. The one of Jesus was not identical to what I saw; "my" Jesus's face, like all the rest of him, was luminous and white, without distinct features. But the pink and purple rays behind the head of Jesus in the portrait were reminiscent of the pinks and purples I had seen in my vision. Maybe the artist had been inspired by their own vision of Jesus.

I wrote Elizabeth Diamond Rose about what had happened. She replied that Jesus had visited her occasionally since 2008. I told Marchiene about my amazing experience, and she said that Jesus had visited her several times as well. And I remembered Suzanne Giesemann described having a visit from Jesus. He has been visiting many people. Elizabeth Diamond Rose thought it was because Jesus cares deeply about humanity and the planet. As, apparently, does the loving, compassionate divine female energy known to Christians as the Virgin Mary, who has been appearing to people (especially children) for centuries.

Wednesday, 26 February 2025

We moved to Tessa and Nigel's lovely house in Girona to stay for 4–5 days while she had back surgery, which was scheduled for today. We had offered to take care of their dog, cat, and fish.

It felt strange to meditate in someone else's home, filled with their energy and their belongings. We created a "bubble" of sacred space on the ground floor next to the bookshelves. That was the only place that felt energetically clear enough.

I sat down to meditate.

>Me: "Oh, Plotinus, it's so good to talk to you!" [I'm teary-eyed.]

>P: "I've been waiting patiently, as always."

>Me: "Can you give me insight into Tessa's condition?"

>P: [Pausing] "It is not for us to know the ins and outs of someone else's life choices, but rest assured, she has many learning lessons presented to her. And to Nigel, with whom she is inextricably linked, in this life and other

lives. Giving and receiving, supporting and being supported. Hurting and helping."

Me: "Oh. ... A panorama of experience."

P: "Exactly."

Me: "What will be the outcome?"

P: "More pain, more suffering, disintegration, testing—the trial by fire of Nigel and all he holds precious."

Me: "Oh. How sad! Is it inevitable?"

P: "Not sad. Educational. And no, nothing is inevitable—except [chuckle] death."

Me: "And rebirth? I want to ask you about reincarnation."

P: "Rebirth is optional. Some of us choose to, others prefer to wait."

Me: "For what?"

P: "A much slower evolution."

Me: "Do soul groups wait to incarnate together? Or can a soul split and be in various places at once?"

P: "Two questions. Not either/or. Soul groups reincarnate together but also apart. Souls can bi-locate—of course—or tri-locate. We are like holograms, able to split off."

Me: "So you can be there—I'm talking to you, Plotinus, existing in a certain afterlife realm—and you could at the same time be reincarnated as someone on this planet?"

P: [Nodding] "Or elsewhere. But you don't really understand the subtleties. It isn't here or there, now, then—it's much more—fluid. You can think about the past and remember it; you can be 'in the present'; or you can imagine the future. We move among the realms like you move from one room to another."

Me: "Whew! A lot to take in."

P: [Nodding] "Most importantly, don't take it too seriously. It's all efforts to *explain what can't be [explained]."*

Me: *[I get an image of quantum choice—x or y—and endless potential.]*

P: [Nodding] "Something like that. Clearly, your attention influences what you perceive—but it's so much simpler and more complicated than 'you' making a choice. Who is 'you'? What 'you' is choosing? Unlimited Oneness is experiencing Itself at every moment with every choice every cell and atom makes. It's all One and indescribable. We are, as your author [Lex Hixon] described it, the effervescent overflow—the champagne bubbles exploding once the cork is pulled. Take the Big Picture and don't get hung up on minutiae."

Me: "OK. ... Can you tell me about the Ascended Masters? My visit with Jesus?"

P: "Ah ... [Smiling thoughtfully] We are many kinds of beings in many realms. Hypatia and I, The Collective, are once-humans who were aware, somewhat conscious in life. Conscious enough in the afterlife to remain present and available—engaged with humans. Like you. I couldn't keep still—I needed to communicate with you!"

Me: "And Jesus?"

P: "Ah ... Some humans have more consciousness—more conscious connection with the Source—than others. I approached it occasionally. Jesus was able to—live in it—or closer to it. He carries a higher vibration. He is 'closer' to the Light. Hence his appearance of luminosity."

Me: "He still cares about the planet, about humans?"

P: [Nodding] "Obviously. That's why he continues to appear to people."

Me: "He said I could call him Jesus, but that 'We are all One in the Light.'"

P: [Nodding] "That is correct. We *are* all One in the Light. Some of us are closer to it than others. Some are in the next room! A dim reflection. Others are so close they are illuminated."

Me: "And the archangels?"

P: "Another dimension. Never human. Configured differently."

Me: "But engaged with humanity?"

P: "Yes. And, also, with beings on other planets. They bring a different energy. Think of all the variety of creatures on Planet Earth—fireflies, frogs, cows, humans, giraffes. It's like that. We are closer to some species than others."

Me: "Are they all good?"

P: [Laughing] "Such a human question! Is a lion killing a wildebeest good? We all have different natures. For some, the improvement of humanity is tantamount—we support your growth and evolution. For others, it is inconsequential. And some are—tricksters, delighting in chaos and havoc."

Me: "Sounds like Trump!"

P: [Nodding]

Me: "Is there a battle between Good and Evil?"

P: "Only as you perceive it on your plane of existence. A very limited perception of either/or, black/white."

Me: "Lots to think about. Thank you."

P: "You are welcome."

Me: "Till next time, then."

P: [Nodding] "Let's make it sooner than later!"

Me: [Smiling] "That's a plan!"

Thursday, 27 February 2025

I had a surprising Messenger exchange with Natalie Fillet, a Dutchwoman I knew from Robert Moss's Active Dreamwork teacher training course six years ago. I had had only minimal contact with her since then.

Natalie was following a trail of breadcrumbs that had led to Cheryl Page. Natalie was on our mailing list, so she had read my article on channeling

Plotinus. She'd watched a video of Cheryl and gone to Cheryl's website, and she saw that I'd written a review of Cheryl's innovative book, *Mystic Richness*. She contacted me to ask what I thought of Cheryl.

She sent the following message. I have lightly edited her and my replies.

"How are your conversations with Plotinus going? I really loved to read your article about it. And of course, would like to hear more. I am interested in doing a new training about communicating 'beyond the veil,' and Cheryl's energy is resonating with me the most at this moment in time. My question is: Can you tell me about your experiences with Cheryl? Do you recommend it? Big hugs, Natalie."

I replied: "Synchronicities abound!! I just finished another visit with Plotinus. Cheryl connected with me five years ago through inner guidance and [her connection with] Mary Magdalene. Cheryl started us on our adventures with channeling by recommending we study with Suzanne Giesemann. We highly recommend Suzanne and her courses. Yes—I trust Cheryl and her work. Just listened to a podcast with her as well. She's on Substack. Any more info you want, just ask! Hugs. Elyn"

Natalie: "Hey Elyn, thanks! I will look on Substack for Cheryl. Saw that she offers a course, where I can try bit by bit. Will do that! What a delight communicating with Plotinus. What do these communications bring (extra?) to your life? Are you going to share this with a broader public? Or are these conversations just for you? Hugs, Natalie."

What great questions to get me to think deeper about this book project!

I replied: "Ah ... yes, I will share with the broader public. He wants that. I've been hesitant to 'come out of the closet' but have done so, first the article, and then an interview last [October] on 'Life with Ghosts – Let's Chat' podcast with Stephen Berkley. He also interviewed Cheryl—she put us in touch. Any questions you'd like me to ask Plotinus?"

I added: "What they have brought to my life is the certainty that consciousness exists after we die in the physical realm. This certainty is not intellectual but gut level now. Evidence has been given by various folks on the Other Side (Hypatia, Pythagoras, and others). Now, if I only knew why I seem to have so many Greeks coming through! That's a question I need to ask for sure. Hugs, Elyn"

Natalie: "I really love to hear this, Elyn. You touched my heart with what it brings to you. (So your gift is also a gift to me, thank you.)"

Later, Natalie wrote: "That's great you are going to share more about your conversations! I guess there are a lot of people who are interested in Plotinus. Sure, what an honor! I do want to ask Plotinus some questions. Need to think of that. Will come back with a few questions.

"The first question that popped up: 1. How cool you chose Elyn as your 'speaking tube' (Elyn, I heard this word in Dutch, it is an old word here, looked it up in Google translate, maybe this old word has a special meaning to you? 'Speaking tube'??)

"2. Do you come through other people also, and have you done this before in history? If so, can you tell us names? Elyn, I will get back to you with other questions."

I replied: "Wonderful comments! Speaking tube! Encouraging me to share more (about Plotinus) for sure. Will ask your question next time I visit with Plotinus. Any more questions to add???"

Talk about synchronicity. Just as I was going to start going through my journal entries and prepare the manuscript about Plotinus, Hypatia, and The Collective, I received a series of messages from Natalie, a woman I last saw nearly six years ago and have had almost no contact with since. A series of messages urging me to write a book about these channeled messages.

Thanks, Plotinus and The Collective, for orchestrating the encouragement!

Friday, February 28, 2025

This day marked the first anniversary of my first, spontaneous conversation with Plotinus. I sat in front of my altar to meditate on the book project. The message that came to me was the (tentative) book title, *Plotinus, Hypatia, and The Collective – Channeled Messages from the Other Side*. Or maybe "from Beyond."

The book would include all the conversations from the first year in chronological order. It would also describe the context of what was happening in my life: the feedback I received from friends, stresses in my relationship with Gary, my terrifying bout with whooping cough, and so on. It would be an accurate account not only of the messages but also of the *experience* of channeling messages from Beyond and how it had transformed me.

The first anniversary seemed like an auspicious day to begin the project. I wrote the following:

"If you had told me that I would be channeling messages from a Greek philosopher who died over 1700 years ago, I'd have said you were nuts! But that's exactly what spontaneously happened to me. With evidence, so I knew I wasn't just making it up."

During meditation that morning, when I asked, "What do I need to know today?" I saw an object that resembled an orange. I asked for this to be the evidential sign that I really was talking with Plotinus and not just having a monologue with my subconscious or the Collective Subconscious. By now, I should have known not to doubt, but …

Later, Gary and I walked into the Old Town, following on a whim a new route that led us down a set of steps we had never taken. At the bottom was a large mural of "The Fool" Tarot card. The Fool's tunic was covered with what looked like oranges. This was the evidence I had asked for. Thank you, Plotinus—or whoever was orchestrating these events.

In honor of this first anniversary, we visited Gipsy again, and I had coffee with Gary and Plotinus. Plotinus spoke through me again, with my permission.

> PS: "I hope this has been [edifying? productive?] for you."
>
> Gary said: "Yes" aloud.
>
> I replied: "Yes," mentally.
>
> PS: "And now begins the second stage. This vessel—this 'speaking tube' [smiling] will now begin to write."
>
> Me: "Is the working title, Plotinus, Hypatia, and The Collective Speak—Channeled Messages from the Beyond, correct?"

PS: [Nodding]. "For now."

[Pause]

[I began taking notes instead of having Plotinus speak through me.]

Me: "Why do I have so many Greeks coming through?"

P: "Because you were Greek."

Me: "Was I Hypatia? Maria the Jewess?"

P: "Does it matter?"

Me: "Yes."

P: [Consulting] "Yes."

[I understood that in some sense, of course, I was them—just as I was everyone. We are all related, all interconnected, all part of the One.]

P: "But more important, you were a Pythia."

Me: "Why more important?"

P: "[It was] your practice for your current work [channeling]."

Me: "Oh. I guess that's obvious. Thank you."

P: "Time now to do the work."

Me: "Yes. This afternoon, another conversation?"

P: "We will be ready."

Then we returned to Tessa and Nigel's home. I wanted to make an offering to express my gratitude to Plotinus, Hypatia, and The Collective, but most of my supplies were at our home. So I offered what I had: a crumb of a chocolate cookie, and lavender and pine essential oils dripped onto the candle wax. I settled into meditation.

Me: "You are here."

P: "Indeed."

Me: "All day, very present."

P: [Nodding]

Me: "It's our first-year anniversary."

P: [Smiling]

Me: "Time to get to work, eh?"

P: "Indeed. You have much to do."

H: "Don't forget me!"

Me: "Of course not! The book title includes your name and The Collective."

H: [Nodding in approval]

Me: "I will formulate more questions, but [at this moment] what do you want people to know, Hypatia?"

H: [Firmly] "That we must learn to live together in harmony. I was brutally murdered by those who wanted domination and power. We see that often in the world. It serves no good—long term, in fact, it delays human progress and development."

Me: "Isn't it a chicken and egg problem? Until there is moral and spiritual progress and development, there won't be harmony."

H: [Dismissively] "An excuse. Here and now, each person is responsible for their actions and progress. They make choices all the time. If they listen to 'the still small voice within,' it will become loud enough to be heard."

Me: "But how to begin?"

H: "With patience, with education, with compassion."

Me: "But—"

H: "Begin with yourself. Be a model for others. You have a saying, 'Be the peace you want to see.' Do that."

Me: "Thank you. … Plotinus, a friend [Natalie] has a question for you."

P: [Nodding]

Me: "Have you spoken through others? And have you incarnated again?"

P: [Nodding] "I have come to others over the centuries. Usually philosophers. Often, they think their ideas are theirs, but they are actually mine."

Me: "Does that bother you?"

P: "Not at all. I hardly need ego gratification on this side of the veil!"

Me: "Can you name one or more of these philosophers?"

P: "Theocrates, Thermopolese(?), Catigulina (?)."

[Just then, the housekeeper walked through the room, and I lost my concentration.]

P: [Continuing] "John Milton. Maynard Keynes. Cosimo Medici. Carlos Mendosa."

Me: "You spoke through them?"

P: [Shaking head] "I spoke to them, and they thought it was their own thoughts."

Me: "Why is it different with me?"

P: "You aren't a philosopher, so it is clear you are not thinking these thoughts."

Me: "And Hypatia? Have you come to others?"

H: [Shaking her head] "I haven't found many receptive to a female guide. A few other women ... you."

Me: "Can someone ask for you to come through to them?"

P and H: [Nodding] "Invitations are readily accepted if the subject is indeed prepared and appropriate."

Me: "I think Gary experienced Plotinus a little bit."

P: [Nodding] "It was a pleasure."

Me: "I want to express my (literally) undying gratitude for the gifts you have given me. I will do my very best to create a book worthy of all your wisdom—a book to help advance humanity—one reader at a time!"

P and H: "Thank you. We have every confidence you will succeed, especially with our help. [Laughter]"

Me: [Smiling] "Thank you!! Goodbye for now. And much love to you both."

P and H: [Surprised, smiling]

I did a Google search for the people Plotinus mentioned and found possible confirmation with John Milton, Maynard Keynes, Cosimo de Medici, and Carlos Mendoza Alvarez. Some of their ideas might, indeed, have been influenced by Plotinus. I couldn't find anything about the three Greeks he had mentioned, but that might be because they were lost to history or because I didn't hear their names correctly.

Saturday - Sunday, 1 - 2 March 2025

I continued working on the introduction to the book. I sent the draft four-page introduction to Natalie, and this was her response (lightly edited and shortened):

"Hi Elyn,

"Oh my gosh, I am in awe of your writing.

"This is amazing—I'm hanging on your every word… in the sense of, "Oh, so this happens to 'ordinary' people, like me." What I love most is your innocence. The doubt you describe makes it all the more believable. All the human elements—your emotions, thoughts, and experiences—come through so clearly.

"The channeling becomes ordinary … in the sense that you describe it as, "What is happening to me? What's going on here?" The urge to check and verify—those are all completely normal human reactions. …

"What speaks to me most in this document:

"The combination of the subject—Plotinus, how he comes through (and others)—along with how it affects you. How you, as a channel/speaking tube, experience this process.

"What also stands out is the authenticity of your experience. The way you move between curiosity, doubt, and eventual acceptance makes it so relatable. It's not a grand, mystical spectacle—it's deeply human. Your descriptions of the process make it tangible, almost as if the reader is experiencing it alongside you.

"Another thing that fascinates me is how the boundaries between the seen and unseen world blur in such an organic way. It doesn't feel forced or sensationalized, but rather like a natural unfolding of something that was already there, waiting to be discovered.

"And then, of course, there's the subtle humor woven throughout—your astonishment, Gary's reactions, the little asides (like the "dirty man" remark about Iamblichus). These details make the text so alive and engaging.

"Perhaps that's why I'm left with the feeling: "Nooo, don't stop! Keep going! What happens next?"

"Your writing is not just a story—it's an invitation. An invitation to explore, to question, to wonder. And that, to me, is what makes it so powerful. Hugs, Natalie"

I replied to Natalie with gratitude for her kind words and asked if I could send her a draft of the manuscript when I finished it. She was enthusiastic and eager to support the project.

I continued to read through the year of journal entries.

Sunday, 9 March 2025

We were still staying at Tessa and Nigel's house. She had required additional surgery, so it wasn't clear how long we would need to stay there. Back-up support was arranged so we could spend the weekend celebrating our friend Barbara's birthday with a group of friends in nearby Sant Martí d'Empúries. We would be staying in two apartments in a remodeled building overlooking the sea, very near the Ruins of Empúries.

We took a bus and got off an hour later at the Ruins of Empúries bus stop. Barbara's husband, Stephen, picked us up, and we settled into the apartment we were sharing with our friend Ani Williams. The three of us had a regular morning meditation practice, so we hoped we could maintain our routine.

Ani is a gifted troubadour/harpist who composes and performs songs that come to her in dreams and at sacred places. She is a sound healer and teacher, and she recently published a book that explores the hidden and forgotten history of this region of the Pyrenees. She told us that the apartment building where we were staying was built over the ruins of a temple dedicated to Artemis of Ephesus, whose cult had been brought there thousands of years ago from what is now Turkey.

> *That morning, after we sent Angelic Reiki to a friend, a voice came through me, saying: "All is well, all will be well. Do not worry about the minutiae. Do not concern yourself about all these tiny details [e.g., figuring out how to stay more conveniently at Tessa and Nigel's]. Flow with the flow. Release. All is well, all will be well."*

Gary said, "Thank you, Plotinus."

The voice said, "I am not Plotinus."

I asked, "Who are you?"

It said, "I am your Oversight/Overseer."

I asked, "Are you an angel?"

"I am an angelic force."

I asked, "What is your name?"

I "heard" something like "Sephora."

This channeling stuff was getting bigger, deeper—higher? Broader? I didn't know. Did it have something to do with meditating on top of the ruins of what had been, in ancient Greek and Roman times, a temple? Did that bring through additional spirit guidance?

I Googled "Sephora." Sephora is primarily a Hebrew female name that means bird. I wondered if the word I heard was, instead, related to the sephirot, singular sephira, on the Kabbalist Tree of Life. Each sephira is an attribute of divine creative life force, which flows through from the unknowable Divine Essence/God into manifestation.

Later, our group explored the Ruins of Empúries with Ani, pausing to meditate and sing near the remains of a temple dedicated to Isis and the ruins of what had been an Asclepion*, an important healing center. The Asclepion was dedicated to the ancient Greek healing god, Asclepius, who had given me advice during several channeling sessions. The statue perched on a pedestal on top of the ruined Asclepion was a copy of the 2,000-year-old marble original, which was in the nearby museum.

After walking through the ruins, we visited the museum. As soon as I saw the statue of Asclepius, I was whacked by the energy radiating from it. Gary caught me and held me steady. I felt dizzy, totally off balance. I wondered if, now that I had a more personal connection with Asclepius, the energy of the statue was much stronger. At any rate, I felt it more strongly.

Ancient people traveled with great devotion and difficulty to be in the presence of a statue of their deity—Artemis of Ephesus, or Serapis, or Isis. Now I wondered what they experienced. Modern pilgrims travel to the shrine of Fatima in Portugal or go to Jerusalem to visit the tomb of Jesus, or to Santiago de Compostela, where St. James the Greater's bones supposedly reside, or to Buddha's birthplace, or Mecca. Maybe there *was* something to the miracles that were reported at such holy sites. Maybe, if you were a devout-enough believer, being in the presence of such sacred energy might have a huge impact. I'd always been skeptical of miracles associated with relics and statues, but now I was reconsidering.

Friday, 14 March 2025

By now, we had stayed at Nigel and Tessa's for 18 days, except for the previous weekend, when we were in Sant Martí d'Empúries. Being in their home took some adjustment. For one thing, we didn't have a private space for meditation. We had created a sacred space on the ground floor next to the library, and that felt energetically clean, but there were lots of interruptions, including cleaning ladies and pets. It just wasn't our home.

I felt uncomfortable opening up to Plotinus in their house. I wasn't sure if it was energetically safe. Time to ask for guidance.

I lit a candle and a stick of palo santo wood incense, and I established sacred space by calling in the seven directions (sky above, land below, East, South, West, North, and the center within).

I asked Plotinus to visit.

> Me: "Is it safe to open up to you here and have a conversation?"

> P: "Be careful. Establish the Golden Dome of Transmutation around you."

> [I always ask Archangel Michael to establish the Golden Dome whenever we do Angel Reiki, but I hadn't thought to ask him to establish it when I meditate.]

> Me: "I will."

> [I do so.]

> P: "That's better."

> [It feels better. I should have remembered as a matter of routine energy hygiene to always create a protected space.]

> Me: "Sorry I haven't visited with you—the circumstances are a bit challenging here."

> P: [Nodding] "Beware—be cautious of extraneous alien energies."

> Me: "Who or what?"

> P: "Past residents. Energies in the land. Millennia of violence and abuse in your town."

> Me: "We are outside the [Roman, medieval, and 17th-century] walls."

> P: "So? Inside, outside, violence knows no boundaries."

> Me: "Are we safe here energetically?"

> P: [Nods] "Do not be afraid. In your normal plane of existence, all is clear and well. It is only when you venture forth [into other dimensions]—'Let sleeping dogs lie.'"

Me: "But it's OK here now with you?"

P: [Nodding] "[With] The Golden Dome of Transmutation, or the Sphere of Art [a process taught by R.J. Stewart]—you are surrounded by the wings of angels; you are perfectly safe. And I can visit you [anywhere]."

Me: "Thank you. I've begun the book."

P: "I have noticed. I am aware."

Me: "I see [in reviewing my journal entries] how I don't ask probing questions. I get an answer and move on."

P: [Nodding] "I wondered when you would notice."

Me: "I'm not used to communicating with the dead!"

P: "I am not dead, obviously."

Me: "I mean—"

P: [Smiling] "I know what you mean."

Me: "What *are* you? What would you call yourself?"

P: "Good question. An ongoing beam of Consciousness honed to a particular frequency, surrounded by a mist of personality and story that remains and retains valence for me. So I talk with you, advise you, remember what I contributed in the way of philosophical insights."

Me: "How long will you be like that?"

P: "As long as I choose—though remember, time is of no essence here."

Me: "At some point, you will shed all of your story?"

P: [Nodding]

Me: "And?"

P: "I will return to the Light."

Me: "Will you reincarnate again?"

P: "I already have, and I will again."

Me: "Why?"

P: "To continue my process of evolution and of service to the world."

Me: "What would you add to The Enneads?"

P: "Nothing. It was complete. I do not revisit the past, though of course I could."

Me: "You could?"

P: [Nodding] "Of course, just as you do in your memories."

Me: "I thought you meant literally."

P: "I do. Past and future are not the same on this [other] side of the reality."

Me: "Oh. [Pause] I want to ask about karma. Does it exist?"

P: "Not as a kind of one-to-one payback, but every action has a reaction, in Newtonian terms. That is how we learn and evolve."

Me: "We humans?"

P: "Not just humans. All sentient beings."

Me: "Cats? Dogs?"

P: [Nodding] "In a much less fine-grained way, yes."

Me: "To become more evolved cats?"

P: "You oversimplify. To become more of what they are meant to be."

Me: "Do cats reincarnate as humans?"

P: "Obviously not. It's a different frequency entirely."

Me: "Oh. … Can you tell me more about my past lives?"

P: "No. I am not omniscient. That is for you to explore. I—we—told you what you already knew. You were a Pythia at Delphi. Obviously, you have a strong connection to ancient Greece."

Me: "Who can tell me more?"

H: "I will attempt to explain."

Me: "Hi, Hypatia!"

H: "Hello, Beloved. You have deep soul connections to this period of the past. You can explore them in your dreams and meditations. I think you call it past-life regression. But why? What does it matter? Suffice to know we are here with you and support your endeavors."

Me: "Ani Williams was delighted to know I was in contact with you, Hypatia."

H: [Nodding] "She is a very interesting soul. I will visit her in her dreams. She does good work. She—like all of you [humans]—sees only partially through the veil, but she has pierced more deeply than most. I applaud her efforts."

Me: "I'll tell her. She'll be happy to know."

H: [Nodding]

Me: "I am working on the book as I can, given the disruptions."

H: "To be of service [to others] is never a disruption. But maintain your focus. I think you have an expression, 'Keep your eyes on the prize'!"

Me: [Laughing] "Indeed. I will do my best. It's been a complicated time."

H: "Life is complicated."

Me: "Easier where you are?"

H: "Different. Simpler. More harmonious. The challenge is accommodating to 'no time' and not simply drifting. It is helpful for us, too, to have a project. And you are one of mine."

Me: "I'm a project?"

H: "Indeed. I guide you on the path of greater awareness and attunement."

Me: "Today is the full moon eclipse."

H: "A powerful and amplifying time to accomplish things. So get to work! [Laughing]"

Me: [Laughing] "I am. I am! Any more advice? About the writing?"

H: "Details are important, but only the salient ones. Minutiae [are] boring and distracting. Hone your words and story well."

Me: "Thank you. I think I'll stop now and write this up before there is another interruption."

H: "A wise plan. We will be watching over you [to give support]."

Me: "Thank you."

H: "Now—go feed that cat!!" [Ziggy is hungry and meowing.]

25 minutes.

I had asked Plotinus once before if he would reincarnate, and he had replied, "No, not likely." Just now, he said he would. The obvious explanation for this apparent inconsistency was that beings on "the Other Side" were still human enough to change their minds.

I sent an excerpt of the conversation to Ani Williams, and she replied:

"What a trip. I have always admired Hypatia, and her comment is encouraging and also surprising to think she knows what I'm up to. But then, of course. When we are in this Earth-density it is wild to have whole conversations with the Other Side. I do them more sporadically, but what a good idea to keep certain more important conversations going."

Friday, 21 March 2025

Tessa and Nigel returned home, and so did we. What a relief to be back in our own space after 3½ weeks. I was so grateful Tessa was recovering, so grateful we could be of service, and so grateful to be back home.

I went out for a walk and ran into María, an old friend. She asked what I was doing these days, and, after hesitating a moment, I said, "I'm writing a book about channeling Plotinus."

María replied, "I remember, you told me about channeling him! So now you are writing a book about it?"

I nodded. "I have a year of channeled conversations. The time has come."

"That long? How time flies! By the way, I have a friend who has invited me to join a monthly channeling session in a town nearby. A group of people get together and ask the channeler questions, and she gives them advice. Do you want to come?"

I was interested in seeing other people channel live, instead of watching recordings on YouTube, but I had some hesitation. "You know, just because someone channels information from the Other Side, that doesn't mean it's good or trustworthy information. It might be, but it might not be. I'd like to know who she is channeling. Just because it's a non-corporeal being doesn't mean it's all-knowing, or even wise."

"I never thought of that," María replied. "You mean, they aren't?"

"Plotinus and Hypatia frequently remind me that they don't know everything. They often call on back-up support to answer my questions. Nor does it mean their advice would always be the best—they don't live in the material plane anymore, so they might not be tuned in to all the complexities."

(I remembered years ago when Elen of the Ways had appeared unbidden in my meditation. She had challenged me to walk her pathways in Wales, and Gary and I said yes. For weeks we followed synchronicities and specific signs to decide where to go next. We soon realized, however, that Elen of the Ways knew nothing about the intricacies and expense of making last-minute hotel reservations and travel arrangements.)

"I never thought of that, but of course they wouldn't be concerned about the details." Maria shook her head. "I think I'd rather trust my own judgment, or the judgment of friends whose opinions I have learned to trust over time, instead of a spirit I don't know anything about."

I nodded in agreement. We chatted some more, and then, after kissing each other on both cheeks (the Spanish greeting and goodbye), we went our separate ways.

Saturday, 29 March 2025

I finished the first edit of my year of journal entries. I was surprised at how little I remembered about the content of the conversations with Plotinus, Hypatia, and The Collective. On reflection, I shouldn't have been surprised. After all, I was channeling information from another realm. Does a "speaking tube" know (or remember) what messages are being sent through it? No.

I was also surprised at how many questions I had asked about my well-being. But, on reflection, I shouldn't have been surprised. Plotinus, Hypatia, and The Collective were offering wisdom for humanity at large—and guidance for me as an individual.

I felt deep gratitude for their help and support, the care and compassion they had so generously given me during the year, the wisdom and advice (sometimes tough, sometimes gentle) they had so graciously offered. I felt so very loved. I knew they were always there—or I should say "here"—and I could call on them whenever I needed. And that was true not just for me. Gary could do so, too. *Everyone* can. They are endlessly patient and always available.

I realized I had many unasked questions and, I presumed, Plotinus and Hypatia had a lot more to say. But my first task was to prepare the manuscript based on my journal entries up to our first anniversary.

As I worked on the manuscript, I felt strangely altered, as if I were tapping into the energy of those beings from the Other Side. I remembered that Plotinus had told me that when two realities touch, it causes "sparks" and energy adjustments.

I also felt like I was undergoing an intense life review, revisiting the tumultuous upheaval of the previous year. As overwhelming as it had been at times, it was a year that had led to the release of many dysfunctional behaviors, to greater compassion, deeper love, and much gratitude. Gary and I were getting along better than we ever had; I basked in his love and support, and he in mine.

Something was puzzling me, however. On various occasions during the previous week, I had suddenly been flooded with memories of Michael, a man with whom I had had a relationship over 40 years ago. I hadn't thought of him in decades, so why was I remembering him now?

Michael was a highly respected, erudite scholar of classical Greek philosophy, of which I knew nothing and had little interest. When we first met at Princeton University (I did my PhD in anthropology there), we had had an instant connection—an immediate recognition of each other and the realization that something important was going to happen between us. And it did. We ended up walking the Camino de Santiago together in 1982 and living together for a year.

Our intense, five-year relationship was difficult and ended badly. But why was I remembering it now, nearly 40 years after it had ended and nearly 20 years after Michael had died? Could there be some connection between Plotinus and Michael?

Suzanne Giesemann says that when you suddenly think of someone who is departed and whom you haven't thought of for a long time, they may be thinking of you from the Other Side. Was Michael trying to communicate with me? If so, why?

What would happen if I "pulled the thread" connected to these resurfacing memories?

I did a Google search and discovered that, long after we had split up, Michael had begun writing about Neoplatonic philosophers—including, of course, Plotinus, the founder of Neoplatonism. Oh!

I remembered our powerful bond. In those days, 40+ years ago, I had had no framework to explain it. As I kept tugging on the thread of memory, suddenly our instant recognition of each other made sense. It was part of a much longer story. Perhaps a repeat of a previous relationship. Or several. Perhaps we had had a past-life connection millennia ago in ancient Greece. After all, if I had had past lives, so had (probably) everybody else—including Michael. There was a thread—or several—that connected Michael to me and to Plotinus.

I suddenly remembered that my very first boyfriend, 60+ years ago, when I was in high school, was a Greek American. At the time, we both lived in a small town in Iowa with very few Greek or Greek American families. Was that yet another thread of connection?

I kept working on the manuscript. I had several trusted readers give me feedback. I expanded and clarified the text. I stopped pulling on the thread of memory. You could even say, I dropped the thread. I had enough to do, trying to weave a coherent tapestry out of the past year's transformative adventures. I forgot about Michael.

I continued to communicate with Plotinus, Hypatia, and The Collective, who asked me to include these additional conversations in Appendix D. They also informed me that publishing this book would not, of course, mean we were finished with our exchanges. They have much wisdom to share, and they plan to continue talking with me as long as I am willing.

Thursday, 1 May 2025

I startled awake during a dream about Michael. In this exceedingly vivid dream, I was sitting on a sofa in a large room, and Michael came and sat next to me in the corner of the sofa. I was surprised to see him. I moved over a little when he indicated he felt squished.

He looked the same as I remembered—thin, with a hawk-like nose, not any older than when I had last seen him. But he was *dead,* wasn't he?

It felt a bit awkward since there were people in the room, watching us, puzzling at us sitting together on the sofa. He turned toward me and kissed me on my mouth. I noticed scratchy stubble and a complete lack of sexual attraction/buzz. We held hands in silence. He had the same tobacco-stained fingers.

It was so long since we had seen each other. 40 years. In this partly lucid dream, I was stunned to be with him again.

I said, "But you're DEAD—you're supposed to be dead!"

He replied, "I can tell you spend much time in the Imaginal Realm."

I said, "You are *not* dead?"

He told me he had disappeared to get out of the "rat race."

Suddenly we were outdoors, and a little child was crying at the end of a long dirt driveway. Two men were trying to help her. One was her father. The little girl was ill and unhappy. I ran over to help. She wanted to see elephants. I called to Michael to help, and he became a circus master to make her stop crying. I knew he would need to do it again to keep her happy.

Michael wanted to know if I was thirsty and needed some water. He was kind and thoughtful. I realized that hadn't been the case when we were together.

I woke up in shock. It felt so real—like a visitation from the Other Side. I immediately recorded the dream in the little notebook I kept beside our bed. I had learned during Active Dreamwork training with Robert Moss that it was important to record the dream as quickly as possible, before it escaped back into dreamland or became distorted by the logical mind.

Lying in bed around 5:45 am, thinking over what had just occurred, I decided I needed to light a candle in remembrance of Michael. Should I light a large candle that would burn for days? A tealight for a few hours? How long did I want it to burn? I realized I was avoiding doing anything, so I got up, put on my robe, and went to my office/workshop/meditation space.

I chose a medium-size beeswax candle, put it on my altar, and sat down to meditate. I took a few deep breaths and tried to relax. As I did so, I suddenly thought: Maybe I could converse with Michael! When the memories had started to resurface, Marchiene had suggested that it would be a good idea to talk to him. I had been hesitant to do so and still was. It was one thing to talk to ancient Greek philosophers whom I had never known, another thing entirely to talk to a dead partner, especially one with whom I had had such a challenging relationship. But now seemed like as good a time as any to try.

I lit the candle, added a few drops of laurel essential oil (laurel was used by the Pythia at the temple at Delphi). I took a deep breath. I asked if Michael had something to say to me about what happened in our relationship. I sensed him approach and heard him communicate psychically. (MF = Michael Frede)

> MF: "We were young then."
>
> Me: "Why did you behave that way?"
>
> MF: "I was troubled. And I didn't know better."
>
> Me: "Is there something you want to say?"
>
> MF: "Only, you are so very loved."

[Wow]

Me: [I suddenly had a flash of knowing] "You are Marsilio Ficino in The Collective!"

MF: [Smiling] "Yes. MF. [The same initials.] You understand now."

Me: "I wondered why he [Marsilio] never spoke."

MF: "Because you were not ready to meet me again."

Me: "Is this real? Give me a sign."

MF: "A grey feather floating down. A lighthouse."

Me: "Were you Marsilio Ficino [in a past life]?"

MF: [Nodding]

Me: "Did you (ultimately) have a good life?"

MF: [Nodding] "At last, in Greece, returning to my ancient homeland."

Me: "How is it to be in The Collective with Plotinus?"

MF: [Laughing] "A delight, I assure you."

Me: "And Hypatia?"

MF: "More of a challenge. [Smiling]"

Me: "Do you have any advice for me?"

MF: "Keep doing what you are doing. Believe in it. Doubt is the work of the devil—the ego, that is."

Me: "Thank you … I loved you very much."

MF: "You loved who you thought I was. We go a long time back."

[I have a vision of a Pythia and her assistant.]

Me: "Illicit love [in the Temple of Delphi]?"

MF: "No. Supportive interactions then, but things went wrong. And did again."

Me: [Nodding] "Why have you come now?"

MF: "To reassure you about the reality of it all. The Imaginal Realm is real—and so is where I abide. Consciousness is never-ending. Personality releases like layers of an onion. You are [everyone is] so very loved. ... You gave me a return to innocence—a return to something I never had. I will always be grateful. I had no better success with my next wife. I had much to learn before I could be content and happy in relationship."

[Michael had been married before he met me, and he married again after we broke up.]

Me: "And were you?"

MF: [Nodding] "Yes, at last. A true partnership—like you and Gary. Much to learn to be true partners."

Me: "Are you buried anywhere?"

MF: "In the sea."

Me: "I 'see' a gravestone with fresh flowers [in Athens]."

MF: "Yes, but I am not there."

[I see the image of an empty grave, a place where people can come to remember him, but he isn't there. I realize that this is an ambiguous statement on his part. 'Not there' physically, or 'not there' because his soul/consciousness is elsewhere?]

Me: "Will you come again?"

MF: "Only if there is need. Today I came to reassure you [that] you are so very loved—and that consciousness is eternal."

Me: "Did you love me then?"

MF: [Nodding] "As best I could."

Me: "I was so afraid of you later."

MF: "I know. I am sorry. I was wounded, and I hurt others. But your fears were what you brought to yourself from my actions. Your fear of confronting your own truths and weaknesses, your own woundedness."

Me: [Nodding, reconsidering how afraid I was of him once he had gone to Berlin for a year and I continued to live in his house in Princeton. I was afraid he would have me evicted. I was afraid of retribution, although I suddenly realized that I had little reason to be afraid of that from him. Clearly, I had a lot to re-examine.] "So, it is time to forgive?"

MF: "Yes."

Me: "I do. I forgive you."

MF: "And I have nothing to forgive [you about]."

Me: [Feeling humbled] "Thank you ... friend? Friends at last?"

MF: [Nodding]

Me: "Any advice about the [Plotinus] manuscript?"

MF: "Keep polishing the mirror of your soul." [That's a Sufi expression.]

Me: "Thank you."

MF: "And remember the Pythia!"

I was stunned. And I couldn't help but wonder: Was this real or was I having an imaginary conversation? After all these months—more than a year—of conversations with Plotinus and Hypatia et al, how could I still doubt? But sometimes I did.

I re-read my notes about the dream. I knew it was exceptional—a *big* dream, a true visitation. I re-read our channeled conversation, and several statements stood out, things I would never have thought of or imagined he would say. For example, Marsilio Ficino = MF = Michael Frede. And "You are so very loved." His pointing out that I had projected onto him my own life history/story, which had made me so afraid of him, and which I was unwilling to examine at the time. He was right. His kindness and gentleness in the conversation, which were not qualities I attributed to him during our relationship.

The doubt came in part because of how easy it was to communicate with him. No long preparation, no lengthy meditation. Just light a candle, take a few deep breaths, ask a question—and there he was.

Was it Michael or was it my over-active imagination? It felt like a real conversation. I was glad I had asked for evidence.

I read several lengthy obituaries and learned that Michael drowned in the sea, on the coast, near Delphi, and was buried in a cemetery in Athens. That seemed to contradict some of what he told me. When I had asked where he was buried, he had said, "at sea," and, also, that he was not in his grave in Athens. But metaphorically, perhaps, it was true. Michael as the "physical being known as Michael" died in the sea, so perhaps he could be said to be buried there. And Michael as the "on-going awareness/consciousness that is Michael" was *not* in a grave in Athens. That was only his body. In that sense, the grave was indeed empty. I'd have to ask him for clarification, if I ever talked to him again.

I turned my attention to him again, and I felt a gentle, loving presence. He told me to forgive myself as well as him. He was right. That was something I needed to do.

I shared all of this with Gary. He assured me that doubt was normal. Most people would be filled with doubt about these encounters.

For me, the doubt was compounded because I had had an intense relationship with Michael, so I wondered if he was saying what I would want him to say? I re-read the channeled conversation and again saw much that I would never have imagined him to say.

I would be on the lookout for a grey feather and a lighthouse.

I shared what had happened with friends, including Nigel. He replied that he'd decided that dreams, fantasy, and reality are interchangeable modes of being. That didn't feel satisfactory to me. To me, it made a difference whether what happened with Michael was my fantasy or a real encounter. Maybe there needed to be a fourth category, the 'imaginal.' Or maybe reality was just a whole lot larger than I used to think, and I hadn't yet updated my understanding to match my lived experience.

I was very emotional. Exhausted, tired, reconfiguring what I thought I knew about my relationship with Michael. Wondering about was it real or my subconscious feeding me lines.

Gary and I went for a walk. Grey pigeon feathers were scattered on the ground, and a flock of grey pigeons scattered as we walked by, but nothing wafted down from the sky. Was that (grey pigeons landing) close enough to count as evidence?

Gary wanted to know if they (Plotinus and Hypatia) knew Michael was Marsilio. I checked in with them, and I knew immediately they knew. They were chuckling at how well the reunion had worked out.

Gary asked if they had planned this as the denouement of the manuscript. I said it didn't work like that.

Plotinus took over (with permission) and spoke aloud through me. "*There are possibilities and what you call probabilities. ... It's a vector, not a certainty.*"

In other words, people and events were brought together (me and Michael), but there were many possible outcomes. It wasn't about the manuscript; it was about the channeling and my development. Communicating with Michael fit in the manuscript if we chose to make it fit. If not, it didn't. This was about me, not the manuscript.

Later that afternoon, I decided to go back into meditation and get more information. The candle was still burning on the altar.

>Me: "Hi, Hypatia, Plotinus, and The Collective!"
>
>They: [Nodding]
>
>Me: "Did you know Michael was Marsilio Ficino?"
>
>P: "Of course. How could we not? We recognize him by his 'soul' vibration."
>
>Me: "So we carry that basic vibration through different reincarnations?"
>
>P: "Just so. As Marchiene said, [each of us is] 'the song God sings.' Each life is a 'riff.'"
>
>Me: "*You* knew!"
>
>H: "Of course. But there was no point in telling you until you were ready."
>
>Me: "Ready as in—?"
>
>P: "Prepared."
>
>Me: "I started remembering him."
>
>H: "Exactly. Those memories were encouraged by him."

Me: "Encouraged?"

H: "Motivated. Sent. Energized. Tweaked. Like striking a harmonic string that causes a similar string to vibrate."

Me. "I see. Why?"

P: "To help complete your healing."

H: "Your recognition of another way to understand your [life] experiences."

Me: "So I'm ready now?"

P: "Apparently. You seem to be taking in the experience [of Michael's visit] and reconfiguring your understanding of the past."

Me: "It's true. Michael, are you there?"

MF: "Actually, I'm not there, I'm here."

Me: "Is there more for me to learn?"

MF: "This time, this life? You are doing well."

Me: "We've had past lives together in Delphi. Were there more?"

MF: "Indeed. In Egypt, when you were a scribe."

Me: "Oh—hence my relationship with Thoth!" [Thoth is the god of scribes, writing, knowledge, magic, the moon.]

MF: "Exactly."

Me: "And what were you, then?" [I wonder—was he my wife? I don't know.]

MF: "Your supervisor. I taught you well and looked after you."

Me: "Did it end well?"

MF: [Pause] "Neutrally. Hence, more opportunities to explore together our relationship, at Delphi, [and in] this life."

Me: "Were there more?"

MF: "Those were the most important."

[Pause]

Me: "How do I know this isn't just my imagination?"

P: "You asked for signs. Did you get them?"

Me: "Maybe. Grey feathers on the ground, a flock of grey pigeons, but not a feather floating. And no lighthouse. Yet."

P: "Be patient."

TC: "To turn this around: why would you think you are making this up?"

Me: "I don't know. … Because—because it was so easy to contact Michael, and he said some things I could have said myself."

P: "Ah."

H: "Of course you could have [said some of those things] because they are true. And you know it. But *would* you have said such things? Had you?"

Me: "No. Michael hasn't been on my mind."

P: "Correct. Now you know why I 'came through' you [at Gipsy Bar]—so you would believe I was real."

Me: "Sigh. Real. Nigel says dreams, fantasy, reality are just different modalities—all valid. I think there should be a fourth for you guys."

P: [Mock offended] "So we aren't real?"

Me: "No—no—I mean material and non-material reality. That's what I mean."

P: [Nodding]

H: "That's clear and concise. But where then is fantasy or dreams? Non-material reality? False non-material reality?"

Me: "Uh. … Doesn't work, does it. Better to think of numerous realms or domains, or a spectrum from physicality to non-material."

P: "Are dreams true? They are meaningful, insightful, silly, peculiar, pointless, frightening—but not 'true.' And fantasy?"

Me: "Easier. Things that never have existed in the physical realm—but perhaps could."

P: "Like: flight, airplanes, teleportation, unicorns."

H: "Not so quickly, Plotinus. Unicorns did exist."

P: "They were misunderstood [that is, mislabeled] creatures [that did exist]."

H: "No, no. They, like dragons, did exist, but not as you imagine, and now they have retreated into other realms—[their] vibrations changed, and they became less 'material.' Ask Elizabeth to explain."

Me: "So I know you are all real because you have given [me] evidence, and [you] tell me things I don't know. But Michael?"

MF: [Sigh] "Do you believe consciousness continues?"

Me: [Nodding]

MF: "I was conscious. I had consciousness. I passed over—so of course I still have consciousness, without a body. Why wouldn't I become part of The Collective? You and I have a very long history. Lives of it. And in this life alone, the Camino, passion, challenges, relationship struggles, heartbreak. Why wouldn't I still be here to watch over you?"

Me: "But it was so easy to talk to you."

MF: "Why should it be hard? The more you communicate with The Other Side, the easier the adaptation of frequencies."

[Pause]

MF: "Go to Delphi—I'll meet you there!"

Me: [Shocked and intrigued] "Oh my! ... Maybe someday."

MF: "Meantime, suffice to know I watch over you, as do Plotinus and Hypatia and others. You are watched over, very loved, cared for. We are as real as ever we were."

P: [Chuckling]

H: [Laughing]

Me: "[You are laughing] because 'real' is a meaningless term?"

They: [Nodding] "Is the Internet real? Is Trump real? If so, which Trump? Is—you get the idea. Even what you call reality is partial and distorted. Incomplete information, inadequate thought processes, distorted thinking."

Me: [Nodding] "I'm tired. I want to cry. This has been very challenging."

They: [Nodding]

Me: "But also pretty amazing. I am very grateful for your love and care. I love you all—all of you, including Michael! [Smiling]"

Friday, 2 May 2025

I needed to rename the book. Natalie urged me to own my part in the story and create a title that honored that, and several other readers of the manuscript also pointed out how the channeling had changed my life. Not only were the messages important; so was my personal, at times reluctant, transformation.

Suddenly, the new title flashed across my inner vision: *The Reluctant Medium – How Channeling Plotinus, Hypatia, and the Collective Transformed My Life*. I ran it by The Collective, and they approved it. In fact, they like it a lot.

During my acupuncture session with Alina, she mentioned that a few days ago they went hiking in the hills in the Garrotxa region near Girona. They visited the small village of Rupit and then went to El Far, a restaurant and sanctuary.

El Far? I almost sat up on the exam table, needles quivering.

I said, "Isn't *far* the Catalan word for lighthouse?"

Alina replied, "Yes, it is. But El Far is not a lighthouse on the coast—it's a huge uplift of rock that's called a *far*—a lighthouse—because it's so prominent and high up, and you can see for miles 360° around, just like from a lighthouse. And there once was a lighthouse there."

This was the second sign I had been told to look for. This was the evidence that the Michael I had communicated with was indeed Michael. Not a figment of my imagination, not a voice from my subconscious. No. It was Michael, continuing to exist as a non-corporeal being on the Other Side. And how appropriately erudite was the evidence: I had to know that *far* was the Catalan word for lighthouse.

I felt humble, grateful, and filled with awe.

The thread of connection that I had begun pulling over a month ago had connected long-dead Greek Neoplatonic philosophers with a recently deceased Greek scholar with whom I had had a tumultuous relationship. I had learned that we had shared past lifetimes in the Temple of Delphi and in ancient Egypt, as well as in Princeton, New Jersey.

I thought about Theseus and the Minotaur, that classic Greek myth about a hero, a ball of thread, and a labyrinth with a half-human, half-bull creature in the center. According to legend, when Theseus entered the labyrinth, he began unwinding a ball of thread so he would be able to find his way back out from the center.

I, however, was following the thread *into* the center and winding it up as I went. And in the center? The life-changing discoveries that we are all interconnected across time, space, and multiple dimensions, that consciousness continues after death, and that Love holds everything together.

Afterword

Plotinus, Hypatia, and The Collective have crucial information that they want everyone to hear. They have given me permission to summarize their messages.

"What you do to others, you do to yourself."

"We are all One. We are all connected. Separation is an illusion. Remember who you truly are: the Light within, connected to everything and everyone. Underneath everything is this foundation of peace, love, compassion, and connection. There is purpose and love in the universe—love *is* the universe."

"We are real. There is more than this petty material world you fight over. There is life after life. Consciousness continues. We are always here, not 'there.' Now is the time—it is of central urgency and importance—for humans to remember to love each other. And not just humans but all living things, plants, animals, the Earth itself."

"These are challenging times for humanity and Planet Earth. Full of potential and possibility to rise out of disharmony, and so fraught with danger if you do not. You must do all you can to alleviate suffering, to restore harmony. Act with loving kindness and compassion."

"The purpose of life is to grow in knowledge and experience—and in Love and Light. To live to your fullest potential. To live from your heart, with heart and love. To feel your unity with The All. To be a blessing to others and send blessings."

"Love one another—and remember to have fun. Play! It's not so serious. You will get another chance. And another. And another."

"You are so very loved."

These messages have transformed my life.

When my brother, Tommy, died in an accident at age 7, my mother was shattered. She said her world was destroyed. If she had known his consciousness continued—and she could, perhaps, maintain some kind of relationship with him—it would have changed her life for the better.

How I act in this world—with more kindness, compassion, and love, with less reactivity, judgmentalness, and impatience—feels even more important, not less. I have a new sense of purpose: what I do in this life, the lessons I learn, the way I behave, matters. The effects of my actions are cumulative.

I can't say that I no longer have any fear of death. But instead of feeling dread at the prospect of dying, I feel curiosity about this great adventure. After all, since I've had past lives, I'll probably have future ones as well.

We are all connected across past, present, and future, and across numerous other realms of existence. Indra's Net isn't an abstract image. Hypatia says, "What you do to others, you do to yourself." We are all nodes in the Net, reflecting each other, linked by vibrating lines of energy. Our connectedness isn't theoretical, it's real. In quantum physics, it's called entanglement.

The awareness that we are all One (like rays coming from the sun) is a call to action. The delusion of separation—that we are individual, disconnected beings—encourages fear, hatred, violence, and despair. The truth is, "What you do to others, you do to yourself." Literally.

When Plotinus says, "You are so very loved," he means *all* of us. We don't have to earn this love or be perfect. This universal, unconditional love is there for us always. In fact, it's the "glue" that holds everything together. Sometimes I feel (figuratively) held in the arms of love; more often, I feel deeply cared for and supported by Spirit.

Beings on the Other Side are eager to help us lead our lives more fully if we ask. Having a relationship with spiritual guides who care about me and give me wise advice is enormously helpful in my day-to-day.

Their guidance isn't a substitute for dealing with my emotional issues, my projections, my "shadow" self. I need skills to improve my everyday interactions, and I need support from Spirit to see the bigger picture. I can use SAGE, which Jake Eagle teaches, to improve my interpersonal relationships. I can use Suzanne Giesemann's The Awakened Way practices to help me release old patterns, return to balance, and stay connected to Spirit as well as matter. There is so much more than this physical, material realm, and we are part of both. Isn't that wonderful!

I am filled with gratitude. Gratitude for the guidance and insights that I have been given. Gratitude that I can share them with you. Gratitude that you can use them to transform your life for the better.

Appendix A – People and Other Beings

In alphabetical order by first name. BCE means "Before Current Era" and CE means "Current Era."

Allan Kardec: The pen name of Hippolyte Léon Denizard Rivail, a French doctor, educator, translator, and writer who lived from 1804–1869. In his early 50s, he became interested in seances, and he began to investigate psychic phenomena. He wrote five volumes known as *The Spiritist Codification* or *The Spirits' Book,* based on conversations with 10 mediums to whom he submitted an extensive list of questions. He is the founder of Spiritism.

Alfred the Great: Famous Anglo-Saxon king (born c. 849, died 899 in Winchester, England). Fought Viking invasions and introduced important administrative, legal, and military reforms in England. Had the reputation of being a learned, merciful, gracious man who encouraged education, including in Early English instead of Latin.

Alina: Friend and acupuncturist.

Anaxagoras: A pre-Socratic Greek philosopher who lived c. 500–428 BCE. Originated the theory of panspermia (life existing everywhere in the universe), was able to predict eclipses, tried to explain rainbows and meteors, and theorized that the sun was a fiery star. Originated the concept of Nous (cosmic Mind) as an ordering force that moved and separated the nearly homogeneous mixture of primary imperishable ingredients that began the universe.

Ani Williams: Gifted troubadour/harpist who composes and performs songs that come to her in dreams and at sacred places. Sound Alchemy teacher, voice analysis expert, and sound healer. Author of *Guardians of the Dragon Path – Ancient Temples of the Pyrenees, The Way of the Stars Camino, A Magdalena Meridian.* https://aniwilliams.com

Ariel Jaenisch Ferrigno: Friend, body therapist, energy healer, teacher, digital artist, and author. https://www.evoluciontir.com/

Asclepius: Greek god of medicine and healing, often shown with a staff entwined with a snake. The staff is similar to the modern caduceus, a symbol of medicine. He was very important in ancient Greek and Roman mythology. Two of his five daughters were Hygieia ("Hygiene") and Panacea ("Panacea"). His shrines were temples of healing called Asclepions or an Asclepeion. People would go there to dream of a cure, which was interpreted by resident priests called Therapeutae. His most important shrine was at Epidaurus and dated to the 4th century BCE.

Athena: Often called Pallas Athena, she is an ancient Greek goddess associated with wisdom, warfare, and handicraft/the arts. One of the Twelve Olympian Gods, patron and protector of Athens. Later syncretized with the Roman goddess Minerva. Usually depicted wearing a helmet and carrying a spear. Other symbols include owls, olive trees, horses, and snakes.

Bernadette: An artist friend with a deep spiritual practice.

Brigid (Saint and Goddess, also known as Brigit, Bride, Bridget): An ancient Celtic goddess, she later morphed into Saint Brigid (c. 451–525 CE), abbess of the important abbey at Kildare, Ireland. Her attributes include patron of wisdom, learning, healing, the hearth, the forge, poetry, livestock and dairy production, beer brewing, and poetry. For centuries, a perpetual fire burned in the Fire Temple outside the Kildare Abbey and was tended by 19 nuns. It was extinguished in the 16th century during the Reformation. Brigid is the patroness of Ireland, and her feast day is February 1, the same day as the Gaelic traditional early spring festival of Imbolc and a day before the Catholic festival of Candlemas.

Caitlín Matthews: A gifted seer, shaman, teacher, writer, singer, oracle reader, and guide to the Celtic wisdom and the Western Mysteries traditions. Author of 85 books, some co-authored with her husband, John Matthews. She is the co-founder of FIOS shamanic training. She and her husband live in Oxford. https://www.hallowquest.org.uk/ and Caitlín Matthews – Hallowquest Sanctuary on Substack.

Carles Torrent Pagès: Catalan friend, painter, sculptor, visionary artist. https://www.torrentpages.net/

Carlos Mendoza-Alvarez (Perhaps the person referred to by Plotinus): Professor of theology. Dominican friar, teacher, scholar. Explores themes relating to social justice—including climate change, human rights, migration, patriarchy, and decolonization. Helps his students reflect on how their education and professional choices will connect with ecological issues and spiritual development. (I couldn't find any evidence that he was a Neoplatonist, but his concern about fostering spiritual development and life awareness could be influenced by Plotinus.)

Cheryl Page: Clinical researcher turned psychic pioneer and medium, Cheryl teaches others to communicate with the great Beyond. An inspiring, creative, and original teacher, she has developed the VIBRATIONSHIP Cross-Veil Communication Method and has recently published the book *Mystic Richness,* a compilation of AI-aided conversations with famous departed people. https://mysticrichness.com/ and on Substack.

Cosimo de Medici: (1389–1464) Very wealthy banker, politician, and statesman in Florence, Italy, during the Italian Renaissance. Patron of arts, architecture, and learning. Established the first public library in Florence, important for the humanist movement during the Italian Renaissance. Commissioned Marsilio Ficino to translate the complete works of Plato into Latin for the first time and attempted to revive Neoplatonism by establishing a Platonic Academy.

Cynthia Ketting: A Catholic friend.

Elen of the Ways: A paleolithic Northern European goddess, often depicted with antlers. She is associated with the land, wild places, and the migration of people and animals, especially deer and reindeer. A guide on the path. Rediscovered by modern paganism in the 1980s; probably related to other ancient antler-bearing deities like Cernunnos. https://celticearthspirit.co.uk/folklore-mythology-culture/brythonic-deities/elen-of-the-ways/

Elizabeth Diamond Rose: Transformational healer, writer, and content provider. www.diamond-coaching.co.uk

Elyn Aviva: Writer, fiber artist, anthropologist, medium/channeler, Imaginaut. PhD in cultural anthropology (Princeton University); dissertation on the contemporary Camino de Santiago. MDiv (Iliff School of Theology). Author of numerous books and articles on powerful places, sacred sites, journey, spiritual quest, and pilgrimage. Chapter in Common Sentience's *Lifetimes.* Books: www.pilgrimsprocess.com. Fiber art: www.fiberalchemy.com.

Celebration! link: https://youtu.be/eCIjtfoBJ98

Plotinus article https://www.yourlifeisatrip.com/home/traveling-to-other-dimensions

YouTube interview: https://youtu.be/YqyoQ6I-gjE?si=Tikqef4LNWw9GJnC

Eric Edmeades: Motivational speaker, coach, and founder of Wildfit, AKA "Food Freedom." https://getwildfit.com/

Evelyn Begody: Navajo teacher, Camino pilgrim, author of *Living with my Dead Husband – a Navajo Woman's Year of Grief.*

Gary White: Elyn Aviva's husband, best friend, coauthor with her of the "Powerful Places in …" series. PhD (Michigan State University), retired Distinguished Professor Emeritus of Music Theory and Composition. Award-winning composer. Dowser, textbook author, spiritual explorer, and Imaginaut.

Books: www.pilgrimsprocess.com.

YouTube interview with Elyn on "Life with Ghosts": YouTube interview: https://youtu.be/YqyoQ6I-gjE?si=Tikqef4LNWw9GJnC.

Celebration! link: https://youtu.be/eCIjtfoBJ98

Henry Corbin: Highly influential 20th-century French philosopher, theologian, and specialist in Iranian studies. Did important work exploring traditional Iranian Islamic mystical philosophers, including Suhrawardi, Ibn Arabi, and Mulla Sadra Shirazi. Explicated the creative imagination and what is known as the Imaginal Realm. According to Corbin, the imagination is the primary way to know Creation.

Hermes: Greek messenger of the gods; ancient god of trade, travel, wealth, luck, fertility, sleep, thieves, and language. One of the 12 Olympian gods and the most mischievous. A guide between the realm of the gods and humans. Credited with inventing fire, the lyre, the alphabet, and dice. Shown wearing winged sandals. The Romans knew him as Mercury.

Hermes Trismegistus: The Greek name ("Hermes Thrice-Greatest") given to the syncretic combination of Hermes and the Egyptian god Thoth. The reputed author of the Hermetic* writings on occult subjects and theology.

Hypatia of Alexandria: (Born c. 350–370, died 415 CE in Alexandria, Egypt.) Important Neoplatonic philosopher, mathematician, and astronomer. Revered as a great teacher and wise counselor. Constructed astrolabes and hydrometers. The first female mathematician whose life is well recorded. She was a Neoplatonist who rejected the teachings of Iamblichus and instead embraced Plotinus's Neoplatonism. Although female, she was highly respected by the scholars and authorities of her time. She never married nor had any interest in so doing. Hypatia was caught up in the political feud between Orestes, the Roman prefect of Alexandria, and Cyril, the bishop of Alexandria. In March 415, she was viciously murdered and ripped apart by a mob of Christians. In modern times, she has become a symbol of women's rights and is viewed as a precursor of the feminist movement.

Iamblichus: (c. 245–c. 325 CE) An Arab-Syrian Neoplatonic philosopher, the biographer of the ancient Greek philosopher/mathematician/mystic Pythagoras. Studied under Porphyry, a pupil of Plotinus. Iamblichus disagreed with Porphyry about theurgy (practices to invoke the presence of the Divine) and held a more strongly pagan perspective. He disagreed with Plotinus's view that posited a separate soul and instead asserted that the soul was embodied in matter—and that matter was as divine as the cosmos.

Jake Eagle: Therapist, mentor, and mindfulness coach we have known and worked with for many years. His Substack is "The Unorthodox Therapist," and his transformative process is called SAGE (Subjective Awareness and Genuine Expression). He is also an author, and is coauthor of *The Power of Awe*. www.sageprocess.com

John and Sally: Acquaintances who visit Girona periodically.

Dr. John Dee: (1527–1608/09) An English mathematician, astrologer/astronomer, teacher, occultist, alchemist, perhaps English spy, Hermeticist*, and advisor to Queen Elizabeth I. Attempted to contact angels and may have done so with the aid of Edward Kelley; at any rate, wrote several books in Enochian, supposedly an angelic language.

John Milton: English poet, pamphleteer, and historian (1608–1674). Drew on Neoplatonic philosophy (the importance of the soul, the pursuit of knowledge, the idea of a higher reality beyond the material world) and Christian theology in his work, *Paradise Lost*. *Paradise Lost* is considered by many to be the greatest epic poem in English.

Jude Currivan: Master's in physics from Oxford, PhD in archaeology from Reading University. A futurist, author, cosmologist, teacher, visionary, and mystic. https://www.judecurrivan.com/

Kathy Gower: Old friend and fellow Camino de Santiago pilgrim.

Khidr (AKA Al-Khidr): An important folk figure in Islam. Described in the Koran as a righteous servant of God possessing great wisdom or mystic knowledge. Also described in various traditions as an angel or as a prophet, a holy being who teaches secret knowledge and aids those in distress. Has been associated with Elijah and St. George, among others. His name comes from the root word for green or verdant, and he is sometimes called "the Green One."

Lee Carroll: Channeler of an entity called Kryon since 1989. www.kryon.com and https://en.wikipedia.org/wiki/Lee_Carroll

Lyn and Bob Sheedy: American expat couple. Friends. She is a skilled animal communicator.

Marchiene Rienstra: Friend, retired interfaith minister, artist, author, voracious reader, trustworthy counselor. MDiv (Calvin Theological Seminary) and MDiv (All Faiths Seminary).

Maria the Jewess: Lived in Egypt, sometime between 0–200 CE. She was the first known alchemist in history and wrote several texts based on her discoveries. Invented processes and apparatuses, including the bain-marie (a water-bath, something like a double boiler). She understood alchemy as resembling sexual reproduction, with different metals being male or female. Carl Jung used her famous quote, "Join the male and the female, and you will find what is sought." Her story became something legendary in later Arabic and Christian writings. Sometimes she is referred to as the sister of Moses and as a contemporary of Jesus.

Marsilio Ficino: An Italian Catholic priest and scholar who lived from 1433–1499 in the Republic of Florence (Italy). One of the most influential humanist philosophers in the early Renaissance. He was an astrologer and translator, the first to translate Plato's writings into Latin. Cosimo de Medici chose him to reestablish Plato's Academy. He translated an important series of Greek texts later called the *Hermetica*, and he also translated the writings of many of the Neoplatonists, including Porphyry, Iamblichus, and Plotinus.

Maynard Keynes: Highly influential English philosopher, scholar, and economist (1883–1946). Brilliant, witty, deeply humane, determined to use economics to improve the lives of the working class and at the same time valuing individual freedom. His early philosophical leanings had a connection to Neoplatonism, most obviously through G.E. Moore's ethical system. Moore emphasized the inherent goodness of certain states of mind, what Keynes referred to as the "religion of love, truth, and beauty." Keynesian economic theories were extremely important and also divisive.

Michael Frede: Prominent scholar and teacher of ancient Greek philosophy (1940–2007). Born in Germany, immigrated to the US, UK, and Greece; died by drowning in the Corinthian Gulf at a beach near Itea, below Delphi, Greece. Specialist in classical Platonic and Aristotelean thought, in post-Aristotelean Hellenistic philosophers, and in early Christian and non-Christian Platonist philosophers, including (especially) Plotinus.

Moses: A legendary, prophetic figure in the Hebrew Bible, the New Testament, and the Koran. It is possible that Moses or a Moses-like figure was born in the Land of Goshen and died at Mount Nebo, Jordan, sometime in the 14th or 13th century BCE. He had a vision of God speaking to him from a burning bush and demanding that he lead God's chosen people (Israel) out of bondage in Egypt. The Exodus describes how he led the Israelites out of slavery. They wandered 40 years before reaching the Promised Land. It is said that God dictated the Ten Commandments to Moses on Mount Sinai, or that he was given (twice) the Ten Commandments written on stone tablets.

Natalie Fillet: Dutch friend, Active Dreamwork practitioner and blogger. www.nataliefillet.com and Natalie Fillet on Substack.

Nigel Ten Fleming: Friend and fellow Imaginaut. Husband of Tessa ten Tusscher. A retired life-science entrepreneur, PhD biochemist, and sculptor who asks probing, science/materialist-based questions.

Paracelsus: (1493–1541) Theophrastus von Hohenheim was his birth name. Swiss physician, alchemist, prophet/seer, and philosopher during the German Renaissance. Traveled widely and was employed at one time as an army surgeon. An important contributor to changing medical practice and theory, he emphasized observation and combined that with received wisdom. He recognized that physicians needed a solid knowledge of chemistry, and he pioneered the medical use of chemicals and minerals. He has been called the Father of Toxicology.

Phyllis Curott: High priestess, witch, author, advocate, podcaster, teacher, and Doctor of Law (JD). One of America's first public witches and a global interfaith activist for eco-spiritual legal rights. Founder of the Temple of Ara. https://www.phylliscurott.com/

Plotinus: (c. 204/205–270 CE) A very important philosopher, born in Roman Egypt, spent time in Alexandria, lived much of his life in Rome, and died in Sicily. He taught both male and female students. Widely considered (with his teacher, Ammonius Saccas) to be the founder of Neoplatonism. His writings have inspired Christian, Jewish, Islamic metaphysicians, and mystics, among others. *The Enneads* were compiled from notes and essays by his student Porphyry. Notable ideas: Emanation of all things from the supreme, transcendent One, a being beyond all attributes, also called "the Alone"; the spiritual triad of the One, Mind/Intelligence, and Soul.

Quotes: "I am striving to give back the Divine in myself to the Divine in the All."

"Life is the flight of the alone to the Alone."

"When we look outside of that on which we depend, we ignore our unity; looking outward, we see many faces; look inward, and all is one head. If a man could but be turned about, he would see at once God and himself and the All."

"We are not separated from spirit, we are in it."

Pythagoras of Samos (Greece): Ancient philosopher, polymath, mystic, and founder of Pythagoreanism, lived c. 570–490 BCE. His teachings influenced Plato, Aristotle, and, hence, Western philosophy. Founded a school in Italy in which initiates were allegedly sworn to secrecy (and for some years, silence) and lived a communal, ascetic lifestyle, which included women and may have included vegetarianism. Credited with many mathematical and scientific discoveries (the five regular solids, Pythagorean musical tuning, the "music of the spheres," the sphericity of the Earth, etc.), some of which were probably discovered by other people. Taught metempsychosis, the "transmigration of souls": upon death, the immortal soul enters a new body.

Pythia of Delphi: High priestess at the Temple of Apollo in Delphi, Greece. Also referred to (in English) as the Pythoness. An oracle who went into trance and made proclamations purported to be coming from the god Apollo. The shrine at Delphi may date back to 1400 BCE, with the Pythian prophecies beginning as early as the 8th century BCE. These oracular proclamations were very important from the end of the 7th century BCE–393 CE. The practice was ended by the Roman emperor Theodosius, who ordered all pagan sanctuaries closed. The oracle was the most prestigious and authoritative Greek oracle, and the Pythia was (were) extremely powerful.

Robert Moss: Historian, author, teacher, storyteller, and founder of the School of Active Dreamwork. As a child in Australia, he had several near-death experiences that profoundly influenced his life and opened him up to perceiving other realms of reality. http://mossdreams.com

R.J. Stewart: Scottish-born composer, musician, author, and teacher of the Western Mysteries, including the Inner Temples Traditions/Inner Convocation (ITIC). Author of numerous books on Underworld and Faery traditions, Celtic mythology, Merlin, Kabbalah, occultism, and ceremonial magic, as well as several oracular decks. http://rjstewart.org

Santiago: Spanish name for St. James the Greater, the first martyred apostle. His bones are supposedly in a casket in the crypt of the cathedral in Santiago de Compostela, Galicia, Spain. In the Middle Ages, pilgrimage to his tomb ranked in importance with pilgrimage to Rome and Jerusalem, and various Caminos de Santiago* developed across Spain and Europe. They led to his presumed burial place in northwestern Spain.

Sarah Thomas: Acupuncturist, healer, educator, and stone-medicine expert. Founder of Upper Clarity School of Stone Medicine. https://www.upperclarity.com/

Stephanie Crystaal: Gary's daughter, a gifted medical intuitive, Pranic* healer, and herbalist. Currently in a four-year university program to become a licensed naturopath. Https://www.facebook.com/positiveenergyhealer3 and positiveenergyhealer@yahoo.com

Stephen Berkley: Doctor of Law (JD), attorney, writer, producer, director of the award-winning film, "Life with Ghosts" https://www.lifewithghosts.com/ Interviews people on his YouTube podcast channel, "Life with Ghosts – Let's Chat!"

Suzanne Giesemann: Retired US Navy commander and aide to the Chairman of the Joint Chiefs of Staff. Highly acclaimed evidential medium, spiritual teacher, author, and podcast presenter. Originator of The Awakened Way. www.suzannegiesemann.com

Synesius of Cyrene: (373 CE–414 CE) In 393 he became an enthusiastic Neoplatonist and disciple of Hypatia. Although not very observant and married, he was elected as the Greek bishop of Ptolemais. He stipulated upon his appointment that he would maintain the right to dissent from orthodox views.

Tessa ten Tusscher: Friend, Imaginaut, PhD psychologist, community-builder, networker, gardener. Wife of Nigel Ten Fleming.

Thoth: Ancient Egyptian god of the moon, wisdom, and writing. Creator of languages, scribe, and adviser of the gods. Depicted as a man with an ibis head or as a baboon. In later Egyptian religion, he was associated with magic and the judgment of the dead. Symbols include the ibis, moon, papyrus scroll, reed pens or stylus, baboon, and scales.

Tim and Gema: Friends of Nigel and Tessa and us.

Appendix B – Concepts

This glossary explains words in the main text that are followed by an * at their first appearance.

*Angelic Reiki: A hands-on (and distant) energy-healing modality channeled by Kevin Core through Archangel Metatron between October 2002 and February 2003 in Yorkshire, England. Further developed and taught by Kevin and his wife, Christine. Combines traditional (Usui) Reiki methods with angelic energies that the practitioner attunes to. It promotes healing and well-being on all levels: physical, mental, emotional, and energetic. https://angelicreikiinternational.com/

Asclepion (AKA Asklepieion, plural Asclepieia): Ancient temple of healing associated with the Greek god of healing, Asclepius. His shrines were temples of healing where people would go to dream of a cure, which would be interpreted by resident priests called Therapeutae. His most important shrine was at Epidaurus and dated to the 4th century BCE.

*BCE: Before Common Era, the modern alternative to BC (Before Christ).

*"Caminante No Hay Camino": Poem by Antonio Machado (Spanish poet, 1875–1939): "Caminante No Hay Camino/ Caminante, son tus huellas/ el camino y nada más;/ Caminante, no hay camino,/ se hace camino al andar./ Al andar se hace el camino,/ y al volver la vista atrás/ se ve la senda que nunca/ se ha de volver a pisar./ Caminante no hay camino/ sino estelas en la mar."

English translation: "Traveler, there is no path." Paraphrased: "Your footprints make the path/ the path is made by walking—you will never travel this way again. There is no path, only the ship's wake in the sea."

*Camino de Santiago: Refers to the Camino Francés and other Caminos de Santiago, pilgrimage routes that lead from various countries in Europe across Spain to the pilgrimage shrine of Santiago de Compostela, the supposed burial place of St. James the Greater, located in the northwestern province of Galicia. The Camino Francés stretches 500 miles across northern Spain. In the Middle Ages, pilgrimage to Santiago was as important as pilgrimage to Rome or Jerusalem. The Camino has experienced a resurgence of popularity in the last 45 years, and hundreds of thousands of pilgrims, spiritual seekers, long-distance hikers, and adventurers travel its network of trails, forest paths, and country roads. Elyn first walked the Camino in 1982 and wrote her PhD dissertation on it. She published the first modern account of an American walking the Camino: *Following the Milky Way* (2nd edition).

*CE: The Common Era, the modern alternative to AD (Anno Domini, the Year of Our Lord).

*Celebration!: Elyn and Gary's uplifting musical event raises the vibration of people and the planet. Elyn wrote the libretto, and Gary composed the music. Link to a partially computer-sound generated version of *Celebration!* with added visual content: https://youtu.be/eCIjtfoBJ98

*Channeling: The act of receiving messages, information, wisdom, or energies from a higher or non-physical source. The recipient (the channeler) is often in an altered state of consciousness. The channeler acts as a conduit for higher Consciousness, spirit guides, departed souls, angels, and so on, who communicate through speaking, writing, or by other means. The channeler may speak in an altered voice or have other physical expressions indicative of the energy/spirit being channeled. Channeling can facilitate deep healing on many levels, provide spiritual guidance, and lead to personal transformation. (See Appendix C.)

*Consciousness: When capitalized, used to refer to an abstract concept that (as Plotinus points out) is impossible to define but perhaps permeates or underlies everything and is prior to everything that exists.

*Continuity of consciousness: The concept that consciousness continues after the death of the body, the physical vehicle through which consciousness is expressed. It continues beyond the limitations of time and space.

*Ein Sof: Jewish mystical concept of God as infinite, ungraspable, incomprehensible, and unknowable. God is prior to any manifestation.

*Evidential medium: A medium who asks for and receives detailed, verifiable evidence from the spirit contacts: names, memories, unique personality traits, and/or life events that prove the messages are from the spirits. Suzanne Giesemann calls these "gold nuggets" or "No Other Explanation" when the information is not known by either the medium or the sitter: for example, the location of a missing bracelet.

*The Golden Verses of Pythagoras: A collection of moral exhortations composed of 71 lines of poetry. Attributed to Pythagorean philosophers. Very popular from late Antiquity through the Renaissance. May have been written as early as the 3rd century BCE, but the first confirmed evidence of the Golden Verses was in the 5th century CE. First translated into Latin in 1494 and into English in 1657. An important resource for Neoplatonists.

*Hermeticism: Philosophical tradition that originated in Hellenistic and Roman Egypt about 2000 years ago. Originally attributed to the god Hermes Trismegistus, a combination of the Greek god Hermes and the Egyptian god Thoth. The collected writings explore the nature of divinity, reality, and spiritual knowledge, and include such topics as alchemy, astrology, and theurgy (ritual practices to evoke deities). It has had an important influence on numerous occult and mystical traditions. The most famous collection is the Greek texts called the *Corpus Hermeticum*, written between 100–300 CE. Another significant text is *The Emerald Tablet*, which was very influential in medieval and Renaissance alchemy.

*Imaginal Realm: Described at length by the French philosopher/Islamicist Henry Corbin, the Imaginal Realm *(Mundus Imaginalis)* relates to the world of dreams, prophecy, oracles, and images—realms that are real but not material. It describes realms of higher and more subtle energies that possess being, objectivity, and creativity. These realms are not imaginary, as in fantasy or false, but rather are an expanded way of understanding/experiencing consciousness. The Imaginal is objectively real—in some ways *more* real than the limited, materialist, physical world.

*Imaginauts: Term coined by Elyn to describe adventurers exploring the non-physical realms, including the Imaginal Realm.

*Indra's Net: A metaphorical description of reality in Hinduism and Buddhism. Refers to an infinite, multidimensional net or web; at every intersection is a multifaceted jewel that reflects every other jewel.

Kabbalah: In Hebrew, it means both "tradition" and "received," as in "received knowledge." A form of Jewish mysticism that explores the nature of God, God's relationship to the universe/creation, and seeks direct experience of this true nature. May have emerged in the 12th century CE, though some practitioners claim that God revealed Kabbalah to Moses. There are many schools of Kabbalah. According to Lurianic Kabbalah, Ein Sof (Limitless/The Infinite/All That Is) withdrew to create space, which created Ohr Ein Sof, the Infinite Light. Or, according to a different interpretation, Ein Sof was progressively constricted to make room for existence. This constriction is called tzimtzum. This resulted in four levels of "worlds": Initiation, Creation, Formation, and Manifestation. Each "world" is a certain level of concealment of the Or Ein Sof. The Tree of Life* is a central image.

*Kinesiology:** The scientific study of human movement and its effects on the body; a holistic therapy based on the body's response to stimuli. Also refers to various techniques used to test a person's muscle strength or weakness when they are exposed to chemical/food challenges, such as sugar or specific vitamins, or when specific questions are asked. The idea is that the muscles become weak when something is not good for that person.

*Magic Square:** A square array of numbers arranged so that the sums of the numbers in each row, column, and main diagonals are the same. Known to Chinese mathematicians as early as the 2nd c. BCE. By the 12th c. CE, the mathematically complex squares were in use in the Middle East. By the Renaissance, they had become important occult objects in European magic.

*Mandorla:** Italian for almond. Also called a vesica piscis, it is formed by a particular intersection of two circles of the same diameter. In religious art, the mandorla is the almond-shaped frame that surrounds certain figures, usually Christ or the Virgin Mary, symbolizing their divine nature. In Eastern Orthodox icons, it depicts sacred moments that transcend time and space.

*Mediumship:** The practice of communicating with the spirits of the dead/non-physical beings. The medium provides evidence of the survival of the human personality or soul beyond physical death. A medium is a psychic who can feel, hear, or see spirits in other dimensions and serves as a facilitator/mediator between realms. A medium is usually contacted by an individual who wants to connect with someone on "the Other Side." Answers are usually detailed and specific to the sitter. Evidential mediums ask for verifiable evidence. (See Appendix C.)

*NDE:** Near-Death Experience. A profound, often life-transforming experience associated with death or near-death. Numerous well-documented cases of NDEs exist in the clinical and popular literature. Common features include: The person appears to leave their body and journey, often through a tunnel, to a light source; they are often greeted by deceased friends and family and may see a spiritual being; they experience a sense of peace and well-being and unconditional love; they may undergo a life review; they are ultimately told it is not their time (or they are given the choice to decide); and they return to their body. The International Association for Near-Death Studies (https://iands.org/) and its Journal of Near-Death Studies are dedicated to studying NDEs.

***Neoplatonism:** Philosophical school based on the work of Plato (c. 428–347 BCE) but further developed in the context of Hellenistic philosophy and religion. Plato's Theory of Forms asserts that ultimate reality exists beyond our physical world. Neoplatonism emphasizes the importance of the soul and spiritual ascent, the goal being to connect with ultimate reality through contemplation and transcending the physical world. It emphasizes the existence of a single, ultimate reality or source—the One, the All, the Good—beyond human comprehension, from which everything emanates. Plotinus (c. 204/5–270 CE) is usually considered its founder.

***Platonic Solids:** The ancient Greek philosopher Plato hypothesized that the classical elements were made of five regular solids that had been discovered before his time (perhaps by Pythagoras). These five geometric forms are the tetrahedron (with 4 faces, associated with Fire), the cube (with 6 faces, associated with Earth), the octahedron (with 8 faces, associated with Air), the dodecahedron (with 12 faces, associated with Ether), and the icosahedron (with 20 faces, associated with Water).

***Pranic Healing:** A holistic energy treatment that uses the body's own energy field and "prana" (life-force energy) to promote physical and emotional healing without physical contact. It uses the body's prana to balance, heal, and harmonize the body.

***Sephirot (AKA sephiroth, sefirot; singular, sephira or sefira):** In Kabbalah*, the 10 attributes or emanations through which Ein Sof* (infinite space, Divinity) reveals itself and continuously creates the physical realm through a downpouring of creative energy, represented by a lightning bolt pattern descending down the Tree of Life*. The Sephirot are usually depicted arranged on three pillars on the Tree of Life and interconnected by 22 paths, often associated with the 22 letters of the Hebrew alphabet. Also created in this descent are the Four Worlds (Emanation, Creation, Formation, and Manifestation/Action), through which this creative energy descends.

*Soul: Regarded as the immaterial, non-physical self, the seat of Consciousness, an aspect of the self that exists outside of the physical body, continues after physical death, and is immortal and pure.

*Spiritism: A religious system that includes belief in reincarnation, the soul's evolution, and the ability of the living to contact the deceased. First described by Allan Kardec, a French doctor/researcher/educator, who became fascinated by séances in mid-19th-century France. He coined the word in 1860 and published five books seminal to Spiritism, compiled as T*he Spiritist Codification* or *The Spirits' Book*.

*Spiritualism: A late-19th century, early-20th century social-religious movement that believes there is continuity of consciousness and people could contact the departed. Although it has faded in popularity, a number of Spiritualism churches and groups are still active, especially in the US and the UK.

*Story of Khidr and Moses: This is a famous teaching story in the Quran (18:65-82), the holy book of Islam. It tells of Khidr, a servant of God who has been given special knowledge. He goes on a journey with Moses, who questions him about the many seemingly unfair or inappropriate actions he sees Khidr do, including sinking a ship, killing a young man, and repaying inhospitality by repairing a wall. Fed up with Moses's questions, Khidr explains the actual circumstances behind the appearances that Moses saw. Khidr always acted in ways that were fair, appropriate, and prevented further harm or greater disaster.

Sufis: A mystical spiritual orientation often associated with Islam but probably in existence much earlier. Sufis seek a personal, direct experience of God using practices like meditation, purification, and zikr (remembrance of God through chanting and movement). There are many different orders of Sufism, each with a different founding father. One well-known order is the (misnamed) Whirling Dervishes, better known as the Mevlevi Order. It originated with Rumi, the famous 13th century CE Persian poet, mystic, and theologian. The Mevlevi form of *zikr (dhikr, remembrance of God) is performed by rhythmically turning ("whirling") in an altered state of consciousness during the Sema ceremony.

*Synchronicity: Meaningful coincidences that seem to be related but lack causal connection. Events that coincide and feel personally significant rather than mere random occurrences. Term introduced by the psychologist Carl Jung.

*Tree of Life: A Kabbalist diagram that represents the 10 Sephirot and 22 paths that unite them, arranged on three pillars and interconnected with 22 paths. The paths are often associated with the 22 Hebrew letters and the 22 Tarot Major Arcana cards. The diagram represents the flow from Nothingness/The One to creation, formation, and, finally, manifestation.

*Wildfit: A way of living developed by Eric Edmeades that encourages conscious, seasonal eating based on the way our African hunting-gathering ancestors ate. Programs support people as they learn to eat consciously, be aware of what triggers cravings, and avoid junk food, sugar, and dairy. The diet includes rotating what you eat depending on your nutritional goals, cycling from plenty of carbohydrates (metaphorically Fall) to shortage/fasting (Winter) to low-carb vegetables and protein (Spring) to fruits and sweet vegetables (Summer). www.getwildfit.com

Zikr (AKA dhikr): Zikr means "remembrance" or "recollection" in Arabic. A form of spiritual practice involving the repeated chanting of phrases or prayers to remember God. Particularly prominent in Sufism. There are many Sufi orders, and each practices its own style of zikr. Sometimes zikr is done alone and seated, with head movements, during recitation of the repeated phrase: for example, in English translation: "There is no God but God," or "In the name of God, the All-Merciful, the Especially Merciful," or one of the 99 names of Allah. Zikr is also done in a group, seated or standing, or circling in unison.

Appendix C – A Brief Introduction to Mediumship and Channeling

"Channeling is the process of revealing information and energy not limited by our conventional notions of space and time that can appear receptive or expressive."

– Excerpt from *The Science of Channeling*, Helané Wahbeh, Director of Research at IONS

The Differences between Mediumship and Channeling

Mediumship and channeling both involve naturally occurring psychic abilities that can be understood as existing on a spectrum from intuition/hunches to telepathy/precognition to deep trance-state/out-of-body experiences. These extrasensory perceptions are known as "the clairs." These include clairsentience (feeling), claircognizance (clear knowing), clairvoyance (clear vision, perhaps of the future), clairaudience (clear hearing), clairempathy (clear emotion), clairgustance (clear tasting), and clairtangency, also known as psychometry (clear touching, "knowing" from holding or touching an object).

Mediumship and channeling both involve receiving messages from beings (angels, spirit guides, ascended masters, departed loved ones, Higher Consciousness) in other dimensions or realms. Purposes range from healing from grief, receiving information, communicating with the departed, personal growth and transformation, spiritual growth, and so on.

The terms overlap, but there are differences.

Briefly, a medium is a facilitator/mediator who conveys messages and images received from other realms to a recipient (the sitter) who has requested information. The information tends to be personal and related to specific questions of the sitter. Often, though not exclusively, the medium is in contact with departed loved ones. The medium can, however, also receive guidance from spirit guides, Higher Consciousness, and so on. Evidential mediums seek verifiable evidence that the communication (and communicator) is valid.

A channeler, on the other hand, channels energies from non-physical beings and allows the information to flow through their physical body. They may go into a deep trance state or remain alert in a state of altered consciousness. They are in contact with beings from many different realms, including nature spirits, angels, ascended masters, guardian spirits, etc. They become a conduit (a "speaker tube") for the transmission of teachings, wisdom, or guidance, often of a more universal nature than personal. These teachings might include general information about the soul's purpose, spiritual development, universal truths, and metaphysical concepts. This content is of interest to a larger audience and not specific to a single individual. They may express the channeling by speaking in an altered voice, by moving their body in different ways, or by writing.

Before a session, the medium/channeler prepares by meditation, prayer, or other means. It's a bit like turning a radio dial to minimize the amount of static. They enter a (lightly or deeply) altered state of consciousness. They connect with energies/beings/departed from other dimensions. They serve as a conduit or facilitator for information to come through by speaking, writing, or other means of expression. They remain connected and receptive to beings/guidance from the Other Side. At the end, they integrate and debrief the sitter/recipient, as appropriate.

We can distinguish between mediums and channelers by the way they communicate. Mediums serve as intermediaries, describing what they see or hear. Channelers serve as conduits for non-corporeal beings by speaking with an altered voice, physical movements, or writing their messages.

We can also distinguish between them by the nature of the messages they communicate. Mediums tend to connect with the departed/personal spirit guide/etc. at the request of an individual sitter to relay information specifically for them. Channelers tend to connect with angelic beings/spirit guides/ascended masters/Higher Consciousness, etc., to bring through information/wisdom/teachings for the spiritual growth of a larger audience.

Mediumship and channeling overlap. Suzanne Giesemann, for example, is a skilled evidential medium who receives messages from the departed and communicates them to her sitters. She sometimes experiences physical sensations related to the departed's manner of death. She also channels messages from her spirit group Sanaya; when she does this, her voice changes. And she has also communicated with the Archangel Michael and with Jesus.

HISTORY

Both mediumship and channeling have a very long history. Although the Bible warns against communicating with spirits, one could say that Moses channeled information from God when he wrote the Ten Commandments on stone tablets. The Hebrew prophets received information and instructions from a non-corporeal being they perceived to be God. According to Muslim tradition, the Quran was gradually revealed by God to the Prophet Muhammad via the Archangel Gabriel; in other words, Muhammad channeled information from a divine realm.

The Egyptians, Greeks, and Romans relied on oracles. The famous Pythia of Delphi (see Appendix A) was a very important oracle believed to channel messages from the god Apollo.

Surveys of modern cultures worldwide report that 90% have a history of mediumship/channeling. In some cultures, entering a deep trance state is a regular form of acceptable, even highly sought-after, religious expression.

In the West, mediumship/channeling gained renewed traction in the 19th century. In the US, in 1848 the Fox sisters in Hydesville, NY, claimed to communicate with spirits via rapping sounds. This set off a furor of interest, and Spiritualism* (a social-religious movement that believes there is continuity of consciousness and that we can contact the departed) soon became quite popular in the US and UK.

Mediums would conduct séances, often involving table-turning, strange noises, the appearance of wispy shapes, and so on. Ouija boards became a way for people to experience what they perceived to be communications from the Other Side. Fraud was rife, and stage magicians created novel ways to deceive the public. Nonetheless, not all mediums or channelers were (or are) fraudulent.

In the mid-1850s, the French educator/researcher using the pen name Allan Kardec began investigating the phenomenon, eventually publishing a seminal series of books based on information he had received in response to questions he asked 10 mediums. The result was the establishment in 1860 of what is known as Spiritism*, a religious system that includes belief in reincarnation, the soul's evolution, and the ability of the living to contact the deceased.

Efforts were made to study the phenomena. The Society for Psychical Research was established in England in 1882 and continues to function (https://www.spr.ac.uk). The American Society for the Study of Psychical Research was founded soon after, in 1885 (http://www.aspr.com/).

In the 20th century, Spiritualism faded in popularity with the public. However, many Spiritualist churches and study groups remain active, especially in the UK and the US.

One early-20th-century channeler gained worldwide fame. The American Edgar Cayce, "the Sleeping Prophet," entered a deep trance state in which he diagnosed ailments and prescribed successful cures for 1000s of people. He also forecasted future events and answered numerous questions about reincarnation, the afterlife, Atlantis, dreams, healing—and much more. He lived from 1877–1945, and his 14,000 channeled messages are available for research at ARE, the Association for Research and Enlightenment, which he founded in 1931. https://edgarcayce.org/

A Google search reveals many other famous (and some infamous) mediums and channelers. Reputable ones include Jane Roberts, who channeled Seth; Tyler Henry (the "Hollywood Medium"); Darryl Anka, who channels Bashar; Esther Hicks, who channels a group of non-physical entities called Abraham; Sheila Gillette, who channels Theo; Lee Harris, who channels "the Zs"; Suzanne Giesemann, who channels the group Sanaya—and many more.

In 1964, the Arthur Findlay College, "the World's Foremost College for the Advancement of Spiritualism and Psychic Sciences," was established in England. Students study Spiritualist philosophy and practices, including mediumship and healing. The College has trained numerous highly respected evidential mediums. https://www.arthurfindlaycollege.org/

Psychic phenomena, near-death experiences (NDEs), and reincarnation have been and continue to be the subject of numerous investigations and many books. Duke University's Parapsychology Laboratory, established in 1930 by J.B. and Louisa Rhine, empirically studied psychic and paranormal experiences. This work continues at the Rhine Research Center (https://www.rhineonline.org/). PEAR (The Princeton Engineering Anomalies Research) was a psychic research program at Princeton University. It was established in 1979 and incorporated in 2007 into the ICRL (International Consciousness Research Laboratories, https://icrl.org/). Research into NDEs and past-life memories is currently being conducted at the University of Virginia School of Medicine, Department of Perceptual Studies (https://med.virginia.edu/perceptual-studies/our-research/near-death-experiences-ndes/).

With the advent of access to modern brain-monitoring technology, many researchers have begun studying channeling and mediumship (and ESP in general) using high-tech equipment. For example, see the research and publications from the Institute of Noetic Sciences (IONS, https://noetic.org/). The University of Arizona Laboratory for Advances in Consciousness and Health in the Department of Psychology explores mediumship, the continuity of consciousness, and psychic phenomena (https://lach.arizona.edu/).

As with anything, one must exercise due diligence. Not all who wander are lost—and not all who claim to be channelers or mediums are. The purpose of this summary is to demonstrate the ubiquity through time and space of human efforts to contact beings "beyond the veil," to communicate with non-physical entities—and, ultimately, to benefit from the undeniable fact that consciousness exists (and continues to exist) in many other realms than our limited, physical world.

Appendix D – More Questions, More Answers

My conversations with Plotinus, Hypatia, and The Collective are ongoing. This book focuses on the first year of communication, but they continue (and will continue) to have much to share with us. At their request, I have included additional conversations in this appendix.

Tuesday, 8 April 2025

I finished a draft of the manuscript, tentatively called *Wisdom from Beyond – Channeling Messages from Plotinus, Hypatia, and The Collective*.

During meditation, I thought about the title and asked if the first part, "Wisdom from Beyond," was OK. I "heard," *"We aren't 'beyond.' We are right here!"*

I thought about it and decided that "from the Other Side" would be equally misleading. Sigh. Then I decided that "beyond the veil" is not here or there. I asked Plotinus if he was happy with the manuscript.

(P = Plotinus, H = Hypatia)

P: "It is good, but can be improved."

[I picked up my notebook and focused on the conversation.]

Me: "How?"

P: "Pay attention to details."

Me: "Punctuation?"

P: "Work toward clarity."

Me: "Hypatia? Suggestions?"

H: "I wondered when you'd ask! [Nodding approval] It is good."

Me: "More Q&A in Appendix D?"

H and P: [Nodding]

Me: "What do you want to say now?"

P: "Dangerous times on your planet. Be wary. Be careful. Do not cause unnecessary harm."

Me: *"Is harm ever necessary?"*

P: *[Nodding] "Sometimes, yes. There is difficulty in change. You have an expression. 'You can't make an omelet without cracking eggs.' An omelet is an excellent metaphor because it is about unity and oneness versus separation."*

Me: *"How do we get through these chaotic times?"*

P: *"Do not fear."*

H: *"Hold tight to your values. Do not weaken."*

P and H: *"You will survive."*

Me: *"Me, or the world?"*

P and H: *"Humanity. A time of purification and clarity, a reset."*

Me: *"The values? The union?"*

P: *"We are all One. We must treat each other with love and compassion."*

H: *"What we do to each other, we do to ourselves."*

Me: *"Is there more you want to say about this?"*

P: *"You must get our message out there."*

Me: *"I'm trying."*

H: *"We will help you."*

E: *"Thank you. May I change the topic?"*

P: *[Nodding]*

E: *"Marchiene wants to know about Plotinus's relationship with gender issues—inequality, patriarchy …"*

P: *[Sighing] "Such a human narrow perspective. Whilst I lived, I did my best not to participate—perpetuate—inequality, but it was unavoidable. I had male and female students and fostered—was guardian to—boys and girls. I cared for all [equally]. However, my society—I believe all—almost all societies are built in inequality."*

H: "Or at the very least, differentiation."

P: [Nodding]

H: "I was trained by my father and treated as an equal at home, but not in society. I had to struggle for recognition and the honor due me. My being female worked against me—but also enabled me to be a valued counselor, a trustworthy confidant. There are always two sides to the coin. And notice, neither Plotinus nor I chose to marry. To do so would have perpetuated the inequality of societal roles."

P: [Nodding]

Me: "Thank you. And on your side of 'the veil'?"

[Laughter]

H: "We are harmonious frequencies—different in many ways, like a symphony—composed of many lines of music, if you will."

P: "That is why we can incarnate as male or female—the differences simply express physically as different genders."

[I have the image of baking: different ratios of ingredients—and sometimes even additional ingredients—produce different products.]

Me: "Did you, Hypatia, volunteer for The Collective or did Plotinus enlist you?"

H: [Laughing]: "It's not like that. We sense different frequencies/harmonies and are attracted. Like two magnets. Is one magnet calling to the other? No. They call each other."

Me: "Ah. ... Plotinus, how long have you been watching over me? Just since the channeling started or long before?"

P: "I've told you before, long before."

Me: "But you said you 'saw our lights' and wanted to enter into the conversation Gary and I were having in Gipsy Bar."

P: "Both are true. As Gary keeps telling you, both/and. I had been watching over you—both of you—and you reached a point in your process of evolving where your lights shown bright and I knew I could communicate with you. I could reach your vibrational level at last. About time! [Smiling]"

Me: "You are joking about time, right?"

P: [Nodding]

Me: "On the Other Side: Do some people continue to 'live' as they did on this side? Playing golf, suburbia, etc.?"

P: [Nodding]: "For some—"

H: "For some, it is a quick transition into non-corporality and its freedom. For others, it is a slow inching forward of releasing old habitual patterns of living. Of course, 'here' there is no hurry, so slow or fast is irrelevant, not value judgments."

Me: "I see. Another question: about the Light that NDErs [Near Death Experiencers] sometimes describe. Can they go into it and cease existing as separate beings? [Is that a choice that we have after death, to go directly 'to the Light'?]"

P and H: [Conferring]

P: [Shaking his head]: "They would learn that it [the Light] keeps moving away as they get closer. It is not time yet for them to merge."

H: "Unless of course they are highly evolved!"

P: [Nodding]

Me: "Thank you! Can I return another day and ask more questions? I have a [long] list."

[I heard the answer to a question I hadn't asked, relating to Natalie.]

P and H: "Of course. That is what we are here for. To answer your questions and provide guidance to you and to humanity. We await our next encounter now that you are making yourself available [to us] again."

Me: "Thank you, thank you! Goodbye for now."

30 minutes.

Wednesday, 9 April 2025

I woke up early, sensing that Plotinus wanted to speak to me. I sat down for my morning meditation, and he came through—I could feel the pressure on my right temple. He wants to make up for all the time I hadn't been asking him questions.

I asked what he thought about the book project.

> P: "You are doing well."

> Me: "I'm trying to. Are there more questions for me to ask?"

> P: "Always you have more."

> Me: "More for you to tell me?"

> P: "We repeat ourselves in our efforts to communicate across the veil, turning our words like an object [of art] that you examine from different directions."

> [I saw an image of someone holding a small statue and turning it around to see it from different perspectives.]

> Me: "Are there artists and composers on your side?"

> P: "There is no need for human-type creativity. We are closer to the Source—the music, the art, flows through us, accessible to all."

> Me: "When I wrote *The Question – A Magical Fable,* where did the images/ideas [come from]? And when I wrote *The Journey – A Novel of Quest,* the characters—where did they come from?"

> P: "From what you call the Imaginal Realm, where all is possible, waiting to be formed from energetic ... concepts ... into interconnected sounds and images."

> Me: "How did I write about two characters I later met [in real life]?"

> P: "Because all is possible, all exists in creative possibility in the Imaginal Realm."

> Me: "[But] they existed here."

P: "Yes, and the possibility of their existing exists elsewhere. I could say 'began elsewhere,' but that creates a false sense of time and movement."

Me: "Did I 'pick up' on their real existences and write about them?"

P: "No, it was not like that. The images you evoked in the cards came through for expression from the Other Realm. You could say they wanted to be expressed, but that, too, is not accurate. There is a force—of longing—[longing] for expression. A 'direction' of formation—that powers, like Dylan Thomas's poem, 'The force that through the … green shoot … drives the flower…'"

Me: "Life force?"

P: "In the broadest sense. There is no difference between human life force and creativity. It is all the same—the expression of the One True Being, the Source of All, expressing itself. It is its nature, though that is a woefully inaccurate description."

Me: "Hmmm. Marchiene wants to ask you about oneness and separation. We are Light, but long to reunite? Separation and unity all at once?"

H: "I'll answer that. Yes. Just as the sun emits rays that are part of it, creating apparent separation while at the same time being of the same substance yet different in—form. The sun ray is not the source [solar nuclear reactions, extruded materiel, etc.] but it is *of* it."

Me: "And the sun ray wants to return to the sun?"

H: "No, the sun ray lacks the self-awareness to long to be reunited. Separation is both true and an illusion. Each human being [metaphorically described as a sun ray] comes from the sun source and yet is a separate expression, with individuality and personality and life experience. Without separation, there can be no evolving, and Source would be completely—static."

Me: "Does Source change?"

P: "Yes."

H: "No. Like a mirror reflecting events, it is untouched."

P: "An inadequate description because it is not a mirror. It is the reflection and the reflected, the substance and the emission—at some level unknowable and unchangeable."

H: "I stand corrected. Words are inadequate to express even our limited understanding."

P: [Nodding]

Me: "A question. Marsilio is part of The Collective?"

P: [Nodding]

Me: "But I've never heard him participate."

P: "Nor has Thoth. They await their time, their appropriate moment."

Me: "What is the meaning of life?"

P: "Whatever you make it."

H: "To be of service."

P: "That is *the* purpose."

H: "The purpose *is* to evolve—but not as you imagine, as a goal to become something. Words fail. We talked about this earlier. Review your notes."

Me: "I remember. We spoke of 'isness' and an acorn becoming a tree."

P and H: [Nodding]

Me: "Marchiene asks what you can and can't do on the other side."

[Laughter]

P and H: "It's such a different realm!"

P: "We can do (almost) anything but choose not to. 'Doing' is much less—"

H: "Relevant."

P: [Nodding]

H: "Although it depends mightily on how removed you are from your 'crossing over.' At first, many people are still caught up in doing—producing—

activities of human life. They are lost without that. But as you gradually release such habitual patterns, you begin to move to the freedom of flow and receptivity."

[I see waves and ocean tides.]

P and H: [Nodding at my mental image]

H: "Imagine yourself as a piece of music. It simply *is*, *delighting (if it could) in its harmoniousness.*"

Me: [Nodding] "Thank you. I will come back with more questions, but now I think I need to rest. I still find these exchanges tiring."

P: "But less so, I hope."

Me: [Nodding]

P: "Bless you. Goodbye."

30 minutes.

I looked up the Dylan Thomas (British poet, 1914–1953) reference. The poem is titled "The force that through the green fuse drives the flower." Here's the first stanza.

"The force that through the green fuse drives the flower
Drives my green age; that blasts the roots of trees
Is my destroyer.
And I am dumb to tell the crooked rose
My youth is bent by the same wintry fever."

Thursday, 10 April 2025

Once again, I woke up early, sensing that Plotinus and company wanted to speak to me.

Me: "I look at the breadcrumb trail of Greeks or Greek themes in my life and wonder if I'm drawing lines between unrelated dots."

H: "Remember Indra's Net? There are many paths and innumerable dots. Some have more affinity—charge—energy—and attraction than others. You are not wrong to draw connections between your Greek connections. Affinity from past lives also factors in."

Me: "Wow. Thank you. Related question: Then—are there soul groups that reincarnate together?"

H: "In some sense all beings—not just humans but more obviously and easily identifiable [as such]—are soul family. Over millennia of birth and rebirth."

Me: "So Michael, Gary, Marchiene—and the soul family I feel gathering in Girona—are all soul family?"

H: [Nods] "You can sense the affinity."

Me: "Hmmm. Why are there soul families?"

[I see an image of a 3-D chessboard.]

H: "To enable even greater learning to all concerned."

Me: "Hmm. OK. So … we switch roles? Play out relationship patterns?"

H: "Indeed. [Nodding]"

Me: "And in the afterlife?"

H: "In a manner of speaking."

P: "We come together through affinity here as well."

Me: "Blood relationship? Actual family on the Other Side?"

P: "Much less so. That is shed—discarded—when we transition."

Me: "So … consciousness continues and personality to some extent, to influence future reincarnations?"

P: [Nodding] "Something like that."

Me: "How? How is the soul modulated to maintain memories or lessons or … ?"

H: [Sigh] "It's not quite like that and impossible to explain. We become more 'frequency' than form. But maintain subtle 'riffs'—"

P: "Perhaps, think of it like a jazz performance with improv and riffs around a central theme. Something like that."

Me: "Hmm. I don't understand."

P and H: [Trying again] "The central core of soul continues always—that ray of the sun—of the One—part."

P: "[It is a part of] the whole, yet living in separation, until it reaches total harmony and Oneness. Meantime, it 'gives off' notes and melodies, melodic lines of experience, that add to the whole—the experience of—well, not the One, but 'the field.' The 'field' becomes richer—a more complex tapestry."

Me: "Oh. I'll try to understand. I'll think about it."

P: "Good idea."

[Pause]

Me: "Does everything have a soul?"

P and H: "Well, not exactly. A rock evolves [changes form over time], of course, but has little capacity for self-reflection. A plastic photo frame, even less so. Things not in their natural state lose their internal harmony—nature—and are truly dead, without soul. Even compost has the possibility for new life—but an acrylic picture frame, not so much."

Me: "What is succinctly your most important message?"

P: "That we are all One."

H: "That what you do to others, you do to yourself. That what you do to yourself, you should always do with love."

P: "There is purpose and love in the universe—love is the universe—the Black Matter, the glue, the magnetism, the gravity—the attraction of one to another—it's love."

H: "Not love as you know it—[not] passion, emotion, devotion."

P: "Something much less personal and also more profound and unchanging. It doesn't fade."

H: "Know that love permeates all."

Me: "And evil? Where's the love?" [Evil seems antipathetic to love.]

P: "Those who 'miss the mark,' dis-resonate, are held in love regardless and gently returned to harmony. We've talked about that."

Me: [Nodding]: "So your central message?"

TC: "We are real. We are always here, not 'there.' Now is the time—it is of central urgency and importance—for humans to remember—you don't need to learn, you need to remember!—to love each other—"

H: "And not [love] just humans but all living things, plants, animals, the Earth itself."

Me: "Or?"

P: We are not doomsayers but, suffice to say, these are dangerous—"

H: "Challenging—"

P: "Times for humanity and Planet Earth."

H: "So full of potential and possibility to rise out of the disharmony."

P: "And so fraught with danger that you will not."

Me: "And then what?"

H: "All souls continue and have other opportunities. But it's a pity to waste so much potential."

P: [Nodding]

Me: "Whew. Lots to think about. Thank you."

P and H: "And you for making yourself available for these conversations."

P: "And for getting the message out there!"

Friday, 11 April 2025

While I was doing my morning meditation, an ibis-headed humanoid holding a writing stylus walked across my inner vision. Thoth! The Egyptian god of writing, wisdom, magic, the moon, and the patron of scribes. He is part of The Collective, but he had never talked to me during our channeled conversations. I had encountered him spontaneously some years before during a meditation, but I hadn't seen him since.

Later, I wrote down the conversation.

Thoth wanted to tell me about the nature of creativity. He explained that all creativity comes from the other realms and that we humans bring it through, like channeling. I asked if that meant we were merely vehicles, mouthpieces parroting what we heard/were told, but he said, "No."

He explained that each artist/writer/creative person expresses in their unique way the concepts/images/frequencies that exist in potential in the other dimensions. Steinbeck was not Shakespeare, was not Tennessee Williams. Picasso was not Dalí. Artists, writers, composers, choreographers—creatives of all kinds—give form to the images/frequencies they hear/perceive. They bring them into manifestation from the Imaginal Realm. Or maybe from All That Is, the Field of Consciousness. Thoth didn't give a name to where these possibilities reside.

Then, much to my surprise, he reached forward and tapped the middle of my forehead with his stylus.

While writing up this exchange with Thoth, I suddenly remembered the 12th-century San Juan de la Peña monastery in Spain that Gary and I had visited years ago. A sculpture on a capital in the cloister shows someone carrying a small hammer and leaning over a reclining man. He is about to hit him on the top of his head. Our guide, well versed in esoteric interpretions, told us that the scene represents a spiritual initiation. The hammer-bearer is about to open the sleeper's higher third eye or "soma" chakra, enhancing their claircognizance: the sudden knowing that something is true without any logical explanation. Some call this intuition or a "gut" feeling.

Thoth did something like that to me with his stylus, but he opened up my third eye, the location of clairvoyance—the ability to perceive or see information or events (including in the future) through clear mental images or visions. I wondered what would happen next. Hopefully, not much. I just didn't have the "bandwidth" for further psychic adventures.

Tuesday, 22 April 2025

I sat at my altar to meditate and talk with Plotinus.

Me: *"It's been too long since I sat down to talk with you!"*

P: *"We are here. We are always here."*

Me: *"I've been working on the book project."*

P: *[Nodding]* *"We know."*

Me: *"What do you think?"*

P and TC: *[Nodding]* *"It is going well."*

Me: *"Suggestions?"*

P: *"Hold true to your intention. To tell the Truth."*

Me: *"I'm trying."*

H: *"You are doing well."*

Me: *"Hi, Hypatia! Welcome!"*

H: *"Thank you, Dear."*

Me: *"In reviewing the messages, I have some questions."*

TC: *[Nodding]*

Me: *"What is mental illness?"*

[Conferring]

P: "A mismatch of frequencies."

H: "Yes. A discordance."

Me: "Physical? Mental?"

P: [Frowning thoughtfully] "The difficulties of language. These [body and mind] are not separate. They impose on each other. They interact."

Me: "Please explain further."

P: "Sometimes the coming-into-form doesn't quite—synchronize—"

H: "Harmonize."

P: [Nodding] "Yes. There is discordance, sometimes greater, sometimes lesser."

Me: "How to help our friends' daughter [who has serious mental health issues]?"

P: [Shaking head] "It's not so easy as 'help.' There are—karmic—influences and impacts. She does what she does, and she teaches her family in the process."

Me: "Oh. But it's so painful for everyone!"

P: [Nodding] "Of course. There is the learning opportunity."

Me: "Can you say more? What causes the mismatch?"

P: [Slowly] "Could be many things. Soul plan before coming in. Past life vectors. What you call karma. Free will. An unplanned imbalance of physical matter. And so on."

Me: "And treatment or cure?"

H: "Totally depending on the individual situation and desired outcome."

Me: "Desired outcome? Normalcy, I presume."

TC: "Exactly. As defined by society."

Me: "I suppose so."

[Silence]

Me: "Another question. The connection between body and soul. You told me the soul comes in after the fetus is formed, but I've heard that the body is within the soul, not the other way around."

P: "Language again. 'Coming into the fetus.' It's not like that, really. [The soul is] 'animating' with consciousness, history of past lives, soul plan, a tiny living receptacle. So of course—"

H: "Of course the soul-form energy is larger than the physical form. It extends through time and space and is immortal, beyond the individual life and times and experience."

Me: "I think I understand. Let me oversimplify. The soul/spirit is an energy 'cloud' that floats around and merges with a tiny bundle of DNA life form, which is also a kind of energy form but more physical. They take on each other's frequency or vibration and merge as one, though not equally in the equation."

P and H: [Nodding] "That will do for now."

Me: "Can you say more about soul family or group?"

[I get an image of swirling masses of color and energy, something like shifting, rippling Northern Lights.]

Me: "The individual souls can be together, reincarnate together, or separately?"

P: [Nodding] "But their attraction to each other increases the probability of their showing up—reincarnating—together. More or less, and more or less frequently."

Me: "What's the purpose?"

TC: "To enhance the opportunities for learning."

H: "It's more efficient."

Me: "OK, I think I understand."

[Pause]

P: "More questions?"

Me: "Always! ... Does Michael want to speak to me?" [In late March, I'd suddenly begun remembering events in our long-ago relationship.]

TC: [Huddle] "He has nothing to say except he is smiling [with pleasure] at your recognition of the length and depth of your attachment to each other and to Plotinus."

Me: "I see! Did he know this when he was alive?"

P: "No. But it's not for nothing—not for chance—he drowned in the sea near Delphi."

Me: "Did we share past lives there?"

TC: [Nodding] "Obviously so."

Me: "More details?"

TC: "None required at present."

Me: "Thank you. But ... I was a Pythia. Was he a Pythia? Or an interpreter?"

P: "He has been both."

Me: "And I?"

H: "Only a Pythia."

Me: "How can you know my past lives?"

H: "They resonate in your energy field. We are trained to read them."

Me: "Where does information—knowledge—come from? Is it stored in the Akashic Records?"

H: "All information is available everywhere. You humans have a limited understanding—as did I—of the workings of the universe. You need to label things."

P: "Humans love their models. And—by the way—I was right about your [taking the] Tree of Life course, was I not?"

H: "Ahem. You label something The Akashic Records, as if they were separate from something else—but it's all there. All here. All available."

Me: "Past and future?"

P and H: [Huddle] "Very complicated. Too complicated to explain. Past, present, and probability is more accurate."

Me: "Oh. ... I'm getting tired."

P and H: "We will leave you now."

Me: "Thank you. Oh—any book title suggestions?"

P: "You have many already. See which one has more 'magnetism'—more attraction. We will help you choose, but the time is not yet ripe."

Me: "Thank you. Goodbye for now."

[P and H bow.]

30 minutes.

Tuesday, 29 April 2025

I was eager to talk with Plotinus and The Collective.

Me: [Feeling weepy to be in contact again.]

P: "We are always here."

Me: "I know. I'm grateful!"

P: "You have questions for us."

Me: [Nodding]

P: "Let us begin."

Me: "Marchiene has various spirit 'Grandmothers' she is in contact with—Elementals, directions, the Other Side."

P: [Nodding]

Me: "Where are they? Where you are?"

P: [Shaking head] "There are many realms here and on Earth. The Elementals and directions she calls on are linked to Planet Earth. Of course, they exist elsewhere, especially the directions are everywhere, but she is connecting to those aspects manifesting on your—once our—planet."

Me: "And the other Grandmothers—the ones who help get things done?"

P: "They are on this side."

[I have an image of a harp player plucking strings.]

P: "Yes, they are able to see and manipulate the Net—the web of interrelationships."

[I see marionettists pulling strings.]

P: "But you are not marionettes being played. You have free will. The Grandmothers and other helpers of their ilk are able to 'harmonize' events—bring disparate events, connections, possibilities into closer proximity."

Me: "Like our moving back to Girona—first Gary proclaiming we had to return for research, then Nuri's dream and messages, and then Booking and Vueling and Carles. [All kinds of synchronicities came one right after the other.]"

P: "Exactly."

H: [Nodding]

Me: "Hi, Hypatia!"

H: "Hello, Dear One!"

Me: "Hypatia, why don't you ever speak through me?"

H: [Shaking head] "There is no need, and I know you don't like it. So why would I?"

Me: "To prove you are here."

H: "Do you doubt it?"

[After a moment, I sense she is going to speak through me. I give my permission. My mouth shifts inside, changing shape. It's a different shape than when Plotinus speaks through me.]

Hypatia speaks through me: "What do you want me to say through you? There is nothing ... no need to say ... Are you satisfied?" [She withdraws.]

[When Hypatia spoke through me, my voice was higher, a little breathless, with a different intonation pattern.]

Me: [Nodding]

[I feel a light pat on my shoulder from her, a sign of affection.]

H: "It is done."

Me: "I've just read a book—My Little Star—[about] a Catholic woman channeling information from St. Michael, the Virgin Mary, and Jesus." *[She does so under the strict supervision of a priest to make sure the beings are who they say they are and are not evil spirits eager to deceive her.]*

P and H: [Nodding]

P: "What is your question?"

Me: "What do you think of that perspective?"

P and H: [Conferring]

P: "It is a closed system from her perspective and gives her a sense of safety."

H: "It excludes all others, of course, such as yourself."

Me: [Nodding] "She'd say I'm either deluded, a fraud, or talking with Satan."

P and H: [Laughing]

P: "It is so easy to demonize the other."

H: "I know that all too well."

Me: "Yes, I know—but—is there a Satan?"

P: "There is no need. Humans create their own evil and their own excuses."

Me: "But you've said we learn more from the evil—"

P: "No, from the bad, the hurtful. If I said evil, I did not mean to personify it."

H: "That is the difference. There are things you think are evil—bad outcomes, harm, terror, violence—but they are not a personified being, a Satan."

P: "We give power to thought forms and enlarge their energy and their reach."

Me: "Like ... egregores?"

P: [Nodding]

H: "Remember—all is illusion—temporary, ephemeral, changing, passing—"

P: "And an opportunity for growth and learning."

Me: "Is there a Heaven? Hell? Purgatory?"

P: "It all depends on what you mean."

H: "Where we 'live' is like Heaven in some ways—exquisite beauty, peace, calm, harmony."

P: "At least for the most part."

H: "Yes, there are other beings around who try at times to disturb our tranquility."

Me: "And the cocoons?"

H: "Swaddled—"

Me: "Beings as well?"

P: [Nodding] "What is Heaven? Perhaps you have Heaven on Earth when all is well and you are loved or doing something you enjoy [such as fiber art, or writing]."

Me: [Nodding] "And Hell? And Purgatory?"

P and H: [Consulting]

P: [Shaking head] "The closest equivalent is the swaddling, but it is not a punishment."

H: "Those who need fear to act properly, need to believe in Hell."

P: "Or Purgatory."

H: "But that's an incomplete—immature—method of development."

P: [Shaking head] "I can't imagine the misuse of imagination that dwells on such suffering and makes alluring images of pain."

[Pause]

Me: "Do I have anything to fear from negative forces?"

P and H: [Shaking heads]

P: "As we told you before, you come from Light and radiate Light—you do not attract those beings."

H: "And their power comes from the attraction you have to them, if you do. Imagine a kind of horrified attraction, if you will, a fascination with fears."

Me: "Whew! Not me! Not mine!"

P: "Exactly!"

H: [Thoughtfully] "These thought-forms persist. We have told you that souls who have crossed over have very different visions—images—of life on this side. Some still live in suburbia."

P: "And some live in what they imagine Hell [to be like], punishing themselves."

Me: "I see."

P: "All is possible here."

Me: "Does it 'leak over' to our world?"

P and H: [Nodding]

H: "Our realms interpenetrate."

Me: "Sigh. Lots to think about."

P: *"Better not. Better to feel the love we have for all of you. Concentrate on love, not fear."*

H: *"Yes—like that prayer you always [recite]—'Where there is hatred, let me sow love …'"*

Me: *"The Saint Francis Prayer."*

H: *"That's the one."*

Me: *"I'm getting tired. Is there more you want to say?"*

P: *"Only this—love one another. Be loved. Be love. Your friend Marchiene said something about 'praying love.' That's it. That's all. That's enough. That's sufficient."*

H: *[Nodding]* *"Indeed. And remember—you are so very loved."*

P: *"As are we all. Good night, my child."*

Me: *"Goodbye, you both—much gratitude."*

35 minutes.

Thursday, 1 May 2025

I woke up dreaming vividly of Michael. It felt like a real visitation from the Other Side. Later that morning, seated at my meditation altar, I decided to try to communicate with him—and I did. Among other things he wanted to tell me, it turned out he is the MF/Marsilio Ficino in The Collective. I asked for evidence to verify it wasn't my imagination, and I received confirmation later that day and the next. I also had a conversation with Plotinus, Hypatia, and Michael. I have included the details of the dream and the channeled exchanges on pp. 238-248.

Saturday, 10 May 2025

Gary and I struggled with creating the cover for the book. We came up with one design—a blue sky with puffy clouds and three barely visible columns from the ruined Temple of Delphi—but it didn't feel right. Too wispy, too ethereal, too ungrounded.

The cover needed to represent the message of the book, so we started over. What was the message of the book? Interconnection across time and space, life after life, and love holding it all together. Closing my eyes, I saw a sunrise sky and an image of interconnecting hearts. Got it!

I'd seen a stained-glass window featuring interconnected hearts years ago in a medieval Spanish hermitage in the Cañon del Río Lobos. We found a picture of it on Google. The center of the five intertwined hearts formed a pentangle, which was important in the Pythagorean tradition. Unfortunately, during the last century, the pentagram was erroneously linked with witchcraft. Using that design might lead people to draw the wrong conclusions about the book. Another Google search, and we found the perfect image: eight interconnecting hearts formed by a single line.

Gary got to work turning the concept into a design. We fiddled with the colors and the font for the text. Once he printed out a satisfactory version, I held it in my hands and went into meditation. I asked The Collective what they thought of it.

> P: *"I don't think the hearts are necessary, but so be it."*
>
> H: *"I'm intrigued by the underlying geometry."*
>
> MF: *"I would prefer it to be more austere."*
>
> Me: *"Well, we can't please everyone. We like it and we're going with it."*
>
> P, H, and MF: *[Nodding in agreement]*
>
> *[A week later. our artist friend Carles offered to design a cover for us. Very modern. No hearts. Plotinus got his wish.]*

Sunday, 11 May 2025

I sat down at my altar to talk with Plotinus.

Me: [Teary-eyed] "I'm so glad you are here! You are such an important part of my life! I think of all the healing [of the past, relationships with Gary and Michael], the learning, the support and care from you this past year!"

[I feel a non-physical hug.]

Me: "I will keep talking to you after the book is done, of course! I will rely on your help and support forever in this life!"

P: "Now, now. All is well. No need to get so emotional. All is well, we will be here."

Me: [Sniffling] "Sometimes I've wondered if I've gone back to sleep because—ironically—you are so easy to reach! Am I just talking to myself? And then I get proof—the grey feathers, the lighthouse—"

H: "It's all right, Dear One. It's a lot to take in. Never fear—you cannot go back to sleep."

P: "Well, you can."

H: [Briskly] "But she won't. She's woke! [Laughing at pun]"

Me: "I'm also tired. Elizabeth says I've integrated the experience, so it's become normalized, [it's] not that I've gone to sleep."

H: [Nodding] "That is correct. Your vibration has shifted higher; we are easier to reach. We are always here, and now the gap is smaller."

P: [Nodding] "It has taken a lot of work—"

Me: "From you, too!"

P: "Less on our parts. Without bodies, we are more flexible."

Me: "I think this will be the last entry in Appendix D—is that correct?"

P and H: [Nodding]

Me: "Is there more for you to say to the readers of this book?"

P: "Trust. Love each other. Trust that all is well and will be well. Remember the larger picture of connectedness. There are no walls between us."

Me: "Hypatia?"

H: "Remember, what you do to others you do to yourself. Love one another. And remember to have fun! Play! It's not so serious. You will get another chance."

P: "And another and another."

H: "What goes around comes around, you say. Remember the circle of life. And death. Birth and rebirth. …"

[Pause]

Me: "Totally different topic."

[They wait.]

Me" "It's about an experience I had a few days ago. Feeling energy coming off the ancient stones in the Barri Vell/Old Town in Girona."

P and H: [Nodding]

Me: "I got a 'knowing' that the energy is like a scent vibration held in the stones. I 'saw' a bloodhound following an invisible scent trail."

P and H: [Nodding]

P: "And your question?"

Me: "Is this related to past lives? Not mine, but in general? Is this why people say they think they've been in a place before when they never have? Our friend Bonney felt in Girona that she'd been here in a past life."

H: "Yes, it could be her soul recognized the scent-vibration from its past. Just like a sudden whiff of perfume may remind you of someone you knew long ago."

Me: "I remember smelling a combination of spices and suddenly being transported back to the market in Sri Lanka where I'd lived for a year when I was 11."

H: "Yes, it's like that. An ancient part of the brain."

Me: "But how does the brain store memories from past lives?"

P: "It doesn't. It's the soul and the configured memories of the personality that are retained life after life."

Me: "Like layers on the onion?"

P: "Exactly."

H: "Well, sort of. Not precisely, but close enough."

Me: [Nodding] "Could it also be just being sensitive to the energies of a place and sensing what happened—like the clair sense of holding an item and knowing something of its history?"

P: "Of course."

H: "Remember, everything is vibration. Like ripples in a pond. Like the Polynesian mariner reading the intersecting ripples."

Me: "Is that how someone can tell the future?"

P: "No one *can* tell the future. They can predict outcomes of possibility, but nothing is fixed."

H: "If they say they can, be wary."

Me: "But what about Nostradamus? He made predictions [centuries in advance]."

P: "The interpretations are similar to the—I can't recall the word—paradroia?—the human mind's ability—" [The correct word is pareidolia.]

H: "Tendency—"

P: "To see faces in rocks, fill in missing pieces. The words of Nostradamus are interpreted to fit events in a similar way."

Me: "What about astrology?"

H: *[Seriously]* "Nothing *predicts the future. It is not fixed.* At least, that is our understanding. All is flux. Even the influence of the stars and planets—they are, after all, living beings with their own—characters—even these are not able to fix the future or predict it beyond a very narrow range and then only probabilities."

Me: "Thank you. Is it all right if I edit this to have this first and your messages at the end? That would read better."

P and H: *[Consulting]* "No. That is not what happened, so, no, it is not all right. It violates the spirt of truth."

Me: "Thank you. I will report it as it occurred."

P and H: *[Nodding]*

[Pause]

Me: "I'm tired again. I know that this is supposed to get easier—and it is in one way—easier to communicate—but I still get tired."

P: "*Of course you do.* You are operating at a higher frequency, and your body is struggling to catch up."

Me: "Is that why I'm eating more carbs?"

P: "No, you are eating more carbs because you like them!"

H: *[Laughing]* "It's true. And we do not judge. We love you."

Me: "I love you too! Goodbye for now."

P and H: *[Waving goodbye]*

Author's Biography

Short Version: Elyn Aviva is a human being who lives in ongoing, interconnected relationship with numerous other beings in the past, present, and future. She wears many labels, including writer, Imaginaut, channeler, pilgrim, artist, mother, wife, sister, daughter, grandmother, explorer of non-physical realms, anthropologist, and friend.

Detailed Version: Elyn investigated the modern-day pilgrimage on the Camino de Santiago for her PhD in cultural anthropology (Princeton University, 1985). Hers was the first anthropological dissertation on the Camino. She walked the Camino in 1982; *Following the Milky Way* (2nd edition) is based on her research. It was the first contemporary American travel narrative about the pilgrimage. She was interviewed for the Smithsonian Channel's 2018 Sacred Sites program on the Camino. Elyn and her husband, Gary White, have walked pilgrimage roads in Spain, France, Ireland, and Cornwall.

Elyn has a deep interest in comparative religion, spiritual development, and the multi-dimensional realms. She has a Master of Divinity degree from Iliff School of Theology (1997) and served the Universalist Church of Denver as an intern minister. She has studied Western Esoteric traditions, Kabbalah, sacred geometry, shamanism, geomancy, conscious dreaming, non-physical healing modalities, and mediumship.

She creates "fiberalchemy" pieces, including free-standing fabric and wire sculptures, felted vessels, masks, and contemporary art quilts. The design concepts come from mythology and the Imaginal Realms.

Elyn has published novels on spiritual journey and quest, as well as numerous articles, most recently on Ancient Origins.net, Ancient Origins Premium.net, and YourLifeIsATrip.com. She and Gary are co-authors of Powerful Places Guidebooks, a transformational travel series that includes nine titles.

Elyn and Gary currently live in Girona, Catalonia (Spain), where they continue to explore the fascinating multi-dimensional universe in which we live. They are grateful for the guidance they have been given that has led them to where they are.

To learn about Elyn's books, go to www.pilgrimsprocess.com and www.powerfulplaces.com. To read some of Elyn's articles, go to www.YourLifeIsATrip.com/home/author/elynaviva, or do a search for Elyn Aviva on https://Ancient-Origins.net. To see Elyn's fiber art, go to www.fiberalchemy.com or Fiberalchemy on Facebook. Also see Elyn Aviva Writes on Facebook.

www.ingramcontent.com/pod-product-compliance
Lightning Source LLC
Chambersburg PA
CBHW070937230426
43666CB00011B/2463